TIME
AND
TIDE

A Story About the Growth of
the Field of Public Relations
in the United States
from the Twenties through the Sixties:
A Participant's Perspective

by Lyle Addison Brookover

LEO AFRICANUS PUBLICATIONS   Washington, D.C.

Lyle a Brookover

Typesetting and design by Chronicle Type & Design in garamond book. Cover
design by Gaal Shepherd.

Brookover, Lyle Addison, 1899-
    Time and Tide

1. Brookover, Lyle Addison, 1899-
2. Public relations consultants—United States—Biography
I. Title
HM263.B675 1985   659.2'0973   85-50082
ISBN 0-933119-00-3

TABLE OF CONTENTS

FOREWORD

My friends, and they are legion, have always said I should write a book about my life. True, it is, I have had many unusual opportunities and adventures. Perhaps they should be gathered into words, I thought to myself.

Lifelong, I have been enchanted with words. The human mind is a storehouse of words to be called forth as you will. Words can start a war, establish a nation, bind a marriage, win or lose a friend.

Words are the transmission belt on which new ideas are carried to a waiting world. There is no limit to the possibilities of use by which words can be made to growl in anger, shout in enthusiasm, or sing and dance with joy. They are always ready to be used, willing to lie down and roll over, if need be.

Think of the magic displayed by an orator who, without manuscript, changes ideas into words for an hour, or the writer who pours his vocabulary into an interesting book so that it may be shared.

Pondering all of this, I decided over 20 years ago to call to duty enough words to tell of the exciting moments, the widely varied personalities, and the panorama of my career. It is my hope that those who have known me in one part of my life can, through reading *Time and Tide* share other stages of my career and meet friends from those days.

Lyle A. Brookover
McLean, Virginia
December, 1984

DEDICATION

My name honors my paternal grandfather, Lyle Brookover, and my maternal grandfather, Addison Kelly. If their spirits are hovering above this earthly scene, I hope my life has not been too much of a disappointment to them. There is a book of genealogy I've read which recounts the emigration of my ancestor, Richard Brookover, from Germany to the New World by way of England in 1620. Our family is related to the Mooreheads and Abbotts, the Monroes, Mercers and Pearces—all good old English names. To the memory of my grandfathers whom I never knew, and all those others, I dedicate this book.

CHAPTER I: 1903-1918
TOTS AND TEENS

My fairly uneventful childhood in Zanesville, Ohio was interrupted by a head-first plunge, at the age of five, into the deep spring which kept our springhouse cool. Since there was no room to turn around, I had to be extricated by the heels by my Uncle Harry Kelly who happened by. He held me up to disgorge and dry out which saved my life.

Wealthy Uncle Harry Kelly's visits from St. Louis were an annual event which brought the outside world into our lives on a hilly, rock-strewn Ohio farm. He brought fame, also, when he drove up through clouds of dust in the first automobile ever seen by our startled neighbors and us.

When my slightly older sister, Laura, led me by the hand to my first day of school, a teen-aged girl 'bully' found great delight in snapping the rubber band which held on my sailor hat. By the day's end, the raw, red welt under my chin brought tears to my mother's eyes. Another day, this budding sadist, jealous of Laura's beautiful brown curls, filled them with cockleburrs. Mother had to cut off the curls to get rid of the burrs which grieved my sister but pleased her tormentor very much.

We had all grades and ages in our one-room schoolhouse; thus, we little ones learned early about life's battles to survive. When I was about ten years of age, I became school janitor. I crunched across the snow on zero degree mornings to shovel coal on the banked fire in the round-bellied stove which kept the room warm all day. My salary was $2 a month: I soon was a capitalist with a bank account.

There were the happy summer days when my dog 'Tippy', barking joyously, helped me to bring in the cows at milking time. Tippy was a brown

1

and white spotted bundle of animation and affection. He thought everything his master did was exactly right and licked his master's hands to tell him so. His formal name was 'Tippecanoe' because he arrived during my study of the history of the presidential campaign when "Tippecanoe and Tyler, too" had been a campaign slogan.

All the boys my age lived at a distance so my dog was my playmate, my pal, my understanding friend. He went everywhere with me: picking blackberries, hunting rabbits, waiting while I did my chores, plunging into the creek when we went to swim. He ran ahead, excitedly wagging his tail, whenever I walked or rode bareback on our chestnut mare. Most of all, I think he loved the day's end when we set off for the hillside pasture. He didn't wait for me, but would search out the cows hidden in little gullies or behind trees and bark at them until they moved toward the pasture gate. He seemed to know as well as I did when we had them all.

One afternoon, Tippy was missing and I had to bring in the cows alone. We searched everywhere; but, it was days later when we learned he had been poisoned by a neighbor because he had run across his field. I didn't cry when they told me; but, that night my pillow was wet with tears. I could not understand the motives which prompted such an act. Nor can I now, years later. Every dog is someone's 'best friend' and Tippy was mine. He lived an unselfish life of devoted service and had done nothing to deserve such a violent death.

Entering my teens, my skill at spelling routed all comers at frequent 'spelling bees.' I became a pint-sized celebrity. One fateful night, I was spelled down by a sassy little girl. I went out back of the building and shed some unmanly tears. Learning came easily to me, much to my sister's disgust, for she had to study hard with much homework. At eleven, I was ready for high school which required passing the Boxwell Examination, named for the state legislator who had fathered the law. Several hundred took the test in Zanesville, our county seat. I was about the youngest and smallest of them all. I still recall a bit of poetry involved somehow in the examination:

> "Alas for him who never sees
> The stars shine through the cypress trees;
> Who, hopeless, lays his dead away,
> Nor waits to see the breaking day
> Across the mournful marbles play . ."

I passed the test and spoke at grammar school graduation exercises in our little country church. I was smartly dressed in white coat and black trousers: I chose as my subject, "There Is Always Room At The Top." How true that still is! Mother had finally yielded to my plea for long pants: we went shopping in town where a bored salesman didn't seem to grasp the importance of the occasion. "Do you dress right or left?" he asked. I had no idea what he meant; so, he explained that the question was in regard to my sexual arrangements. I certainly felt sexy when I stepped out in one of the latest models for young men.

Mother loved music: she taught me to run the scales on our small parlor organ so well that I was asked to play the organ in the Methodist church. My great delight was to play a little faster than the choir sang and come out a bar or so ahead. Later, I bought a violin and took lessons. But, that interest waned. Then came voice lessons. That enthusiasm was also short-lived. Kreisler and John McCormick must have breathed easier to have this threat of competition removed.

I was fifteen when the Ohio Department of Agriculture offered free trips to Washington to youngsters who grew the most corn on an acre of ground in the various districts. I entered the contest, planted my corn, hoed and tended it with loving care. A torrential rain one summer night flooded the field: in the morning, the shoulder-high corn was flattened to the ground.

I went along the rows and set each stalk upright, saying a little prayer meanwhile. When the field was harvested a few weeks later, I had won! Imagine the thrill of boarding my first pullman car for the overnight trip with fifteen other winners to the nation's capital. (One winner was a girl, decades before Women's Lib!)

We were welcomed, photographed, saw Congress in session and money being printed, climbed the Washington Monument, visited the Lincoln Memorial, heard Secretary of State William Jennings Bryan give an inspiring address, were graciously received by the first Mrs. Woodrow Wilson at the White House (the President was ill with a cold,) and took a steamer to George Washington's home and burial place at Mount Vernon, shepherded by my congressman, the Honorable George White of Marietta.

I fell in love with Washington and vowed I'd be back as I stood on Pennsylvania Avenue and gazed at the Capitol dome, shining in the distance. At last, we departed for Philadelphia where we marveled at the Liberty Bell, Independence Hall, the elegant Bellevue-Stratford Hotel. I had my first glimpse of theater in the play "Little Women" at the Adelphi Theater.

Home and 'broadened by travel,' I finished high school with honors. Along came a salesman for business training at Meredith College in Zanesville who promised me a direct path to brilliant success in accounting work. I signed up, over my father's protest that I was sure to come to grief in the big, bad city.

Two incidents stand out with great clarity in memory of this period. I'd spend weekends on the farm, travelling back and forth to Zanesville on the Ohio River and Western Railroad, then the only remaining narrow-guage railroad in America (it is long since abandoned.)

One Sunday evening as the train approached, Mother walked with me down the road to Brookover Station (named for our forebears who had bought the land from the Indians and whose descendants lived there when the road was built.) We were talking busily with Mother advising me to study hard and avoid temptation. Before we crossed the track to the platform, we said good-bye. As I waited to board the train, Mother thought of something more to tell me. Hastening across the track, she caught her foot in the rail and fell prostrate at my feet. The locomotive's bell clanged wildly, smoke gushed from its stack and the train slowed its race toward us, only yards away now. The engineer and fireman stared horror-stricken from the cab, knowing they could not stop in time. Instinctively, I reached down from the three-foot high platform and grasped Mother's hands. She was small, but she weighed 125 pounds or more: I was not strong and, at no ordinary moment would I have tried to lift her three inches, let alone, three feet!

But now, with superhuman strength which certainly came through Divine intercession, I pulled her from the track only seconds before the engine slid by and the train jolted to a stop. With the way clear, the train moved up so the passenger coaches could reach the plattform. By this time, the crew was agog and passengers were gaping from the windows. I was speechless: so was Mother.

Assured that she was unhurt, I reluctantly boarded the train for a most jittery journey. When I arrived in town and dashed to a telephone, my heart began to beat more normally when I heard Mother's calm voice saying: "Oh, I'm all right, but I doubt if I can sleep well tonight." I was so shaken that my sleep was troubled for several nights.

Another weekend, a neighbor kindly offered to drive me back to school on Monday morning. As we raced along in his open car, my hat blew off and away. I rose as my friend slowed down and placed my hand on the car door which swung open. I fell from the car, landing on my feet, but momentum carried me forward. I fell and struck the side of my head on the concrete pavement.

The next thing I remember was the screaming siren on the ambulance in which I was being rushed to Bethesda Hospital. An examination revealed a skull fracture and a broken collar-bone. I remained mostly unconscious; but, I awakened once to hear the doctor say: "I don't think it's worthwhile to set his collar-bone. I don't think he'll make it."

With that encouragement, I drifted off again! Hours later, I roused up to find my parents anxiously watching over me. My ear was bleeding and I had a splitting headache. The bleeding (which continued for two days) was a saving grace. My youth and will to live did the rest. Daily battles with

4

a cross nurse who got soap in my eyes whenever she bathed my face provided a challenge. In two weeks, I was home again with a humming in my ear which lasted for months, and a disfigured shoulder.

Graduated at last and morally undamaged, I entered my first job as cost accountant in a casket factory where I had excellent opportunity to ponder on the brevity of human existence. Weary of the silk linings and knowledge of what seemed unfair profits at the expense of the bereaved, I betook myself to another job— enlisting classified ads for a daily newspaper. From thence to a clerkship in the Pennsylvania Railroad office where I learned the joy of traveling on a pass. Every chance I got, I was off to Cincinnati, Chicago, or somewhere, sometimes riding all night, red-eyed and cinder-strewn, but getting a larger look at life.

Eva Kelly Brookover

CHAPTER II: 1918
THE CALL TO WAR

When the German Kaiser's U-boats started sinking American ships and World War I began with a formal declaration of war by the United States Congress (the old-fashioned way), I felt an old-time urge to help defend my country's people and property and enlisted in the Army.

My parents opposed my getting into the war until it seemed I might soon be drafted. I didn't wish to be drafted: more than sixty years later, I still feel that, in a country which prides itself on freedom for the individual, a draft system which forces into military service young men who don't want to serve is morally wrong. I do feel, however, that able young men should **want** to enlist as I did, and for the same reason. Universal military service for a short period of youth is probably a fair requirement of those so fortunate as to be born in "the land of the free and home of the brave."

What Dad and Mother didn't know was that I had slipped off to a Navy recruiting office in Columbus and taken a physical test which had come to naught. When I stepped into a box of chalk, bare-footed, and then took a few steps on a clean floor, my hopes of "seeing the world" as a Navy guest were shattered completely. "You have flat feet," the recruiting officer said flatly.

My flat feet and I went off to a college unit, the Student Army Training Corps at Bethany College, West Virginia. With several hundred other patriots, I took my first faltering steps toward becoming an army officer. "Forward march" and "squads right" were a new language learned in weary hours on the drill field. Interspersed with these were hours in the classroom where we battled with college subjects with some essentially military studies thrown in.

On the field, I was a six feet tall, skinny corporal with seven other men calling me their leader. In classes, I led in sanitation and hygiene. I did well in Spanish language classes taught by a dark-eyed senora, as well as algebra. But, when it came to trigonometry, I had no alternative but to sit next to the brightest student in that subject on examination day.

We bitched cheerfully about the quarters, the officers and the food. One reason for the latter was the wartime scarcity of such edibles as sugar and salt. Hot cereal for breakfast without these was a rugged diet—I can almost taste that cereal today!

One chilly evening, after hours of rigorous drill, we lined up for mess and waited for the mess hall doors to open (they were kept locked untill the meal was ready.) After a long wait during which we sang, cursed, and moved ever closer together, the door was thrown open suddenly. Everybody shoved forward. The first fifty or so men fell like dominoes into the room, knocking over chairs, tables loaded with food and even a few startled K.P.'s.

Mess was called off at once: those toward the front of the line were ordered to report to headquarters; the others, to their quarters. When I faced the stern inquisitors and gave my name, rank, and serial number, the presiding major shot at me the first question:

"Corporal Brookover, did you push in the mess line?"

"Certainly, sir," I replied.

"Why did you do that?" he asked.

"Because everyone behind me was pushing and I could not help myself."

I thought the officers looked surprised. One said: "All the others said they didn't push!"

I was given my freedom with a kind word of commendation for telling the truth. Since everyone else was confined to quarters, I had no one to roam about with until bedtime.

We were scheduled to go to Officers' Training School at Fort Oglethorpe, Georgia on December 15, but the war ended—four days too soon! The earlier report of a false armistice fired our commanding officer, a hard-bitten major, into ordering an all-day march 26 miles down the mountain to the small town of Wellsburg. The flu epidemic was at its peak: there was no one in the streets to cheer as we limped by. Back at camp after dark, we soaked our blistered feet and crawled off to bed **before** the bugle sounded.

I got an honorable discharge in time to be home for Christmas. I found both my parents had nearly died from flu. My sister had been summoned home from her war job of nurse's training at East Liverpool Hospital.

Shortly after, I came down with flu myself; but, I recovered fairly quickly.

A highlight of my stay at Bethany (in no way associated with winning the war) was being pledged to Beta Theta Pi fraternity. I was singled out for this honor from among three hundred soldiers by a senior student and Beta, Admiral Dewey Wolfe. While singing with brothers at the fraternity house:

"Oh, start the loving cup around,
Nor pass a brother by _____ "

and the many other songs for which Beta is famous, I could forget the trials of a soldier's life and be happy again. I wanted more than anything in the world to go back and become a full-fledged Beta. But, my Father refused financial help, saying: "All those fraternities teach you is to drink, smoke, gamble and run after women." Many times I wished I had defied him and gone back. I could have earned my way.

I dated an Alpha Xi Delta sorority girl in Bethany and later, one of the sisters at Ohio State University in Columbus. With them, I attended many of their charming dinner parties and dances.

At the time, I was doing what the boys call 'playing the field' for I always thought the practice of 'going steady' was like going into a well-stocked library, selecting one book and reading it over and over again; meanwhile, passing up all the other challenging volumes, beautifully bound and printed, any one of which you might find more attractive than your first choice.

Along came my twenty-first birthday: Sister thought I must have a birthday party. We invited most of the young people we knew, among them a half-dozen of my 'current favorites.' Well, it is easy to guess what happened! Each of my 'dates' assumed that I was her special escort for the evening. I got into a frightful mess! I aged considerably during those hours and, as Kipling so tidily phrased it, 'learned about women' from Betty and Almeda, Lulu and Marie, and Olive and Anne—all at the same party and all madly in love (?) with me.

All of them married quite well and are, presumably, living happily ever after while I continue playing. I still correspond with Olive, Anne and Almeda who are now widows and wonderful friends.

The next 'happening' was an operation for appendicitis. On the evening of my second day in the hospital, Dorothy drove up in her red sports car (a snappy Apperson) wearing a red dress and hat and carrying an armful of red roses. Her call on me threw the hospital into a turmoil: the lady superintendent came in to inquire casually about the glamorous visitor. (Women do have a bit of curiosity in their make-up, you know.)

Following my hospital stay, I recuperated at home in a state of depression so deep that I refused to talk to anyone, even my family. One evening the telephone rang: the city editor of the *Times-Recorder* (our morning newspaper) was asking if I would like to join the staff. That was the tonic I needed! I accepted at once, becoming a cub reporter waiting to read his own byline on his first front page story.

When my coverage of the annual Chamber of Commerce banquet made headlines—on a night when news was scarce—I mistakenly thought I had reached the top. finding his favorite author on the front page is as stimulating to a reporter—even a veteran- as applause is to an actor or opera star. That's why there are so many young men who aspire to journalism!

In 1921, I was elected national president of my high school fraternity, Alpha Pi, at a convention in Cedar Point, Ohio and re-elected in 1922 at Cincinnati. I served two terms, relinquishing the office at a national convention in my home town of Zanesville on a day when the funeral train bearing the body of President Harding passed through as it rolled eastward from San Francisco to a state funeral in Washington. Alpha Pi had many chapters in Ohio: others were in Chicago, Indianapolis, and Philadelphia. Our ancient Greek ritual was most impressive; our handclasps were secret and binding, and our social purpose was highlighted by formal dancing parties at festive seasons.

The time came to move along: I migrated to Clarksburg, West Virginia and joined the advertising department of the *Exponent* with an occasional news assignment from the city room. The Advertising Club picked me up; shortly, I was named to head the 'pep' committee.

I was able to secure for one of our programs the celebrated cartoonist, George McManus, who spent a day in Clarksburg. He delighted the school children with drawings of "Jiggs and Maggie" and autographs. He regaled us at dinner that evening by doing quick sketches in color and enjoyed himself hugely at a party afterwards in his honor.

When I drove him to the station at midnight to see him off for New York, he said: "Watch my cartoons for the next two or three weeks." Sure enough, presently there appeared one in which Jiggs told Maggie, "I met the nicest guy in Clarksburg the other day and he said . . . ."

"Playing the Field"

CHAPTER III: 1924
WORLD'S ADVERTISING CONGRESS

In 1924, the Club named me as a delegate to the World's Advertising Congress. I made my first ocean journey on the *SS Republic*, landing at Southampton. The Congress was held at Wembley Exposition outside London. The scene itself was fascinating, a British Empire show featuring exhibits from dominions in all parts of the world.

The Prince of Wales (later King Edward and, still later—thanks to Wally—the Duke of Windsor) welcomed 1,900 Americans and many hundreds from other nations to the Congress. At a private luncheon afterwards, a young American lady from Nashville, Tennessee crashed the party because of Prince Edward. When the Crown Prince learned about her presence, he insisted that she be permitted to remain. Thus, he proved that he was all that we democratic Americans expected a royal personage to be.

We were royally entertained during our stay: a fabulous luncheon at the ancient Guild Hall, attended by the Lord Mayor of London, smothered in robes, plumes and medals; also, by Lords Riddell and Reading and a toastmaster in brilliant robes who proposed the toasts and told us when we could smoke. At a luncheon in the Picadilly Hotel, smartly-uniformed waiters brought in mar tinis on large silver trays—just like in the movies. A different wine was served with each course, much to my undoing. We also enjoyed a party hosted by the Duke of Connaught at the Connaught Club, a splendid formal concert at Albert Hall, and a brilliant ball given by Gordon Selfridge at his mansion in Belgravia. He was the American merchant prince who owned a huge department store in London.

At the Selfridge ball, I danced with Nora B. Imber, the 20 years old, statuesque blond daughter of Sir Horace Imber, publisher of the *Daily Chronicle*. When she lamented the fact that we were seeing more of the London sights than she ever had, I asked her to join me the next day. She agreed: we lunched at the Cheshire Cheese and visited the historic Tower of London where the Crown Jewels are displayed. Those sights were new to her; but, promptly at four o'clock, she begged to be excused and dashed off to Waterloo Station as she, "positively must be home in the country by teatime."

After a bit of correspondence, I had visions of marriage and my becoming a British journalist—all in the family, of course. Those dreams faded quickly when I received holiday greetings from Nora signed "Mrs." something or another.

The Royal Family let it be known that we delegates would be welcome at a morning levee at Buckingham Palace. They avoided the embarassment of having a royal command declined by advising that "those who wished to attend" would receive invitations. I was one of the few Americans who had brought both dress suit and tuxedo; but, I was not about to go to the trouble of renting a morning coat, knee britches, pumps with silver buckles—all of which needed to be worn! I had some satisfaction, however, in knowing I **could** have met the King and Queen. I also had fun watching the uproar among my colleagues who **did** go.

One joyous day was spent at Haver Castle in Kent where our trains were met by 'tally-ho's' which carried us to the castle and a welcome by Major John Jacob Astor, M.P. and publisher of the *London Times* and his most charming wife, Lady Violet. After being shown the grounds and told the story of the castle's occupancy by King Henry VIII and various ladies, including Anne Boleyn, I was sorry that Anne could not have been there to greet us. Her bedroom is a memorable sight.

A bountiful luncheon was served in the shade of green-and-white striped marquees on the grounds. After the final toasts, Lady Violet rose and made the most perfect, polished speech I'd ever heard a lady give, before or since. There was time for another stroll in the beautiful grounds: I got lost in the garden maze where a path led into tall shrubbery and wound to the center where there was a sparkling fountain. The amazing part is how one finds ones way out again! The voices of friends, heard over the shrubbery, finally rescued me.

I was fortunate in receiving invitations for post-Congress visits to Ireland and France. I had made a friend at the Congress, Charles McConnell who owned McConnell Advertising Service, Ltd. in Dublin (whose firm has since celebrated its Golden 50th Anniversary). It was then the only Irish company which had a "brawnch" in London and Charlie was properly proud of that.

Our party traveled by train to Holyhead, crossed the Irish Sea by steamer and landed at Kingstown where I was warmly greeted by friend Charlie and Mrs. McConnell. They whisked me from the dock to the Grosvenor Hotel by car and asked me to register and have my luggage sent to my room. The warmth of Irish hospitality may be measured when I say that I saw my room for the first time at four the next morning. Delightful sightseeing, luncheon, dinner, supper clubs and dancing, with a dash of Irish whiskey now and then filled in the hours between.

The next day, we were off to the lakes of Killarney, the most enchanting spot one can imagine where red-cheeked carsmen row you across mirror-like waters, surrounded by low emerald hills. They shout to the hills and, when the echoes answer, they say: "Now, you'll believe there are little men and women (leprechauns) in those hills."

We were shown through Muckross Abbey, a beautiful and very old mansion beside the lakes, then owned by John McCormack, the Irish-American tenor whose fame was world-wide. He was not present, but a small army of dignified servants made us welcome. One American woman, the wife of a wealthy advertising man, distinguished herself by swiping a large handful of notepaper from a writing table as we passed through the private rooms. The shops with tempting displays of Irish linens lured us for hasty shopping before catching our traian back to Dublin.

That evening, sitting back to back, high in a charabanc and well-fortified with Irish whiskey, several friends and I journeyed to the hotel where the President of Ireland, Liam T. Cosgrave (a small, graying, dignified man) was guest of honor at a formal dinner. He greeted each of us with a cordial word of welcome. Our descent from the jaunting car at the hotel entrance (and before the crowd of citizens) was much less than formal, I fear, but it was pure fun.

Another day, we drove through Phoenix Park where some of the best horsemanship in the world is continuously on view. The Irish are great horse lovers and equestrian skill is commonplace. Our drive ended at the mansion of Governor-General Timothy Healy, representative of the British Crown, who gave us afternoon levee with many hundreds in attendance. Under gay marquees on the lawn, waiters dispensed food and drinks while a red-coated band provided stirring tunes. Passing through the reception line, I strolled to the beverage tent at the moment when our host had just given the band a respite. The band members were soon gathering around me to quench their thirst. One asked me a question and, in a moment, I was in the center of the group, eager to talk to an American.

"Would we be able to get jobs with a band if we came to America?" asked one.

"Would it be easy to get a job on the New York police force?" asked another.

"What does it cost to go to America, and how much money would I need to live on until I get a job?" asked a third.

The questions, friendly and respectful, continued until I was astonished. "Do all of you want to go to America?", I asked them. "Don't any of you want to stay in Ireland?".

They explained that it was very difficult to make much money there and that all the Irish were so poor. They had heard about fabulous opportunities in the New World. Many had friends already over here. I was a bit depressed by the evident poverty on every hand in Ireland; but, I was delighted by the irrepressible good cheer. Little old ladies on the street would place a bit of heather in one's lapel, saying, "This will bring you good luck." they were grateful for tips—although they had not asked for money—and I feared this was their only livelihood.

Back across the Irish Sea (renowned in song and story) we took a night train to London. We were delayed on a siding while the red and gold Royal Train flashed by, apparently destined for a royal vacation spot in Scotland—a summer castle rather than a cottage!

Soon we entrained again for the journey to France. Before boarding the cross-Channel ferry, we enjoyed a good look at the 'White Cliffs of Dover', commemorated in the beautiful war-time song.

The wonderful and varied program arranged by our French hosts included a flying exhibition by the French Air Force at Le Bourget (where Charles Lindbergh would, three years later, make his landing after his historic solo flight across the Atlantic in a single-engine plane). Aviation was, at that time, quite new. We looked forward with enthusiasm to the air show.

The day's events gave interesting proof that speaking a country's language is a great advantage when traveling. My companion for the day was Irene Haskell, a charming advertising delegate from Chicago who was quite fluent in French.

After a daring exhibition by the French pilots (which was greeted then by roars of applause but would be quite unimpressive by today's standards), announcement came over the loud speaker that some of the international guests would be taken aloft for brief flights. Irene and I were determined to be among those to go, as neither of us had flown before. Names were called out; of course, the more distinguished visitors were chosen first. We became impatient, as time was slipping by. Irene finally approached one of the aviators and held a spirited conversation with him in French. She returned to tell me our names would be called out next. He had been eager to put **her** name on the list but not mine. When she told him she could not go without her 'brother', our names were called together.

The Handley-Paige plane had a rear entrance with a tall step-ladder to

16

the door. My 'sister' went safely up and I followed. Just as I was about to step inside, the ladder started to fall. I almost did a 'split' in mid-air—without previous ballet training!

Unfortunately, I was carrying the lady's umbrella and an armload of her tourist folders and programs, as well as my own. Thus unbalanced and unable to grab ahold of anything but air, I made an ignominious descent to the muddy field before thousands of people. Not willing to let a broken leg nor arm deter me—I wasn't going to miss the chance to fly—I painfully gathered up myself, umbrella and literature, and climbed that treacherous ladder once more.

Aboard, I settled into a seat beside Irene and assured her that I was not badly hurt. We climbed above the Paris rooftops and flew as far as the English Channel. The trip was thrilling, indeed, its novelty increased by my unhinged state.

Back at the airfield, as we raced to a landing, I could not believe the plane and landing strip were going to meet on agreeable terms. My heart almost stopped beating as the earth shot up toward us. Somehow, we made it. Safely down, I took the bus to my Paris hotel where I quickly stripped to examine my bruises. They were plentiful, but the adventure into the 'wild blue yonder' was more than worth all the black and blue marks!

Nor, did my injuries prevent my donning white tie and tails that evening to see "The Woman of Navarre" and an exciting ballet at the Paris Opera. It was such fun, on the Promenade, to say (with elaborate casualness), "Oh, yes, we flew today at Le Bourget."

President Doumerge honored the delegates with a great dinner at Elysee Palace which I did not attend. Thus, I fortunately missed being blamed for the theft of the gold palace spoons, missing after the dinner and apparently stolen by some disgraceful guest. I had plenty of ribbing about the incident afterwards, but my alibi was airtight.

One whole day in France was spent at glorious Versailles where we were shown throughout the Palace, the Hall of Mirrors, the Petit Trianon, and the unforgettable gardens where the fountains were playing just for our benefit. As evening came, we settled on a garden slope and watched, across a small lake, the most dazzling display of fireworks I'd ever seen.

There was time for night club gaiety—the Folies Bergere and The Lido—and a mammoth reception by the American Chamber of Commerce. The latter, at midday, almost caused me to miss the Folies. I'd made a novice's mistake of taking martinis first, and then switching to champagne.

I was staying at Hotel Continentale whose proprietor, Maurice Barrier, had married a San Francisco girl. She devoted herself to pleasing their American guests. One night, she and I dined at Chateau d'Armenonville (a lovely spot in the Bois), went on to Le Paroquet where Josephine Baker and a nude chorus were appearing (danced there awhile), and moved on to Zelli's, a cafe very popular with American collegiates. Monsieur Barrier was there with a lovely companion. He eventually came to our table alone, bowed low and asked, "May I have this dance with my wife?" I was slightly unnerved, but managed to stagger over to dance with his lady friend.

Toward morning Elise Barrier and I visited Les Halles, the great market where all Paris got its food supplies. Rosy-cheeked farm lads and girls were arranging their vegetables and other goodies temptingly, calling to one another in high spirits. At a food stand, we enjoyed 'jambon and cafe au lait'—a huge ham sandwich and coffee which was half hot milk—then left for the hotel as the sun was rising. As I said good-night to Elise in the lobby, Maurice arrived and bade me a pleasant good-morning.

Reluctantly, as all travelers do, I bade farewell to Paris, took the boat train to Cherbourg and the journey home on the giant *Leviathan,* queen of the seas at the time. Everyone complained that she sailed too fast for the entire crossing was one festive house party. Fortunately, my cabin mate was one of the U.S. swimming team, returning from the Olympic Games in Paris.

We made dining arrangements to be seated with the rest of the Olympic swimmers, including Duke Kahanamoku of Hawaii. He was then the world's champion swimmer and one of the nicest and finest gentlemen I've ever met. The girls on board wanted to see an exhibition of Olympic talent and they were told I was the diving champion. As a result, I didn't dare go near the ship's swimming pool, much as I wanted to. It would have been an Olympian disaster, had I tried!

Most of us had bought champagne in Cherbourg: we had gala parties at our tables every night that lasted for hours. We had the run of the ship, although we were cabin class passengers. The Olympic colors opened all doors. There were so many unfamiliar, but eager, hands extended for tips as we left the ship , that I generously bankrupted myself. When my roommate, Ralph Breyer, and I settled into our room at Hotel Martinique, we both had to wire home for funds. The group had a lavish farewell dinner before parting company; but, all agreed it was dull, compared to Europe—Prohibition, naturally!

On returning to Clarksburg, I found I'd missed one of the biggest days in that city's history—the homecoming of John W. Davis to accept the Democratic nomination for President of the United States. What fun that would have been, for I knew his sister Emma quite well ! She lived in the old family mansion and I had visited her frequently with a mutual friend, Mrs. Corinne Lockman.

Mrs. Lockman was a rare and splendid personage who largely influenced my life at that time. We were mutually interested in culture, the arts and the outside world, but exiled to a sleepy, small city whose leading families were mostly coal and oil 'nouveau riche'. While she was three times my age, her spirit was as blithe as mine. We were great pals, going around together to the limited social activities of the town, ignoring the whispered comments which were plentiful!

She was American Red Cross representative for that area. Also, she served the Veterans Administration and various other welfare groups. A close friend of President Wilson's daughter, Eleanor, she had come from a fine French background, studied music, became an opera star, made a most unfortunate marriage, reared a daughter, and then embrked upon a welfare career.

She was tireless in efforts to aid the poor, the alien, and the unfortunate. Veterans were a special concern. When organization funds ran out, her own purse provided financial assistance many times.

With a tall, commanding figure always smartly attired, snowy hair always beautifully groomed, and large dark eyes that spoke of pity and understanding, Corinne Lockman was at home in any situation from the White House to the opposite extreme. Later on, she came to Washington: I invited her to accompany me to a large formal reception the Secretary of State, Frank B. Kellogg—called 'nervous Nellie' by the press—was giving at the Pan American Union for visiting Latin journalists.

"Why didn't you write me!" she wailed. "I've brought no dresses suitable to wear to such a party. But, I'll go anyhow," she added.

She wore a large hat and an expensive daytime dress, standing out strangely amidst the low-cut, floor length evening gowns. But, she was surrounded all evening by friends won by her gaity and charm. She also accompanied me to the White House reception on New Year's Day.

Shortly afterward, she made a trip to the West Coast to visit her daughter and Navy son-in-law. On the return journey, several cars of the train fell over a mountainside, and she was killed. I lost a wise counselor, an inspiring philosopher, and a noble friend!

CHAPTER IV: 1925
THE LURE OF THE PRESS

Restlessly, I moved from West Virginia to Columbus, Ohio where I did promotional advertising for the *Columbus Dispatch*. From there I moved to Springfield and then back to Zanesville. I was becoming stimulated by tales of the great Florida Boom and decided that Florida was the place for me to make my fortune.

Stopping over in Washington, D.C. enroute, my cousin, Will McGarry flouted my plans. "This is the place for an ambitious newspaperman," he said. "The Florida 'boom' will be a 'bust' by the time you get there." (He was right about the Florida 'boom'!)

He convinced me, and I stayed on within sight of the Capitol Dome, my lodestar. (Remember, I'd promised myself ten years before that I would be back!) Shortly, I landed in the Washington Bureau of the *Cleveland Plain Dealer* and became a member of the National Press Gallery and the National Press Club.

I soon met on pleasant terms all the leading news correspondents. Among them, I decided Richard Oulihan of the *New York Times* was my ideal journalist. Tall, handsome, urbane, impeccably groomed, a confidant of those in power, he was kind and helpful to a greenhorn like me. There were my bureau colleagues, Walker Buel and James Wright, both most gifted writers and very helpful; Roy Roberts of the *Kansas City Star*; Ulric Bell of the *Louisville Courier-Journal*; Carter Field of the *New York Herald-Tribune*; and many others, all successful in **our** profession. What an atmosphere for a fledgling to grow in!

During those years, I came to know personally almost all the senators

21

and scores of congressmen. Senators Reed of Missouri, Borah of Idaho and Taft of Ohio stood out among them all.

I stood nearby as President Coolidge laid the cornerstone of the new 14 story National Press Building. Congress had to pass a bill to give us the extra story, as the height of Washington buildings was limited by law to 12 stories then. One evening later, as I entered Poli's Theater with Congressman and Mrs. Brooks Fletcher of Ohio to attend a play, we were walking up the long esplanade when we heard White House aides calling, "Make way for the President." At that moment, Mrs. Fletcher stepped out of one of her white evening slippers and it rolled back down the ramp, stopping just at the feet of the First Lady, Grace Coolidge, entering with the President.

Mrs. Coolidge smiled sympathetically as an aide retrieved the shoe. He presented it to Mrs. Fletcher with a bow. On that occasion, as always, Mrs. Coolidge was serene, gracious, every inch the First Lady—perhaps the most outstanding one until that time to occupy that exalted post.

Lunching in the Capitol restaurants amongst senators and congressmen was a lively experience. I often enjoyed watching the venerable Theodore Burton of Ohio having his daily lunch of crackers and milk at a nearby table. Mr. Burton was involved in my first front page banner-line story in the 'P.D.' It was about a Senate hearing on diversion of Great Lakes water at Chicago. Burton, former Secretary of War Newton D. Baker, and City Manager William R. Hopkins of Cleveland were battling for Cleveland's rights.

Even more exciting that year than Gene Tunney's win of the world's heavyweight boxing championship by beating Jack Dempsey was my first attendance at a Gridiron Dinner. This traditional banquet of Washington journalists is the most famous event of its kind, open only to invited guests. Invitations are not available for the asking—no matter who is doing the asking! The guest list that year was headed by Vice President Charles G. Dawes; others were Secretary of State Kellogg and the other nine Cabinet members, Speaker of the House Nicholas Longworth and a shoal of senators and congressmen and the ambassadors of Germany and Brazil. John Philip Sousa was present to lead the U.S. Marine Band in his new composition, the "Gridiron March."

After the dinner, many of the guests repaired to the 'little green house on K Street', famous during the Harding administration as a hide-out for the President and his closest friends for 'recreational purposes.' The old mansion was owned by the utilities magnate, Henry L. Dougherty: that evening's party was a swinger which lasted until dawn. Highlights were songs by Speaker Longworth and his side-kick, Congressman Maurice Crumpacker of Oregon. They brought down the house with a sentimental presentation of "The Little Old Red Drawers That Maggie Wore." Longworth, the suave, immaculate Cincinnati millionaire husband of 'Teddy' Roosevelt's daughter, 'Princess Alice' had a fine voice. Crumpacker, a genial giant of a man, joined in with a rich rolling bass to make a duo which one could never forget.

During that evening, Governor Albert C. Ritchie of Maryland, a serious contendor for the Democratic nomination for president, was confronted by a prominent newspaper publisher and worshipful admirer, who was driven by his consumption of refreshments to extol Ritchie as the "... one and only, all-time, exactly right man for the country's welfare ..."

To this unexpected eulogy, the governor listened with considerable patience and a far-off look in his eyes. When the torrent of words subsided, he made what seemed the perfect response. "You may be right," he said.

My correspondence for the *Plain Dealer* included a column on the activities of the Ohio delegation in Congress. I made a daily round of the offices of two senators and twenty-two representatives. Some of them produced a minimum of news, due to an evident fear of 'press comment' back home. Others were not only friendly, but quite willing to help me write my column. Among them were Representatives Brooks Fletcher of Marion and Roy Fitzgerald of Dayton. The latter headed the House Committee on Revision of the Laws. I became interested in his attempts to codify the terrifying mass of laws passed by each succeeding Congress. I wrote a feature story, "Ten Laws That Grew Into Millions" which Fitzgerald inserted in full in the *Congressional Record*.

Fifty years later, that story is still apt and perhaps worthy of being read by a newer generation. I have included it at the end of this chapter.

I also wrote a feature, "Congress Is Like A Schoolroom," and another, "Re-Discovering The Nations' Laws" which were published in my own paper, the *PD* , and several other big city papers. (At space rates, this was a way to get rich slowly!) I even made the *Toronto Daily Star* in Canada.

Congressman Fletcher, a heavy-set man with wavy black hair and piercing eyes whose voice was loud, erudition profound, and whose great hope, it seemed was to be an up-dated William Jennings Bryan, gave me constant urging and inspiration to write bigger and better stories.

My daily visits to the Speaker's Office brought me to the notice of his amazing wife, the late Alice Roosevelt Longworth, of whom it was said that if she walked into a room with five hundred people present, everyone would instantly stop talking, such was her personal magnetism. Imagine my youthful delight when one day, after I had chatted with her and Mrs. James Begg, wife of the Congressman from Sandusky, Ohio, and left the room, she remarked to Mrs. Begg— who duly reported to me—"That young man is the best dressed newspaperman in the Press Gallery."

Lunching at the Press Club one Saturday afternoon, we were all delighted when 'Nick' Longworth strolled in accompanied by the famous rope trick artist and comedian, Will Rogers. They took a corner table: we hardly gave them time to finish lunch when some 25 of us crowded round to hear a conversation punctuated by roars of laughter. Will was telling of his current visit to the White House and how he slipped bits of meat under the table to the White House collies. President Coolidge's frugality was an open secret: Will claimed the dogs were slowly starving on the White House diet.

I have been many times impressed with the desire of thousands—yes, it must be millions— of Americans to shake hands with our President. Yet, the Coolidge hand-clasp, somewhat like picking up merchandise in a fish market, left something to be desired. However, my dear friend, Lucille Hershey from Columbus, Ohio, was appearing in a Washington theater in "The Vagabond King." I became a 'stage-door Johnny': over a late supper, she told me of her great desire to meet the President.

It was arranged: at the appointed hour, I escorted Lucille to the White House. We joined a line headed for the President's Office. As we passed along, an aide announced her name. Mr. Colidge, with hardly a glance at Lucille, reached for her hand and murmered something or other, meanwhile passing her along with an arm movement that most experienced reception line clebrities use to keep the line moving. Lucille was auburn-haired with a vivid face, beautiful figure and glorious voice. I felt she rated a little more show of enthusiasm—and there was none. But, she was happy over a dream realized and the attendant publicity which the incident received. (See *Times-Recorder* clipping at end of this chapter.)

Another incident which stands out in memories of those days was an invitation to a concert at Dumbarton Oaks, the magnificent Georgetown estate owned by the late Ambassador and Mrs. Robert Woods Bliss. They were very public spirited: thousands of people enjoyed their lovely gardens at almost every season. (The mansion and gardens were eventually given to Harvard University as a study center. The planning meetings for the United Nations took place here.)

After the concert, refreshments were served in the immense drawing room. I found myself standing beside the inspiring Episcopal Bishop of Washington, James Freeman, and his wife. It was he who had dreamed of a great cathedral in the capital city. With only a million or so dollars raised toward this goal, he started work to make his dream come true. He was unquestionably the greatest churchman I shall ever know. Now, nearly sixty years later and with many millions of dollars expended on construction (and after Bishop Freeman has long since passed away), the National Cathedral of St. Peter and St. Paul is nearly finished. Dean Francis Sayre, a relative of President Wilson, completed a tour of over thirty years at the Cathedral during which much of the progress was made. On several occasions, I met Dean Sayre and found him to be a witty, cultured and charming man, as well as an inspirational leader and priest.

****

A thrill of a different sort came to me one day when I encountered my friend, Lieut. Elwood 'Pete' Quesada of the Army Air Corps, in the National Press Club. He said that since I now had a reserve commission in the Army, I should come out to Bolling Field and let him show me a few flying tricks. I accepted with some misgivings: I was not reassured when I saw the two-seater, open cockpit plane in which I was to leave the earth for my second flight.

Pete treated me to all the Air Corps knew about flying, including 'dog fighting' and other spectaculars. Flying upside down, however, was the worst of all. He would look back occasionally with a fiendish grin; however, I never did let him know how happy I was to put my feet back on solid ground!

EVENTS

LYLE BROOKOVER IS HOBNOBBING WITH THE GREAT

According to a dispatch from Washington, D. C., Lyle Brookover, formerly of this city, seems to be hobnobbing with President Coolidge and other notables at Washington, D. C. The story is as follows:

"Miss Lucille Hershey, a very talented Columbus girl, has been receiving unusual social attention here and her visit no doubt will leave very pleasant recollections. Miss Hershey is a daughter of A. W. Hershey, head of the Hershey-Rice Co. and proprietor of the Seneca hotel at Columbus. She is a comedy star in the cast of the "Vagabond King" in the company playing Washington and plays next to the leading part, although this is only her second year with the troupe.

"Miss Hershey was introduced to President Coolidge by Lyle A. Brookover of the Cleveland Plain Dealer's Washington bureau and she was so thrilled over meeting the president that when she passed out of the receiving line she turned to her escort and said:

"I am not going to wash my hand all day."

President Coolidge might have said that it is not often he gets an opportunity to shake hands with as interesting a person as Miss Hershey Her father and mother visited Mr. Coolidge at his old family home in Vermont when he was running for the vice presidency in 1920 and they were anxious to have her meet the president.

Representative and Mrs. Brooks Fletcher had Miss Hershey with them on a trip at Mt. Vernon and Mr. Brookover was host at a dinner party at the National Press club in her honor."

Times-Recorder
January 17, 1927

25

Second commission: Thirtieth Statutes, 58, act of June 4, 1897. Commissioners: (1) A. C. Thompson (Ohio, afterwards United States district judge at Cincinnati), (2) A. C. Botkin (Montana), and (3) David B. Culbertson (Texas), who were succeeded by (1) David K. Watson (Ohio), (2) W. D. Bynum (Indiana), (3) John L. Lott (Ohio).

Salaries and expenses of this commission under the indefinite appropriation (30 Stat. 58) are explained in the following letter from the Comptroller General of the United States:

COMPTROLLER GENERAL OF THE UNITED STATES,
Washington, February 3, 1931.

Hon. ROY G. FITZGERALD,
Chairman Committee on Revision of the Laws,
House of Representatives.

MY DEAR MR. CHAIRMAN: With further reference to your communication of December 3, 1930, wherein you request certain data in regard to expenditures under the act of June 4, 1897 (30 Stat. 58), made by the commissioners, authorized under the act to revise and codify the criminal and penal laws of the United States, I have to advise the records of this office for the fiscal years 1898 to 1907, inclusive, show that the total sum of $204,498.84 was expended therefor.

There is furnished below a tabulated report of the expenses during each fiscal year:

Miscellaneous expenses

Fiscal year	Commissioners' salaries	Expenses, clerk hire	Miscellaneous expenses
1898	$14,836.94	$5,882.21	$1,545.70
1899	15,000.00	5,400.00	1,283.55
1900	14,258.25	5,400.00	1,057.84
1901	15,233.52	5,400.00	1,155.38
1902	15,000.00	5,400.00	1,472.44
1903	15,000.00	5,325.00	1,592.20
1904	15,000.00	5,141.00	1,616.37
1905	15,000.00	5,400.00	1,468.27
1906	14,805.55	5,190.00	1,628.81
1907	6,874.98	1,462.50	760.33
	141,009.24	49,910.71	13,578.89
			49,910.71
			141,009.24
Total			204,498.84

Sincerely yours,

J. R. McCARL,
Comptroller General of the United States.

Result: Criminal Code enacted March 4, 1909 (35 Stat. 1088); Judicial Code enacted March 3, 1911 (36 Stat. 1087).

Commission worked 10 years, submitted its final report to Congress on December 15, 1906. Under the acts of June 4, 1897 (supra); March 3, 1899 (30 Stat. 1116); and March 3, 1901 (31 Stat. 1181), the commission was empowered to revise and codify the criminal and penal laws of the United States, the laws concerning the judiciary and practice of the courts of the United States, and, finally, all the laws of the United States of a general and permanent nature, respectively.

Four separate editions of the commission's revision presented in 1906, 1908, 1909, 1910, and 1914 were not adopted by Congress.

REVISION AND CODIFICATION, 1919-1924

Revisers and codifiers: (1) Dr. William L. Burdick, Kansas; (2) Hon. John L. Lott, Ohio; (3) G. K. Richardson, Massachusetts; (4) J. Wallace Bryan, Maryland; (5) M. J. Keys, New York; (6) Hon. Clinton O. Bunn, Oklahoma; (7) Prof. Joseph H. Beale, Massachusetts; and (8) Prof. Austin W. Scott, Massachusetts.

These codifiers prepared a codification of all general and permanent laws of the United States.

Result: Passage by House of H. R. 9389, Sixty-sixth Congress; passage by House of H. R. 19, Sixty-seventh Congress; and passage by House of H. R. 12, Sixty-eighth Congress.

No action taken by the Senate on any of the above bills.

Salaries (contingent fund of House)	$13,779.96
Printing and binding	35,235.97
Total	49,015.93

ADOPTION OF UNITED STATES CODE AND SYSTEM OF CUMULATIVE CODIFICATION, 1925-1931

Compilers and employees: (1) West Publishing Co., Minnesota, and (2) Edward Thompson Co., New York (11 lawyer experts, 40 clerical assistants).

Work began in July, 1925; United States Code adopted June 30, 1926 (44 Stat. L., pt. 1). Cumulative codification system adopted May 29, 1928; March 2, 1929 (U. S. C. sup. title 1, c. 3).

Salaries and expenses for code (two companies) (Senate contingent fund)	$10,000.00
Code index, Public Act 222, Sixty-ninth Congress	5,000.00
Clerical expenses (House contingent fund)	1,050.00
U. S. C., Sup. II, Public Act 1034, Seventieth Congress	5,000.00
U. S. C., Sup. III, Public Act 78, Seventy-first Congress	5,000.00
Printing (U. S. Code)	38,258.20
Total	64,308.20

Compilers: (1) Harry A. Hegarty, (2) Edwin A. Mooers, and (3) Howard Boyd.

Result: First complete code of laws for the District of Columbia (containing all British and Maryland laws in force in District). Compilers worked four years (August, 1926–August, 1930).

Salaries: Public Act 222, Sixty-ninth Congress; Public Act 631, Sixty-ninth Congress; Public Act 2, Seventieth Congress; Public Act 386, Seventieth Congress	$19,152
Index, District of Columbia Code, Public Act 1034, Seventieth Congress	5,848
Total	25,000

A former Washington newspaper writer, Mr. Lyle A. Brookover, who has taken interest in the work and history of the committee, and who has made researches and has a real grasp of the problems before the committee, has said:

TEN LAWS THAT GREW INTO MILLIONS

(By Lyle A. Brookover)

Eighteen thousand five hundred and seventy-nine proposed laws have been tossed into the hoppers of the Seventy-first Congress of the United States. They are in the form of Senate and House bills and joint resolutions of both bodies.

This assembly, it seems, would sustain our boast of Congress as the "greatest lawmaking body in the world." The mill grinds slowly, but too much legislation will come out.

Laws are at one time a great blessing and a costly plague of modern civilization. Thus the United States gains most of the blessings and suffers most the plagues.

In ancient days the activities of a great race of people were controlled by the Ten Commandments. These required approximately 132 words to set forth 10 fundamental rules of human conduct.

To-day, we find the general and permanent laws of this Republic published in a new codification which has 1,705 pages, fine print, devoted to actual statutes. The laws included were those in force at the opening of the Sixty-ninth Congress. By the end of that session the codification bill was passed. Passed also were new laws which filled 250 more pages of the published volume, as an appendix.

Parallel reference tables, an index, the Declaration of Independence, the Constitution, and other organic laws of the Nation boost the total number of pages to 2,453. The book weighs 10½ pounds.

The grand total of words used is 5,212,416. Twenty-two and one fourth tons of type metal were used in publication by the Government Printing Office.

Twenty-eight thousand two hundred and fifty copies were printed and widely distributed. Outside official circles, they were sold for $4 per copy, probably the greatest value, from a tonnage standpoint, in all the history of book selling.

Commercial law publishers divided the 50 titles, ranging alphabetically, perhaps significantly, from "Agriculture " to " War," into pocket-size volumes, with annotations.

In a foreword to these small volumes, former United States Senator George Wharton Pepper points out, " Mahomet need no longer seek the mountain. The mountain has distributed itself into foothills and all of them have come to him."

The hefty volume of codified law is available as the tangible result of over 10 years' labor by the Revision of the Laws Committee of the House of Representatives. It was condensed from a previous mass of some 25 volumes. They were one good reason why " lawyers grow gray."

Human nature has come unchanged through 3,000 years. Life is more complicated now, it is admitted. The intricacies of government, commerce, and social relations of 120,000,000 Americans offer little comparison to the daily lives of the races of that bygone day.

Yet there are the same human impulses to " worship idols," to " break the Sabbath Day," to " lie, steal, covet, kill, commit adultery, dishonor parents," and " ignore Divinity."

Scarcely recognizable in their present form, these same 10 laws still stand. So-called " civilization " has required an estimated addition of 2,400,000 more laws by Federal, State, and city governments of this Nation.

And this Solonic trinity tosses out some 40,000 more new laws each year, with an attitude approaching abandon.

Governing us with laws as few, as to the point as the tablets handed down at Mount Sinai is an ideal hardly to be realized. Steps are being taken toward it by a group, feeble in its minority.

In 1874 the Revised Statutes of the United States became law. This compilation was thought to be comprehensive revision of all Federal laws then on record and in force.

Then followed a half century in which every member of every legislative body in the country seems to have given ear to the slightest whim of his constituency. During this period the organized minorities burst into flower, each seeking, through devious channels, the lawmaker's favor. Strange measures, of vital interest to a favored few, appeared as laws which never passed to govern all.

In 1926 the United States Code was adopted by Congress. Included within its covers were an estimated 5,000 separate enactments of general and permanent law, over 12,000 sections. Fifty thousand acts and joint resolutions have received the presidential pen since George Washington signed the first act of Congress, June 1, 1789.

The first act signed by President Washington was one regulating the time and manner of administering oaths as required by the sixth article to the Constitution, to Members of the Senate and House, members of the several State legislatures, and executive officers of the Federal Government and of the States. It was the first legislation of the Congress of the United States.

The new code did not eliminate or revise. It simply gathered all the laws of the land, overlapping, unnecessary, ridiculous, obsolete ones included, under distinct classifications and headings preparatory to revision. An advantage already gained is that the laws can at least be found.

Chairman Roy G. Fitzgerald, of the revision committee, who introduced the bill enacting the Code, declared that it could be rewritten more clearly with one-half the words used.

Perhaps if it were written in one-tenth or one-twentieth its cluttering legal phrases a mere human being might gain some idea of what he must and must not do by law. "Ignorantia legis neminem excusat."

It is not strange that lawyers and judges find it necessary to set the ether waves on end with torrents of legal interpretation before a final verdict can be arrived at by juries.

The law must be defined. Supreme Court Justice Holmes says "the history of what the law has been is necessary to the knowledge of what the law is."

The great minds of England have differed in the definition. Coke, great English jurist, declared "law is the perfection of reason," while Tennyson saw it as "a codeless myriad of precedent."

Imagine opposing lawyers explaining this act, which is a part of the newly published code:

"No person, firm, or corporation, or officer, agent, or employee thereof shall forge, counterfeit, simulate, or falsely represent, or shall without proper authority use, fail to use, or detach, or shall knowingly or wrongfully alter, deface, or destroy, or fail to deface or destroy, any of the marks, stamps, tags, labels, or other identification devices provided for in sections 71 to 94, inclusive, of this title, or in and as directed by the rules and regulations prescribed hereunder by the Secretary of Agriculture, on any carcasses, parts of carcasses, or the food product or containers thereof, subject to the provisions of such sections or any certificate in relation thereto, authorized or required by such sections or by the said rules and regulations of the Secretary of Agriculture."

FEDERAL DEPARTMENTS SHARE THE WORK OF REVISION

Each of the 10 Federal Government departments has been invited to study the code for sections of departmental interest, which might be rewritten or repealed. Each was furnished, as a beginning, with comments upon 200 or more sections that appeared at first glance to be useless and out of date.

The law establishing the code declared that it can be proven wrong in only one way, by going back of it to the original law, and showing inconsistency.

Later, an act was passed to put new-born laws into supplemental volumes, one to be issued at the end of each congressional session. As additional supplements are issued, preceding ones are thrown away. Thus one code book and one supplement will contain all laws of general and permanent effect at all times.

The same act authorized new editions of the code not oftener than every five years.

The revision committee then set to work on the District of Columbia Code. Research in assembling the District laws was infinitely harder than preparing the Federal Code.

The District of Columbia as created by the First Congress consisted of a portion of Virginia and a portion of Maryland. It is, of course, governed by Congress, which has provided that the common law; all British statutes in force in Maryland on February 27, 1801; the principles of equity and admiralty; and all general acts of Congress that are of application to the District, shall control.

This means that—

The maxims and principles of equity as developed in the court of chancery;

The common law as it existed in 1776;

And all the laws of the legislature, not only of the State of Maryland, from 1776 to 1800, but the laws of colonial Maryland government up to the year 1800, together with the acts of Congress that apply, comprise the great body of law in the District.

In other words, the State courts of Maryland and Virginia administer their own State laws and the Federal courts the Federal laws, but all of those laws are under the jurisdiction of the courts here.

The confusion and uncertainty arising under these conditions is obvious and deplorable.

Is it any wonder that 15 previous attempts at codification of the District laws have fallen a bit short of their mark?

Workers on the District Code found many examples of amusing and antiquated legislation.

There is in force a British statute passed in the fourth year of the reign of King George II (1731) providing that whosoever offends against the law requiring all pleadings in the courts to be "in the English tongue and language only, and not in Latin or French, or any other tongue or language whatsoever, and in words at length, and not abbreviated shall for every such offense forfeit and pay $133.33 to any person who shall sue for the same."

—— 23 ——

Imagine the trouble that might be caused by anyone who should "try and collect" in view of the thousands of times Latin phrases are used in court papers.

Another law (shades of Sir William Blackstone) dug up from the past reads as though patterned after the Holy Scriptures; passed during the ninth year of the reign of Henry III (1225—over 700 years ago); and in the style of that day, nearly a century before Chaucer, it relates to dower and the right of quarantine of widows as follows:

"* * * and she shall tarry in the chief house of her husband by 40 days after the death of her husband, within which days her dower shall be assigned her (if it were not assigned her before) or that the house be a castle; * * * and for her dower shall be assigned unto her the third part of all the lands of her husband, which were his during coverture, except she were endowed of less at the church door."

Whoever wins more than $26.67 in a gambling game, being convicted, shall forfeit five times the value of his winnings. At least, an act passed in the ninth year of Queen Anne's reign back in 1710 so recites.

Authority for this code of general and permanent laws in force in the District of Columbia was granted by Congress in 1929. It is about to come from the press with the laws carefully classified, titled, and indexed.

"If present ideas are realized," says Chairman Fitzgerald, "after the repeal of obsolete statutes and the harmonizing of discordant features by perfecting amendments, the whole body of the code may be revised and the law stated in simple, precise language in an effort to approach an ideal of legislative expression."

The next vigorous step was in February this year, when the Revision of the Laws Committee introduced a bill which seeks to repeal 98 sections of the Federal Code. These sections are laws affecting the Departments of War, Navy, and the Interior, and their repeal was recommended by these departments.

If this bill passes, these laws would be indicated as repealed in the next supplement. With the next edition of the complete code they would be dropped permanently.

These three departments will continue their work of recommending laws for rewriting or repeal. The reports of preliminary work of the other seven departments are eagerly awaited by the House committee. It is hoped that hundreds of "deadwood" laws may be removed in this manner.

Hundreds of statutes set forth in the code have been virtually repealed by later enactments, but they are still there. Some 40 have been declared invalid by the United States Supreme Court, therefore are laws no longer. They are still there. Thousands have been nullified by implication or because of inconsistency.

LAW REVISION NOT A NEW SUBJECT

The Revision of the Laws Committee may well take new courage in its efforts through studying the work of the first such committee recorded in history's pages—that established in 528 A. D. by the Roman Emperor Justinian.

In the first year of his reign Justinian appointed Tribonian, a statesman of his court, to establish a code of Roman law. With 16 chosen associates Tribonian set to work.

They found the law which had been accumulating for 20 centuries comprised in 2,000 books, or, stated according to the Roman method of computation, in 3,000,000 sentences.

It is probable that this matter, if printed in law volumes such as are now used, would fill from 300 to 500 volumes.

In 534 A. D., the codification being completed, the emperor decreed that no resort should be had to the earlier writings, nor any comparison be made with them. Commentators were forbidden to disfigure the new with explanations, and lawyers were forbidden to cite the old. The imperial authority was sufficient to sink into oblivion nearly all the previously existing sources of law, but the new statutes which the emperor himself found it necessary to establish in order to explain, complete, and amend the law rapidly accumulated throughout his long reign.

And so it goes today. The worthy Representatives who have pored over the laws for years in their work on the revision committee offer new laws to Congress faster than old ones are being repealed.

Since the Seventy-first Congress convened in special session a year ago, Chairman Fitzgerald has submitted 163 measures for the consideration of his fellow-legislators. His 12 associates on the committee have asked for passage of a total of 262 bills, a grand total of 445. Representative Lamar Jeffers deserves special mention. He has only asked for passage of six bills.

Chairman Fitzgerald has seen fit to serve his Ohio constituency throughout four terms by vigorous lawmaking efforts which have gained for him a reputation as one of the leading law "makers" in the lower House. In justice to him it may be said that of his general bills many have been soundly based on public benefit, such as the codification bill, workmen's compensation, war veteran relief, and similar subjects.

Also, his district being the site of the national military home, Wright Field, and other Federal institutions brings an avalanche of requests to his office for private bills and special legislation.

We have dealt mostly thus far with general and permanent legislation. Congress also indulges its love for lawmaking in private bills for individual pensions, correcting military records, compensation for injuries, construction of bridges in congressional districts, and such like.

Halfway between private and general laws are those dealing with national parks and reservations and with Federal affairs of the District of Columbia, of national but not individual interest.

Then there are the appropriation acts providing funds to run the Government. About 15 of these each Congress cover some 300 pages of the statutes published after the sessions.

The tariff bills are not to be overlooked. The one just born of great travail holds great possibilities for argument and legal interpretation in its 535 pages.

There are so many laws and so many agencies of enforcement that mental chaos and eventual insanity surely would be the portion of any well-intentioned citizen who tried to obey them all.

Lack of knowledge of existing law coupled with frightful carelessness on the part of lawmakers has given rise to absurdities such as these:

In 1893 Congress passed an act which was signed by the President authorizing the sale of the old Chicago post office to the "lowest and best bidder." This slip was later discovered and corrected.

One Senator tried to amend the Ohio code relating to public railroad crossings of highways. His bill cited the section of Ohio rather than Federal law.

The House passed a bill proposing to amend sections of the Compiled Statutes of the United States—a private compilation! The Senate was about to pass this measure when it was discovered and a concurrent resolution of the House instructed the Clerk to strike out the language of the engrossed bill.

Several times Congress has passed an act " proposing " to amend an earlier law.

It has even attempted to amend an act that had not been enacted.

Congress once tried to amend a law which had been repealed seven years before. Comparison has been made of this futile gesture to " trying to hang a picture on a wall that had been torn down."

STATES AND CITIES FOLLOW SUIT

State and city governments are awakening to the menace of too much legislation. They are following the Federal lead in attempting to codify and clarify their laws.

A former Governor of Virginia suggested that all State legislatures be convened in special session for the express purpose of repealing all bad laws. His suggestion met with instant and favorable editorial comment from the press of the entire country.

The Ohio Legislature has an active committee at work on its code, with the result that bills were passed in 1927 and 1929 repealing 1,054 old and superseded statutes. Still more repeals will be sought in 1931.

New Hampshire's Legislature distinguished itself at its 1930 session by adjourning without enacting a single law. The New Jersey Legislature met, repealed scores of laws, and " adjourned."

The city of Cedar Rapids, Iowa, has just completed codification of its ordinances. They are grouped in a volume, said to be both thorough and simple, in 94 chapters, under 18 titles. The work was regarded there as " one of the first steps toward good municipal housekeeping."

On every hand the old idea that a legislator is elected for the one purpose of getting more laws, is becoming passe. The highest needs of any constituency may be best served by caution in lawmaking, rather than speed. The majority has no lobby other than the voice of the people. That voice should be heard in such volume as to drown the cries of vicious minorities for special privilege.

Improvement of the phrasing of legal measures is a subject on which every legislator might render magnificent service. Why should laws for the masses be made so ponderous that they must be revised, rewritten, amended, interpreted, appealed, explained, and fought over before one single criminal be lodged in his cell?

The present legal system, unfortunately, spends so much time in fighting civil cases where property rights are involved, and prohibition cases which deal with a moral issue, that criminals have little fear of the law ever getting around to their affairs.

As the tangle of legislation knots more closely about us, we discover its boon companions—difficulty of enforcement and apathy toward crime.

More laws—less obedience. The criminally inclined (and they are usually " smart " people) know that the law which should punish them, instead of going straight to the point, has devious wordings and loopholes which will ensnare judge and jury, who listen to legislative counsel of both the individual and the State in a web of stupefying interpretation and high-sounding phrases.

A law is broken, and the criminal relies on the very law itself to set him free.

A prisoner in court is one of two things—guilty or innocent. That fact is lost sight of entirely as the great pastime of legal jousting goes on. Unlike our other sports this game has no closed season. Its effect can be only harmful to the cause of justice and to the good of all.

Swift punishment for crime is relegated to the limbo of forgotten things. The public mind changes in tempo accordingly.

The newspapers carry the story of an awful crime. Human passions are aroused, momentarily, by pity for the victim and a desire for punishment of the criminal. But as the courts wrangle day after day over points of law, it follows naturally that we humans, who become bored so easily, yawn and say, " Well, let's go to the movies," or " Turn on the radio."

Untold masses of clerks and armies of struggling lawyers rise up to call the Congress blessed, for without its generosity of laws,

No. 65——24

couched in entangling and bewildering phrases, they would have to seek new jobs.

One doubtful merit of this pyramid of legal verbosity is its beneficial effect upon the unemployment problem. Such compliment also might be paid to an earthquake or a hurricane which sets men to work in reconstruction.

We can not sidestep the rule of " vis major," nor evade th eacts of Providence, but we can limit the acts of Congress.

How can we correct this evil? Set the whole united force of public opinion, and there is no greater force, to the task of limiting new laws until enforcement catches up with what we now have; weed out, condense, and rewrite the old ones until they are in form and number such as may be understood and obeyed by all; put our belief anew in the majority principle and see that a safe majority is demanding each new law.

The congressional committee and other agencies pioneering in the work of simplifying the law should have the support of the entire membership of every legislative body in the land. They should be assisted by the bench and bar, the press, and every citizen. Huge sums of money, sinister influences, are working toward the other extreme. In this free country laws should not be for sale.

The Hon. James A. Reed, himself an able lawyer and a peerless cross-examiner, declared just before retiring from the United States Senate in 1929 that " we have enough laws now to govern us for the next 10,000 years." Anyone who gives cursory thought to this problem will agree that a " lawmaker's holiday " is much to be desired.

Ten thousand years seem a long time. It would be " some holiday." But perhaps he's right.

It may be of interest to call attention to some of the difficulties encountered in connection with the new code for the District of Columbia. Therefore, I present some correspondence had with a member of the District bar, Harry S. Barger, Esq., relative to criticism of the code:

WASHINGTON, D. C., August 21, 1930.

Hon. ROY G. FITZGERALD,
    Chairman Committee on Revision of the Laws,
        House of Representatives, Washington, D. C.

Subject: The New Code of the District of Columbia.

DEAR SIR: You have been good enough to solicit suggestions and indications of errors in connection with the labors of your committee in the captioned matter, and the undersigned takes the liberty of submitting the following:

By the act of May 29, 1928, New Code, title 1, section 1, page 1, Congress directed the preparation under the supervision of your committee, of a " consolidation and codification of the laws * * * relating to or in force in the District of Columbia," and not a revision of those laws. It very clearly appears from an examination of the results of the labors of your committee that there has been attempted a complete revision of the laws, and it equally apparent that the attempt and the result are far beyond the authority conferred by Congress.

Section 1 of the 1901 code provides that " the common law, all British statutes in force in Maryland on the 21st day of February, 1801," etc., should remain in force in the District of Columbia, except as they may be inconsistent with or replaced by some provision of that code. Chapter 60, sections 1639 et sequence, of the 1901 code provides that " all acts and parts of acts of the General Assembly of the State of Maryland general and permanent in their nature," etc., are repealed, with certain enumerated exceptions. It is noted (1) that the new code omits the clause " All British statutes," etc., as contained in the 1901 code, and (2) so far as the writer has been able to find, the entire provisions of chapter 60 of the 1901 code have been deleted. Furthermore, numerous statutes of Maryland have been carried forward, notwithstanding they seem to be general and permanent in their character, and not within the exceptions contained in the chapter of the 1901 code relating to repeals.

Inquiry made of one of the members of the bar who assisted your committee in the preparation of the new code elicited the information that acts regarded as having been repealed or superseded have been omitted, as well as acts regarded as obsolete and inconsistent, and that where there was doubt whether a given act has been repealed or was obsolete or inconsistent it was included.

Certainly an attempt has been made at a revision rather than a " consolidation and codification " of the laws " relating to or in force in the District of Columbia," and it is respectfully suggested that, since the authority conferred by Congress has been so far exceeded, the new code can not be regarded as official or as a correct statement of the law " relating to or in force in the District of Columbia." Congress assuredly did not authorize a revision, and it is certain that Congress could not have authorized your committee or any person or persons working under its direction to make a revision, even if it had so desired. Revision must be the act of Congress the same as any other enactment.

Very truly yours,
                                        H. S. BARGER.

———

DAYTON, OHIO, October 6, 1930.

HARRY S. BARGER, Esq.,
    Lawyer, National Press Building, Washington, D. C.

DEAR MR. BARGER: Your letter of August 21, with reference to the new Code of the District of Columbia, has just come to my attention upon my return from Europe, where I went as an American delegate to the Interparliamentary Union conference.

CHAPTER V: 1926
PLAIN DEALER CITY ROOM

Presently the Congress adjourned and I was off to Cleveland and assignments in the '*PD*' city room. Among the first was one to cover a Mardi Gras parade which was glorified by the presence of a Ziegfeld Follies star, Luise Blackburn. Nearness to such glamor almost overwhelmed me; in the course of a brief interview, I felt myself falling in love. Perhaps fortunately for both of us, Broadway called her back quickly and our casual correspondence died on the vine.

Suddenly Cleveland was agog with the impending visit of Queen Marie of Romania who was touring the United States. The City Council got into a hassle over whether or not to wear morning coats, striped trousers and high hats to greet her. The Hollenden Hotel tenderly placed white satin on the commode seats in the royal suite. The Romanian Consul resigned in a huff over what he considered insult to Romanian-Americans of Cleveland (who were quite numerous) by not placing them on the reception committee.

The royal morning dawned: Queen Marie suddenly decided to go home because the King was ill. (He had been before she left, but the apparent real reason for her decision was constant wrangling over details with her companions on the Royal Train.) In her stead, Cleveland received Prince Nicholas, at 33 her youngest son, who arrived in black suit and derby hat, tired and seemingly bored, but still able to smile at a group of pretty Romanian-American girls. The offical committee went to the Union Station: the Prince's private car was switched to another track and arrived at the B&O station across town.

When order was restored and the Prince, tall, thin and weary, emerged from his bedroom to face us eager reporters, we stood in the royal presence until he was seated. "Who will have the first question?"he asked and added, "I think it should be the young lady," referring to the only woman in the gang, Harriett Parsons of the *PD*.

This was Harriett's big moment. Leaning forward, in a breathless voice she inquired, "How does it feel to be a prince?" We male rporters could have cheerfully wrung her neck.

Nicholas was at a loss for a moment: the question was hardly what he had expected. Casting a cool glance at her, and with his haughty face showing no warmth whatever, he replied, "Being a prince has its advantages and disadvantages." He finished the interview with a muted appeal for friendly relations between our two countries and an explanation that his mother, the Queen, was truly concerned over her husband's illness.

Later came genial Prince William of Sweden, loud-voiced, quick-mannered, with blue eyes and a distinguished face. He asked the press to "get comfortable" as his interview began. He was distinguished for many things and had hunted big game in Teddy Roosevelt's paths in Africa. He had been booked by Louis J. Alber, Cleveland impressario, to give 50 travel lectures in the United States: Prince William went home $50,000 richer from the tour. His reception at the Cleveland Museum of Natural History was brilliant. Afterward, his chauffeur couldn't be found. So, His Royal Highness hopped into a police car for the ride back to the Hotel Statler.

Marion Talley, the little girl from Kansas City who made a bombshell debut at the Metropolitan Opera House in New York, was next in the line of distinguished visitors I covered when she arrived in Cleveland on a concert tour. Arriving at her hotel suite, I found a small family group consisting of her mother, sister Florence, and the almost-diva aged only 20. It was an unusual setting for one who had achieved fame, suddenly or otherwise! Mama cooked Marion's meals, checked for 'ladders' in her hosiery, and watched protectively over her 'two baby girls.' I wrote that ". . . Marion doesn't smoke, drink, dance, use powder or rouge, doesn't like jazz music, society, isn't interested in men or fashionable clothes, and has no hobby except her music." Mother Talley told me later she liked my story the best of all that had been written about Marion. They were plentiful for she was something of a phenomenon for awhile until the public decided she wasn't a great singer after all. She ultimately gave up singing, made an unfortunate marriage (it was understood), and disappeared from public view.

Another vocalist I wrote about was Bessie Brown, tall and handsome blues singer who appeared in Palais d'Or, a colored cabaret. She nightly provided songs delightful to listen to, wrote intelligent and enjoyable poetry back stage between numbers, and, from her earnings, provided her daughter with a college education. My story and picture was the first such coverage of a colored entertainer in the history of the *PD* A friend and I went to hear Bessie often: she'd come to our table and read her latest verses. On Thanksgiving Day, she came to us with a beautiful cake she had baked especially for us.

Maude Adams, the memorable Peter Pan (but whom I had seen only once on the stage as the Portia in "Merchant of Venice.") came to town. I was called in by the 'Big Boss', Avery Hopwood, who confided that Maude was one woman who could excite him almost to a frenzy. He urged me to try my utmost to get a good story from her. I chased her all day, from one place to another, never quite finding her, until I learned she was stopping at the palacial mansion of Matthew Brush, electrical industry millionaire. I was detained at the door by a haughty butler who explained, "Miss Adams is seeing no one."

Naturally, I haunted the place until late evening, chased the limousine which emerged to the Union Station, and at last found the sleeping car where she was settled, the porter said, in a lower berth to New York. My proffer of folding money interested the porter in taking a note to the lady. He returned, alas, with the message that she was sorry, but was too tired to see me.

Returning to the city room, I composed a fanciful bit about the spirit of Peter Pan hovering over the Hotel Hollenden where Maude Adams had stayed many years before, and how the real Maude had tapped her feet to the dining room music the evening before while she dreamed of past glories. Mr. Hopwood was appeased, but disappointed.

About that time, the 'Lone Eagle' flew to Paris: when he was nearly there, almost the entire '*PD*' staff gathered around the wire service desks, waiting for news of his landing. Later, when he arrived at Cleveland on his triumphant tour, the city desk gave me a peremptory and exciting order, "Follow Lindberg!" I hired a taxi and kept pace with his movements through the day. At the banquet in Hotel Cleveland, he was cold and surly, having previously refused to receive the press. When he left to spend the night with his mentor and host in Paris (Myron T. Herrick, U.S. Ambassador to France now at his estate in Chagrin Valley), I ordered my driver to keep directly behind the Ambassador's limousine. A great crowd had gathered outside the hotel to see Lindberg: my driver apparently felt this was his one great chance for glory. He shot forward, blowing his horn, and parted the throng—by the mercy of God, killing no one in the process. Lining up with the official car, we roared out to the country, arriving at the brick mansion one minute behind Lindbergh. But, the iron gates were closing and police stood by with orders to admit no one. The mansion was ablaze with lights and I could hear music playing—but that was all.

Three other incidents stand out in this period of city room activity. The ore boats that ply Lake Erie bringing iron ore to the steel mills of Cleveland give young men a chance for vacation jobs on the crew. One young man, upon arriving in port, invited his girl friend aboard to see the ship. She fell overboard and was drowned. I was assigned to visit her home to get the details and her picture. Her family had not yet heard of the tragedy when I arrived.

Her sister was reluctantly giving me information and the picture when her brother, a big hulk of a man, came in. When he learned of my errand, he almost literally threw me out. Thus, I returned to the city room empty-handed.

A mystery had arisen about the rumored departure of one Mr. Victor, head of the huge May Company department store. I was sent to interview him and find out 'what was cooking.' I waited from mid-afternoon to closing time in his busy outer office. Finally, the great man came out: upon my identifying myself, he apologized for keeping me waiting! He invited me into his luxurious private office, seated me and completely shattered the mystery. He said he was tired and going to the Alps in Switzerland where he "could pick edelweiss and lie in the sun and listen to the tinkle of the sheep bells."

I led off that story with this quote and it made the front page. This was a triumph any young reporter will understand.

The *Plain Dealer's* star reporter, the late Roelif Loveland, was my best friend and one I shall never forget. He and his dear wife joined my friend Gene Perry and me to attend the glamorous Cleveland Arts Ball one evening. We enjoyed the antics of the mob of gaily costumed and non-costumed (this was before nudity became so casual) merrymakers until nearly dawn. On our way home for a night-cap, Lovey declared, "I feel so good, I'd like to give everyone $500."

When the World Series in baseball was on, I was asked to get a crowd reaction story at the huge score board in Public Square. Enroute, another reporter, Bob Gage, lured me into his car as he was going out into the country for a story. I had 'lots of time.' We drove and drove and finally got lost. About the time the ball game was over, I saw a sign which said "20 miles to Cleveland." Needless to say, I was red-faced when the city editor asked me for my 'crowd reaction' story.

Back to Washington for a brief session of Congress and a reporters' trip to Philadelphia with Secretary of Commerce Herbert Hoover who was to speak at the launching of the Lurline *S.S.Malolo* at the Cramp shipyards. We traveled in a special car: upon arrival, we were met by a distinguished group and rushed through the city at 60 miles an hour with a large motorcycle escort. Ever since, I've felt that was the best way to get through traffic. I always like to see motorcycles leading the way.

Later, when Hoover was President, I enjoyed meeting him and Mrs. Hoover at the 50th Anniversary Dinner of the American Red Cross in 1931. On another occasion, I accompanied a large delegation of Clevelanders to the White House to invite Mr. Hoover to some Cleveland occasion. Photographs of the group were taken on the South Lawn. When the aides shouted, "Make way for the President," I was caught with nowhere to make way except by stepping backward into a petunia bed. Thus awkwardly poised, I was astonished when the President came abreast on that sultry day, stopped to mop his brow and said, "It certainly got hotter by degrees today!" This was especially so since these exact words were my father's favorite comment on a hot summer day.

When the First Lady, Mrs. Lou Hoover, appeared as the honor guest at the dedication ceremony of Phoebe Hearst School in northwest Washington, an attractive group of schoolgirls approached and presented her with a huge bouquet of American Beauty roses. She took them in her arms, **stems up**, and held them that way until the ceremony was over. She was undoubtedly a splendid woman, robust in stature, but somewhat retiring in manner, and this *faux pas* seemed characteristic of her.

****

The only other similar incident I recall was when Clare Booth Luce arrived in Trenton many years later to speak at a United Service to China Rally. Upon descending from the Air Force plane, she was presented with a large branch of orchids by her Trenton hosts. As she walked to a waiting limouusine, she trailed the orchids in the dust—whether in disgust, disdain for the giver, or sheer carelessness, I shall never know. Later, she snubbed the Air Force and flew back to Washington with Admiral Mark Mitscher in a Navy plane.

****

Again I returned to Cleveland and covered the state American Legion convention in Elyria. A kind hotel manager offered me his desk to get some sleep while the exhuberant veterans howled through the night outside. Soon after, I launched on state-wide coverage of the campaign of Atlee Pomerene as Democratic candidate for return to the U.S. Senate. I accompanied the candidate and his gracious wife for six weeks, traveling in a chauffeurred Cadillac limousine loaned by one of Pomerene's ardent admirers. That car probably lost the candidate quite a few votes in the poorer rural districts. We visited every county seat, and some villages between. Mrs. Pomerene won many friends by her simplicity and gracious manner. In press interviews she said, "My husband is my hobby."

Ed Gableman of the *Cincinnati Enquirer* joined our party for the final days. He and I had plenty of advice to offer the Senator at private sessions in our hotel rooms late at night. His frequent saying was that "no man was ever defeated by a speech he didn't make." For this reason, he'd smilingly decline some of our bravura suggestions.

Prior to a large rally in Toledo, Ohio, two prominent Democratic Party women joined the party to try to win some of the women's votes. They were Mrs. Izetta Jewel Brown of West Virginia and Mrs. Eleanor Bailey Johnson of my hometown of Zanesville. Before the meetings, Mr. Pomerene would give Ed and me the highlights of his speech and we would file an advance story. On this one occasion, we filed and adjourned to the Hotel Secor: by this time we knew, short of a riot, the story would be unchanged.

While thus pleasantly engaged, it developed that each of us wanted to go to Cleveland that night, not wanting to wait for the limousine trip the next day. Ed was short of cash but assumed I had plenty as we were both on generous expense accounts. I thought he had money so was not concerned about my flat wallet. As we compared notes, we were dismayed. Just as we emerged from the bar, the two lady Democrats descended the broad staircase to the lobby, glamorous in orchids, evening gowns and jewels.

Noting our dejected looks, they inquired as to the cause. When we explained, both purses flew open simultaneously and our troubles were over. This memory was good for many laughs in after years.

CHAPTER VI: 1928
FREELANCING

Mr. Pomerene was defeated and shortly after I left the *Plain Dealer* to free lance in writing and public relations. The fact that I was involved in a heavy romance at this time possibly turned my thoughts to poetry, with this result:

Life-Tides
By Gene Lisle

To the still-water shoals I was carried
By the tides of life, running free:
I was drifting, though time never tarried,
'Til love caught you and brought you to me.
Since that fair day we first smiled together,
When our heart strings vibrated in tune,
I've sailed always through sunshiny weather,
Darkness changed to the white light of noon.
Through the fog-banks of doubt that beset me,
Your bright spirit sends rescuing beams;
Shore nor sea will not let you forget me,
Thoughts of you bring sweet peace to my dreams.
Let us wish that the tides of affection,
Might continue for always to flow;
While your eyes in their starry reflection,
Speak the love which we already know.

One frosty morning, as I strolled on the roof of Quad Hall, the bachelor residence where I lived, I looked across the city to the graceful Terminal Tower. As if guided by unseen hands, I suddenly rushed down the stairs to my typewriter and composed, in an hour or so, a poem, "Tower Moods," which was published in several places. I shall take the liberty to quote:

Dost laugh at man who builded you,
Sky-piercing stone and steel?
O'er the great city, stretched beneath,
Dost sense of conquest feel?
Rich jeweled crown of industry,
That holds the present stage,
Somehow I know that, looking down
Your heart holds youth and age.
In crystal air you proudly hold,
That queenly head on high;
Disdaining modern man's applause,
To higher gods you cry.
Traditions old, researches new;
To each you suavely bow;
Grey-veiled in smoke or Erie's fog—
Oh, I could love you now!
In bitter storm and slashing gale,
Staunch, fearless, hid from sight;
To know you're there gives mortals strength,
To battle through the night.
A stately link 'twixt earth and heaven,
Calm rule your fev'rish world;
To mark your very topmost reach,
Red, white and blue unfurled.
In early morn, at dusty eve,
Thou ever-present tower,
The sight of you can lift me up,
Make rich each passing hour.

I wrote some other bits, and several articles for trade publications (particularly the Cleveland Trust Company monthly magazine) and handled press relations for a variety of clients: a flower show, a dog show, a road show of highway builders' machinery, and a radio show. Cleveland had a fine new public auditorium which was excellent for such events.

The radio show came soon after Gertrude 'Trudy' Ederle had conquered the English Channel: we got the bright idea to bring her to Cleveland as the drawing card for the show. She came, ungainly, unhappy—like a fish out of water. She could not meet the public graciously; she could not broadcast well; she was not glamourous in face nor figure nor dress. **BUT,** she could swim the English Channel which no woman had been able to do before.

Red Grange, the Illini 'galloping ghost' of football fame, was appearing in an exhibition game the weekend before Trudy was there: his public relations men and Trudy's (with my help) dreamed up a perfect feature story. We would get the two celebrities together and suggest the beginning of a romance. Well, it was tough going, for both flacks were concerned over which star would get the most benefit from the publicity. We got Trudy out to the football game; but, Red Grange's mentor kept him away from her throughout the afternoon. Thus, a great story died!

Next came a livestock show at the Cleveland stockyards. As a feature to offset the dreariness of fat steers, I dreamed up a dairymaid contest, **NEVER** guessing what a whirlwind I was creating! Who would think that, in metropolitan Cleveland, there would be literally hundreds of girls who could, and would, milk a cow in public for a big cash prize? The ethnic groups from Middle Europe who are very populous in Cleveland furnished many contestants, striking in their national costumes. This produced a keen rivalry for each knew exactly what she was doing! The gimmick was good for many columns of publicity and dozens of pictures.

In the midst of this uproar, word came from home in Zanesville that my father had broken his leg and was in serious condition. I raced down to visit him at the hospital. As I dashed back the next morning (I was scheduled to speak about the livestock show before the Cleveland Chamber of Commerce), my car struck some loose gravel and landed upside down in a ditch. Somehow, I caught a train and managed to arrive in Cleveland in time to make my speech—only to be told that my father had passed away. I managed the speech and, with minutes to spare, caught a train back home for the funeral.

CHAPTER VII: 1928
THE WILLIS CAMPAIGN

Surviving that holocaust with no serious damage, I was snooping around in New York when a telegram came from Charlie Jones, assistant to Senator Frank B. Willis of Ohio, whom I knew well. He wanted me to come out at once to Columbus, Ohio to handle publicity for the Senator's campaign for the Republican nomination for President. He wasn't exactly in the Presidential race as yet, but he was campaigning for Ohio's delegates to the Republican national convention in an effort to stop the snow-balling campaign of Herbert Hoover. For several weeks, we put out releases extolling the Willis record and attacking Hoover's, with uncertain results.

On March 30th, Senator Willis came from Washington to give an important address, his homecoming to the town of Delaware (seat of Ohio Wesleyan University) where he lived. I had prepared some notes for his speech and we went over them together. He finished the draft: copies were mimeographed to hand to the press in late afternoon. When the reporters came in, all were planning to go hear the speech. Since it was my birthday and they had their advance copies, I was preparing to celebrate by attending "George White's Scandals," then playing a one-night stand at a local theater. When I told the gang I was not going to Delaware, they simply picked me up and carried me out to one of their cars and started off.

There was a huge dinner for the Senator, followed by a big parade with red fires marking the route to the college auditorium where the meeting was scheduled. I took my place in one of the front rows where the Senator smiled down at me when he walked on stage. There were the usual introductions, high school and college music groups and a men's chorus which sang, "The End of a Perfect Day." Moments before Willis was to be introduced, I noticed a change come over his face. He rose and walked into the wings where, minutes later, he breathed his last. I reached his side in time to hear the final fluttering of life ebbing from his body.

In the ensuing pandemonium, the audience was dismissed. Charlie Jones and I retired to our hotel to plan our next moves. Charlie was shocked almost beyond bearing, for he'd served the Senator long and faithfully: naturally, he felt a great sense of personal loss. There was no one there who had authority to act. To Charlie fell the sad task of notifying Willis' wife and daughter back in Washington. I had many problems with the press and long distance calls to make.

Late that night, we found ourselves at the center of a violent controversy between the two leading undertakers of the town over who could claim the 'distinguished remains.' Mrs. Willis had been too shocked to discuss any details so Charlie had no help in deciding the matter. The debate waxed hot: many claims to preference were advanced by each disputant, punctuated by unpleasant attacks on each other. finally, from the depths of his agony and despair, Charlie cried, "Why don't you two flip a coin if you can't settle this quarrel any other way?" A nickle was tossed: the matter was settled.

The funeral was to be held in the college chapel with its very limited seating capacity: I think about 1200 seats. As all politicos are ardent in their attendance at political funerals— to see and be seen—it was certain that thousands of people would want to attend. A seating plan was arranged: with the help of some young people, tickets were numbered and readied for distribution. There were nearly 100 each of reporters and photographers whom I had to look after. The tickets for the other attendees were in my care also.

Early in the day, the Congressional committee arrived from Washington. Then, the governor of Ohio and his retinue claimed their seats, and so on through the hours. With a long line of persons waiting hopefully, I gave out what I thought were the last of the tickets, and began saying, "Sorry, but there are no more seats." We had arranged an overflow room where the services could be heard.

I had just turned one more claimant away when the leading Republican from my hometown, Mr. Frank Ransbottom, a pottery millionaire whom I had viewed with awe as a youth, came up and greeted me warmly. He asked for two seats with the assurance that I certainly couldn't turn him down. I fished in an inner coat pocket where, to my surprise, I found the last two. My reputation was enhanced at once with that one Republican!

No sooner had the echoes of the Willis tragedy died away when a call came from—**DEMOCRATIC** state headquarters. "Why don't you come

40

over and help us defeat Hoover?" The question was apt, for I was out of work: I accepted, with no feelings of guilt nor improper conduct. I had no commitment to either party, except to do what I was being paid for. I went to work at once and soon was immersed in another aspect of the 1928 elections—to nominate and elect Governor Al Smith of New York.

It was continually mentioned in our offices that Mr. Hoover had let his name be used as a Democratic candidate for President in some states, notably Michigan. It was decided to send me to Lansing, the Michigan State capital, to see what I could find out. I scouted around there and found the printing company which had published the state ballots in 1920. An appeal to the head of the firm was rebuffed quite coldly, so I waited and watched until that gentleman went out to lunch. I hurried in and found an agreeable young employee and asked him if he could find a copy of the 1920 ballots in the files. A short search produced what I wanted. I resisted hugging him, walking out with an enthusiastic "Thank you! Thank you very much!"

Here in cold type was the name 'Herbert Hoover' leading the list of DEMOCRATIC candidates on the state primary ballot for President in 1920! I could hardly wait to get back to Columbus. I was promptly dispatched to campaign headquarters in New York where James Raskob and James J. Hoey were advised of my coming with my precious message. I turned the ballot over to Mr. Hoey who was cordial and expressed his thanks. I then returned to Ohio. Imagine our surprise when national headquarters never sprang the surprise on Mr. Hoover! To this day, I don't know why. Bill Donaldson, House Press Gallery superintendent who, upon hearing this story later, ever afterward called me 'Raskob' instead of my own name.

****

The late Senator Willis had most kindly assisted me previously in getting an Army Reserve commission. I had been called to active duty in 1928 as a Second Lieutenant at the first combined air-ground maneuvers ever held by armed forces of the United States. The Red army and air fleet was based at Columbus airport: the Blue army and air, at Wright-Patterson air field in Dayton. I flew in some of the maneuvers and, in general, learned a lot and had quite a time. The fact that, among dozens of officers present, I was the only one wearing a black suit and black felt hat made me outstanding—almost too much so! On a dull night, when the top G-2 was away from his desk, I wrote a realistic battle release which delighted the reporters and almost lost me my commission!!

****

That year, for the first time, I attended the Kentucky Derby and watched the great victory of Reigh Count, owned by Mrs. J.D. Hertz and ridden by jockey C. Lang. After the races, my friends and I went on to Lexington, staying overnight at a fraternity house where they were holding a ball of some kind. One brother stood on his head on the lawn until they finally decided to go out and pull him down.

I've enjoyed watching the Virginia Gold Cup steeplechase at Warrenton for many years. Another annual sports event which I have always followed is the Army-Navy football game at Philadelphia and elsewhere.

****

At the Cleveland Air Races in 1929, I ran into an old pal, Johnny Winefordner, with whom I had double-dated in high school days. He was in the Army Air Corps as a fighter pilot stationed at Selfridge Field. His unit had flown in for the races. We had quite a reunion. When we parted, he to go back to Selfridge and I to go on to Chicago, he said, "Why don't you fly down with me to Zanesville next week-end?" I agreed that that was a wonderful idea. He left telling me to let him know where to pick me up for the journey.

One morning later, on the elevated going into town, I opened the *Chicago Tribune*: there on the front page was the story of the fatal crash of Johnny's plane at a celebration in South Dakota. I made the journey home in time to attend Johnny's funeral. The philosophy that has always sustained me at times like that is the beautiful saying that "Death is the birthday in eternity of a one-time pilgrim of earth."

My short public relations stint for the Road Show in Cleveland paid off quite handsomely when I got a telegram from the director of the American Road Builders' Association, Mr. Charles M. Upham, asking me to come back to Washington to take the position of director of publicity for their organization. My father had passed away recently: I gathered up my sister, arranged for Mother to come later, and embarked upon another chapter of life in the Nation's capital.

CHAPTER VIII:1930
THE ROAD BUILDERS

I had hardly settled down to the new job when an invitation came for us to participate in a National Highway Congress in Mexico. Our party of honorary delegates (about 30 in number) set forth in a special pullman car to St. Louis: then, we travelled on the "Sunshine Limited" to the border where our car was attached to a Mexican National Railways train to the capital city. We had stopped in San Antonio long enough for us to go uptown to a hotel to have a shower bath as the train had no such facilities.

We moved slowly across the hot Mexican desert to the industrialized city of Monterey, noted for the production of fine beer. Then, we climbed high into the mountains, stopping at San Luis Potosi where the station platforms were crowded with natives selling flowers, fruits, greasy legs of fried chicken, and bags of opals—for 60 cents American!

We were housed in an old Spanish hotel, the Mancera, where no one spoke English. The rooms were arranged in galleries around a large patio. I had a bedroom, small reception room crowded with furniture, and an impressive Spanish-tiled bathroom where the plumbing worked! Each morning I stood at my window to look across at the snow-clad volcano, Popocateptl, and breathed deeply of the stimulating mountain air. We were wakened by a concert of cocks crowing, in the heart of the city.

Convention sessions were held in the large Opera House which is slow-ly sinking a few inches each year. The city lies in the bed of an ancient volcano at an altitude of 8,000 feet. It is surrounded by mountains which rise to 14,000 feet on the road to Cuernavaca: the terrain is unstable. We

43

were handsomely entertained by government authorities, climaxing in a reception at Chapultepec Castle where we were greeted by President Pascual Ortiz Rubio. We were taken to the old capital of Puebla, the fascinating city of Oaxaca, the floating gardens of Xochimilco, and to the Pyramids of Teotihuacan where I climbed the Pyramid of the Sun with Gustav Pabst, son of the prominent Milwaukee brewing family.

Motoring through the mountains with many hairpin turns with dashing young Mexicans at the wheel provided us with many a thrill. We were guests at the national pastime, bull fighting, a number of fiestas, banquets, displays of horsemanship, dancing and fronton (jai-alai). One late night, as I hurried across the park to my hotel, I was confronted by two Chinamen carrying a coffin on top of their heads. Mexico certainly is colorful!

Time to go, and we entrained for Vera Cruz. As we circled down the mountain, we could see the railroad track in seven curves below us. At desert level, it was dusty and hot. Delicious sun-ripened bananas, pineapples and melons were brought aboard and served iced for our pleasure. At Vera Cruz, an army of urchins descended on our luggage. But, our greatest concern was to get quickly to a shower. We dined late on the public square outside our hotel, besieged by boys who shined our shoes while we ate, fire-swallowers who entertained us and newsboys who tried to sell us three-weeks old newspapers from the States.

We crossed to Havana on the Ward Line steamer "San Jacinto." Below decks, I came upon an extraordinary man, General Rafael de Nogales, a revolutionary leader and soldier of fortune. A sometimes general who apparently took part in all Latin American and other uprisings, he was traveling clandestinely, for he might not be permitted to enter Cuba if he were identified. He admitted liking the ladies and showed me the little alarm watch which he carried on all 'romantic missions', set to ring at the proper time for him to leave. In my library, I have Nogales' exciting book, *Memoirs of a Soldier of Fortune.*

Cuban hospitality all but exceeded that of Mexico. After a few days of sightseeing and entertainment, all of us readily agreed to come back the following year for the dedication of the new Capitol and the opening of the fine new 300-mile Carretara Central, the central highway from Pinar del Rio to Santiago de Cuba.

I went down a month early to write some stories, and was provided with a government car and chauffeur, guest cards to the Country Club, the Yacht Club and the Jockey Club. All doors were opened for me. I toured the new highway for its entire course, was shown through the new palace with a large diamond zero milestone in the foyer, and greeted by President Machado. Of him, the Cubans said, "All presidents raid the treasury, but Machado has also given us something for our money." They were justly proud of the beautiful capitol and the highway.

A large group arrived from the States for the ceremonials and the entertainment was magnificent in every detail, including centerpieces of red, white and blue flowers at every party honoring the Americans. I wrote and sold a number of travel articles upon my return to Washington.

****

The bonus Army had descended upon Washington when we got back. I spent several evenings at their encampment upon the Anacostia Flats, listening to and sympathizing with these veterans of World War One who felt their government was not recognizing their patriotism by denying them a bonus. Cabinet officers and prominent citizens moved quietly among the huts at times, for everyone had sympathy for them and the orderly conduct of their protest. There were no broken windows, burned buildings nor hurled obscenities such as we have witnessed since. They simply settled down to wait, under conditions of privation, until Congress saw fit to act.

There were revolutionaries among them: a fiery newspaper was rumored to be funded by Communist sources. The citizenry became increasingly alarmed by the invaders. President Hoover finally ordered Army Chief of Staff, General Douglas McArthur, to rout them from their camp and escort them to the city limits, meanwhile burning their pitiful huts and cabins so they couldn't come back. Colonel Dwight D. Eisenhower was one of the officers who carried out the President's orders. I still remember the red sky over Anacostia the night these veterans marched through Washington with the Army, politely but firmly, showing them 'the way to go home.'

****

The road shows were the largest industrial exhibits in the country at that time. I handled press relations for the annual exhibits in Atlantic City, Detroit, and St. Louis. I took care of all the newspaper and magazine writers, issued press releases covering the displays, convention sessions and other features, and published a daily convention newspaper which had to be under the delegates' hotel doors before they rose in the mornings.

In Atlantic City, I had to dash to Philadelphia at the end of a harried day, make up the newspaper and wait for it to be published so I could take it back. The Philadelphia city engineer provided a car and chauffeur to rush me, with my burden, back to the shore. The first morning, the limousine broke down just before dawn on the desolate marshes, miles from anywhere.

One of my sidelines was to greet the bootleggers in every city who appeared to regard the press office as the best 'point of contact' with the convention. I gave the press a dinner at each city: in Atlantic City, they reciprocated with a dinner for me where I mixed baked clams and gin in quantities which had a horrible result for me!

I returned there two years later to cover a United States Chamber of Commerce convention. After a night meeting, as I strolled home to my hotel, I saw a shabby young man, apparently near to tears, standing in a doorway. I stopped and spoke to him: he said he was terribly hungry. I preferred to feed him rather than give him money; so, I took him to a nearby restaurant. He wolfed his food, meanwhile telling me a sad tale about his mother's death.

I noticed two men come in and sit near us. As we left, they did also: outside, they stopped my friend to question him, then turned to ask me for identification and to explain how I happened to be with this lad. I had plenty of credentials so the officers believed my story. They took me over to show me the contents of the young man's traveling bag—it was filled with burglar tools! Police had been watching, trying to catch him as he was one of the 'Legs' Diamond gang, notorious burglars. My press friends the next day bemoaned the fact that the detectives had not brought me to jail, for they would have really 'fixed me up.'

About this time, I had gone to a New Year's Eve party where I spent some time with two foreign service officers of the U.S. government. They insisted I should be in the foreign service and prevailed upon me to take the examination. Upon my return from Mexico, I found a six weeks old, special delivery letter with very official looking contents, informing me that I had been appointed to station in Mukden, Manchuria. While I was not aware that fierce fighting would break out there at almost the moment I was scheduled to arrive, I thought the post was too far away and too undesirable. So, I risked my future by turning it down.

The Department of Commerce was not angry, apparently: they offered me Bogota, Columbia instead. On taking the required physical tests, I was found underweight for life in such a high altitude. Their final offer was Caracas, Venezuela: just as I was packing to go, Mother became critically ill. I again begged off and was assigned to the Foreign Construction Division of the Bureau of Foreign and Domestic Commerce.

Then the new President, Franklin D. Roosevelt, named 'Dirty Dan ' Roper (or so he was named by the press) as Secretary of Commerce. Roper proved his political sagacity by conducting the most rapacious, inhuman wholesale housecleaning that he was capable of. I was not much concerned as my fellow workers faded away, as I had voted for Roosevelt. Eventually, however, I was summoned to the personnel office: the director bluntly said, "I forgot to fire you." Thus ended my **career** in the foreign service.

I turn my back on the ocean so as to be surprised when my ship comes in. Lyle A Brookover

On the Boardwalk

CHAPTER IX:1935
UPI/NRA

The following day, I received a call from the late,great journalist, Raymond Clapper, then head of the Washington bureau of United Press Associations. I went to work at once for the wire service, beginning my duties with assignment to Quantico where the Marines were mobilizing a regiment for possible duty to quell an uprising in Cuba.

After several days of waiting and watching troop trains pull in with Marines assembling for another foray into Latin-land, the threatened revolution fell apart. I said farewell to many new friends (Marine Corps generals, lesser officers and privates) and came back to cover a quieter, but substantial revolution—the emergence of Roosevelt's New Deal.

Assigned to cover the National Recovery Association, I was soon dealing with another general, the NRA head Hugh 'Ironpants' Johnson (see photo at end of chapter.) His omnipresent aide and secretary, 'Bobby Robinson', scavenged the Commerce Department offices for rugs and furniture for her boss's office.

The NRA Blue Eagle screamed from the front pages of all the daily newspapers for many weeks as industry and labor leaders met with the government to formulate codes of business ethics and co- operation to help the nation climb out of the Great Depression. Summoned to the testy general's office one morning because of a story I had written which displeased him, he proceeded to chew me out—with Bobby beaming approval. He then smiled and shook hands as he dismissed me.

When the famous lawyer, Clarence Darrow, was called in to analyze NRA operations from a legal standpoint, we became quite good friends.

Johnson and Darrow were at loggerheads and getting nowhere. One night I 'took a flyer' on a story that they would meet the next day to talk things over. It was a 'scoop' that earned me plaudits from *UP* bigwigs. It created such a furore that before the next day was over, the two **actually did** go for a ride together in General Johnson's limousine. Darrow lost his hat, but not his composure.

The Blue Eagle soon after lost all its feathers through the Supreme Court's so-called 'sick chicken' decision. General Johnson's glory faded into history.

Meanwhile, I'd had daily contact with the top NRA deputies (Averill Harriman, Donald Nelson, Leon Anderson) and the active participants on labor's side (William Green, Phil Murray, Sidney Hillman and John L. Lewis). Later, I came to know George Meany, Green's successor, and David McDonald, head of the powerful Steelworkers' union.

During the liquidation period, Harriman took over. Though he received the press daily, the story had lost its punch. One day, he greeted us with the announcement that the only news was that he was returning to business affairs in New York. He added that he would like to entertain us at dinner before he left. No one expressed any thanks or regrets: no one accepted what seemed a genuine invitation. We simply filed out and went back to the press room.

Thinking it over, I became ashamed of our collective rudeness. I went to Marshall Coles (my guide, confidant, and friend in the press office) and asked her to express my apologies to Mr. Harriman. Also, to say that I should like him to be my guest for lunch at the National Press Club before he departed. That invitation was accepted and a date was set. Although he had already departed for New York, he made a quick plane trip back to keep his commitment: he was a most gracious guest.

Talking in NRA corridors one day with the dramatic, bushy-browed John L. Lewis, I was galvanized into action by his comment, "I'm going to take my union (the United Mine Workers) out of the American Federation of Labor." I dashed off a bulletin and story to the United Press. Lewis made good on his statement: he established the Congress of Industrial Organizations (C.I.O.) which organized its unions on an industry-wide basis, as opposed to the A.F. of L. system of craft unions.

While covering cabinet departments of the New Deal, I came to know well the first female cabinet member, 'Madam' Perkins, Secretary of Labor. I dined at her home and still have her autographed picture. Her Assistant Secretary, Edward F. McGrady (an able, genial Irishman) was one of my favorite 'bigshots' and, of other newsmen as well.

Postmaster General 'Jim' Farley intrigued us all by his astute political mind and by his ability to call our names correctly after only brief introductions. Secretary of Agriculture Wallace's press meetings were noted for his dream-like, visionary disclosures on agriculture, economy and world affairs. Later, when he was Vice-President, I had the privilege of introducing him at a National Press Club Pan-American Dinner.

I became a member of the White House Correspondents' Association and attended White House Press conferences where I occasionally bulletined a story concerning the NRA. I was charmed at a White House reception by the knack of the President and First Lady in personalizing each welcome in the receiving line. A feature of all such gatherings is the interminable time one waits to be admitted and received. Once inside, the glamor is unforgettable: the Roosevelt hospitality was generous and cordial.

When Franklin Roosevelt was elected, the Press Club gave him a dinner. When he entered and slowly hobbled across the foyer to the ballroom, I marveled to myself that, in all this broad land with its millions of citizens, we should choose so handicapped a man to be our leader. That evening, I became acquainted with John Charles Thomas and Morton Downey who entertained the President.

Two terms later, the Press Club again entertained Roosevelt: that time, it was world-famous violinist Fritz Kreisler who walked shyly out on stage, violin under his arm, and asked, "What do you want me to play, Mr. President?" After he had regaled us with several magnificently played classical numbers, the dinner was over. Those of us near Kreisler suggested an after-dinner drink. Kreisler readily agreed: it was my great privilege to sit beside him as we downed our bourbon-and-sodas.

He spoke of his childhood and of how he had played outside his father's cobbler shop in Austria, quite early forsaking childish games for his violin. When he prepared to leave, I secured his wraps and walking stick and escorted him to the elevator. We parted with a hearty handshake: I was in a daze the rest of the evening.

During my *UP* years, I came to have great affection for Ernie Pyle, illustrious reporter and war correspondent, GI's hero who would die under enemy fire at Iwo Jima. Ernie and I had many fine gab fests: one of our favorite topics was the vast and varied knowledge required of a reporter—in sharp contrast to the small amount of his pay check! The American Newspaper Guild was organized at this time and was trying to remedy this situation. I joined the Guild and was a delegate to its first large national meeting in Cleveland where I helped frame a constitution. Our president, Heywood Broun, rode herd on some stormy, all-night sessions, fortified by a jug of gin which was ever-handy. Other newspaper colleagues who were close friends included Harold 'Tommy' Thompson of the *UP* and Joseph Miller of the Associated Press. I was Thompson's sidekick at NRA, saw him through a divorce and remarriage, and off to Tokyo as a foreign correspondent for *UP*. Later, he became a vice-president for Arabian-

American Oil Company—quite a rise in the world financially—and has since retired. Miller and I were bitter rivals on many a story, but good friends after hours. I flew to Boston to be best man at his wedding to Elinor Lord, an actress and socialite. Much partying followed the austere church reception. I slept a few hours at the Harvard Club and flew home the next day through a thunderstorm so violent that all on board were ill—except me. I was saved by a hang-over so bad that I couldn't feel any worse.

Another long night I recall was that of the Senate filibuster by colorful Senator Huey Long of Louisiana. I sat in the press gallery through the night, watching and listening as the 'Louisiana lion' chewed betel nuts and spewed out the fragments on the Senate floor, by way of punctuating his rambling discourse. I stood sometime later beside the marble shaft which rises majestically over his grave in the shadow of the Capitol in Baton Rouge and remembered that night and other events in the martyred senator's career.

Major George Leonard Berry, longtime head of the International Printing Pressmen's Union, was one of the deputies stranded by the submergence of the NRA Blue Eagle. He stayed on for a time while the effort was being made to salvage something from the large organization—and the surprising number of codes which had been formulated to eliminate unfair competition to steel manufacture, coal mining, automobile and motion picture production, textiles, and dozens of other business groups, ranging in size almost down to button hole makers.

Major Berry conceived the idea of forming an industrial council which would do the job that NRA had failed to do. President Roosevelt thought highly of the scheme and appointed Berry, 'Co-ordinator of Industrial Co-operation,' a title that gives pause. The indefatigable major went to work setting up an independent bureaucratic organization.

Since he had joined NRA some months before, I'd come to know him and like him. He called me in and told me of his plans. "I want you to come with me as a public relations adviser," he said, naming a salary that topped the *UP* by several points. I liked his ideas and the title sounded good. Without further parley, I became a bureaucrat, complete with secretary and other helpers, sitting in on big-wheel conferences—sometimes at the White House. I even had special license tags for my car during Roosevelt's second inauguration.

The day I resigned from *UP*, I went with Major Berry and was roundly lambasted by Raymond Clapper, my former boss who was now writing a column, for carrying 'water on both shoulders.' I was handing out press releases for the new organization before anyone had heard of my leaving the wire service. My *UP* superiors were kind enough to urge me not to leave, telling me they were considering sending me to Moscow as a correspondent. But I felt, to use a phrase, that the die had been cast.

It soon appeared that the timing was wrong for the Major's new venture. Business was recovering somewhat from the Great Depression: big business was disenchanted by the collapse of the NRA and becoming equally so with other aspects of Roosevelt's New Deal. The Industrial Council gathered a smattering of important people from both industry and labor, as well as a horde of hangers-on and 'loose nuts' of various descriptions. The first meeting ended in an uproar and a field day for reporters. Major Berry lost his temper and challenged his hecklers to "step outside" where he'd settle with them. None of the real leaders of industry took part: even labor leaders were skeptical.

As a sort of side-show to this operation, Major Berry (with the cooperation of John L. Lewis and Sidney Hillman) founded labor's Non-Partisan League—with the avowed purpose of re-electing FDR in 1936. Even though this effort succeeded in its purpose, Roosevelt cooled off toward his C. of I.C.: we "co-ordinators" were no longer summoned to the White House. My rude awakening to what was going on in the country came when I went to Cincinnati to address an international conference of display advertising men. My passionate plea for industrial cooperation was met by severe heckling and raucous and disparging shouts of "He's a New Dealer!" Roosevelt's stock was finding few promoters in that crowd.

A huge dinner was organized in Major Berry's honor by his friends, hundreds of whom crowded the Willard Hotel ballroom to feast and hear laudatory speeches. A short time later, the honored guest returned to his barony in Tennessee, the Pressman's Home for retired unionists, the union headquarters and his large holdings in real estate. He returned to Washington almost immediately after, having been appointed by the Tennessee governor to fill an unexpired term in the Senate.

While my feet were still in the government trough, the Democratic party convention was held in Philadelphia. My friend, James Robb of American Airlines, came by to see if I wanted an airline ticket to attend.

"A big shot like you certainly should be present," he argued, so convincingly, that I finally agreed to go. Jim and his associate, AA office manager Herbert Ford, arranged a reservation and rushed me out to the airport—only to find the plane had taxied from the strip and was poised for take-off at the end of the runway. They telephoned out to the pilot to hold it and drove me out to the plane where I was hoisted aboard, to the complete amazement of the other passengers. Needless to say, I was the object of interest and comment on that short journey. Arriving at the convention, I plunged at once into a series of banquets, luncheons, hotel suite parties and the conventtion sessions— the first I had attended since 1924 when I was present at the New York Democratic convention on my way to Europe.

Shortly thereafter, I was honored by being named an 'Admiral of the Flagship Fleet' by American Airlines. A luncheon and an imposing certificate go with the honor which is very nice. (Amusingly enough, 20 years later they forgot to consult their records and named me again. The result was another nice luncheon and another, and much larger, certificate!)

During the Berry era, I provided myself with an interesting sideline by opening a concert bureau to present Latin American artists. Old-timers will remember this was the time of the 'Good Neighbor' policy: my co-impresario, Arnaldo Conti Berenguer, and I were right in the swim. Arnaldo's grandfather was a conductor at La Scala opera in Milan: his mother was a long-time harpist with the New York Philharmonic so his musical credentials were correct. I found the concert bureau, Beren-Brook Artists, was an excellent way to siphon off any surplus cash from my generous government salary!

We presented a number of concerts, but always seemed to end up in the red. With the patronage of a goodly number of Washington diplomats and socialites (such as Princess Margaret Draper Boncompanyi) we presented pianists, violinists, vocalists, and dancers from Latin American countries. Finally, we took on the Mexican Tipica orchestra which was a large and well-known attraction. When we stood in the back of the house that night and surveyed the large crowd, I thought, "At last we'll have a profit!" No such luck.

We then booked Giovanni Martinelli, a good friend of my partner's mother. He came to town, was generously wined and dined by old friends, while the summer's worst thunderstorm drenched our customers hurrying to Constitution Hall. Forty-five minutes past the announced hour, the great tenor arrived in 'mellow state' and gave a masterful and folksy evening of music, marked by a choice of encores for which his accompanist did not have the music, and by a number of delightful conversational asides from the artist. I felt well-repaid by the warmly autographed photograph Martinelli presented me the next day before leaving.

We also presented the one and only Ted Shawn and his company of male dancers who were so good that I presented them again a few weeks later in Lynchburg, Virginia. In each audience, we had skeptics who had to be won over to acceptance of male dancers: but, the splendid work of this company (which required athletic condition and skill) won them many friends. I had known Ted for many years and had always regarded him as a great artist who has contributed much more than any other man to the world's beautiful art of the dance. I also knew and admired Ruth St. Denis, the other half of the Denis-Shawn dance group, and Mary Howry, my dear friend who toured the world with this group.

I was quite active at this time in the Arts Club of Washington. Hugo Inden, a gifted German painter, and Hans Kindler, founder and conductor for many years of the National Symphony Orchestra who lived at the Club, helped me with many projects. We staged a very profitable Spanish Fiesta, featuring the 'flamenco circle' with a 'duena' surrounded by family members and friends who each rose and danced or sang in turn.

To our astonishment, from the packed house one after another, strangers rose and joined the circle, some proving to have greater talent than the members of our chosen group.

Madame Juliet Chautemps, wife of the former Premier of France and a brilliant pianist, was a club member. One evening, I gave a dinner for 28 guests. I thought, since all were friends, I would not need place cards. How wrong that was! After cocktails, we adjourned to the dining table and a panic ensued. All the guests seemed to choose the same chair! My composure was later somewhat restored when Mme. Chautemps graciously sat down at the piano and played a beautiful concert at my invitation.

Another sideline at this time was my work for the noted Arctic Explorer, Lincoln Ellsworth who felt that he had been poorly treated by our government in recognition of his brave feats. He wanted to get a military commission and a medal. He was an exciting personality, but very difficult at times. Appeals to the Army and Marine Corps were unavailing; but, the Navy gave him a reserve Lieutenant Commander's commission. Congress finally awarded him a gold medal: we had fun getting a design that suited Ellsworth from the U.S. Mint. My friend Nellie Tayloe Ross, former governor of Wyoming, was the Mint Director at the time. When the medal was to be presented at the White House, Mr. Ellsworth asked me to have the President entertain him and his wife at luncheon. That was too large an order for me; but, the pictures of the medal presentation appeared in most of the nation's press while the Ellsworth's went elsewhere for lunch. (See clipping at end of chapter.)

One bright Saturday, I took Mother, who loved horses, over to the exclusive Madeira School in Virginia far a horse show. Upon returning home, I learned that my secretary, Gladys 'Shug' Redman had been urgently trying to reach me. I called her at home: she said she had had a man on her hands all day who was anxious to give me a job. Since the 'Berry Bureau' was about to expire, I listened with some interest.

The man—who proved to be Carleton Putnam, president of Chicago and Southern Airlines—was staying at the Shoreham. I went to see him after dinner: we talked, with me mostly listening, until 2 A.M. He was a most unusual man, completely sold on himself and his airline, its hopes and plans for the future which he wanted me to share.

He'd heard an enthusiastic description of my talents and, without having met me, apparently decided I was the man he wanted to help him make his dreams come true. I was wary about leaving Washington and going out to St. Louis to live—and also not too certain that the future was going to be as rosy as he predicted! He insisted that I fly out and visit the line, sometimes known as 'the Mississippi Valley Route' from Chicago to New Orleans.

Gen. Hugh S. Johnson Tells About NRA

Denied Commission

LINCOLN ELLSWORTH

NO COMMISSION FOR ELLSWORTH

WASHINGTON, Aug. 19. (AP)— The House Military Committee made public yesterday a War Department letter opposing a bill to make Lincoln Ellsworth, Arctic explorer, a lieutenant-colonel in the Officers' Reserve Corps.

Ellsworth, 57, was commander and navigator of the Amudsen-Ellsworth polar flying expedition. He applied for a Reserve Officer's commission last February, the Department said, but was turned down. Representative Sutphin (D.-N. J.) asked Congress to make the appointment.

"While the War Department was deeply appreciative of the patriotic tender of his (Ellsworth's) services and keenly aware of his splendid record of achievement," the Department said in reference to Sutphin's bill, "yet it did not feel that under the regulations as now administered, he could be appointed to a grade commensurate with his age or in keeping with his prominence in civilian life."

Deviation from the regulations to make individual appointments, the Department said, would tend to be "destructive to the morale" of the Reserve Corps.

Ellsworth Commission, August, 1935

CHAPTER X: 1937
CHICAGO & SOUTHERN/NEW ORLEANS

A few days later we flew together to St. Louis where I visited the company headquarters. The next day we flew to New Orleans, a city I'd long wanted to see because of its historic past and reputed Spanish-French-Creole charm. During our first day there, Herman Deutsch, a distinguished maggazine writer and journalist with the *Times-Picayune*, spent some time with us, regaling us with stories of the city's colorful past. The phone rang: Marguerite Clark Williams was calling to invite Mr. Putnam to a formal dinner party she was having that evening.

He demurred, saying he had a companion from Washington with him, to which Marguerite replied, "He must be a gentleman if he is traveling with you. Wouldn't it be safe to bring him along?" To the argument that neither of us had brought evening attire, she insisted that that didn't matter in the least. She was without question the leading hostess in the city, living then in a spacious mansion on St. Charles street with a very large staff of servants. Since her home was considered New Orleans' finest, I thought I was doing rather well on my first night in town.

Arriving for cocktails (and I was wearing a brown business suit and tan shoes) we were greeted by our hostess, a diminutive lady with an all-enveloping smile and sparkling personality. She introduced us to an impressive group of formally dressed gentlemen and ladies. Marguerite tactfully explained who we were and that we were flying through on business. But, Carleton said in an aside to me, "They'll probably think we are a couple of private detectives engaged by Marguerite to guard the ladies' jewelry for the evening." There were PLENTY of diamonds to protect!

I was enchanted with Marguerite who was the widow of Harry Williams, a wealthy Southwesterner who had been a pioneer in the budding age of aviation, but who had been killed in a tragic plane crash a few years earlier. As a movie acttress in the period of silent films, she had been a contemporary of Mary Pickford and the first to enact the role of Princess Snow White. As I succumbed to her charms, I realized I was merely joining a vast company of her admirers all over the country. One of the most touching memories I have of her is of her placing a fresh rose before her late husband's photograph in the drawing room each morning. She was gracious to everyone; but, I was most fortunate to have my affection for her returned in large measure.

She and her circle of friends made that year of my life one of the most delightful and exciting that I was ever to know. They urged me to take an apartment in the French Quarter. Through Marguerite's influence, I was able to bypass a long waiting list and secure a lovely high-ceilinged living room, bedroom and Spanish-tiled bath in the Pontalba apartments (said to be the oldest apartment buildings in the United States) facing the equestrian statue of General Jackson in the Place d'Armes. I would go out through my elegant wrought iron door in the mornings to get some fresh air and pay the General a visit.

I had been named business manager of the Chicago and Southern Airlines with duties including public relations and supervision of ticket offices and personnel. As my office was in St. Louis, I was constantly flying up and down the Valley. I was described in the local press as "a local citizen who commutes 600 miles by air to his office."

The weekend I took possession of my new quarters, I flew in from St. Louis on Friday evening. Saturday, I joined Marguerite and friends for a sumptuous luncheon in one of the city's celebrated restaurants; thence, to a box at the Ole Miss-LSU football game. From there, we proceeded to a large cocktail party in an elegant home in the Garden District where an orchestra, hidden in the greenery, was playing 'Truckin' on Down', a favorite of those times.

When I expressed concern, as evening came on, that I had not as yet received my apartment key, I was assured that all had been taken care of. So, I crossed the threshold of my new home for the first time to find some 75 of my new friends enjoying themselves, a butler and maid dispensing beverages and turkey, ham and other foods from a flower-laden buffet! What a joyous way for my stay in New Orleans to begin!

Among the many wonderful new friends I made was Hildegarde Lyons, society editor of the *Times-Picayune*. She and I became partners: I escorted her to just about every important society dinner, ball and debutante party that season. There were many choice small dinners at 'Duke' Arnaud's, the Three Sisters, Antoine's and other famous eating places. I tried famous Antoine's to provide the meals we served aloft (which would have been a great drawing card for the airlines) but they refused. I still think this was bad judgement on their part.

My friends voted me membership in the Southern Yacht Club, although I was woefully lacking in yachting lore and equipment. Many happy hours were spent at club dinners and dances, or offshore in the yachts of others. I had guests down from Washington at the holidays. Ed and Avis McIntyre closed their Bourbon House Bar to the public and invited their intimates for a New Year's Eve frolic, presided over by the genial Swedish bartender, Eric, who had only one upper front tooth and was always smiling. One of my guests astonished the sophisticated New Orleanians by appearing in a full-length ermine evening wrap; but, she hadn't known the party was to be held in a saloon.

Two activities of special interest were my frequent visits to our Jackson, Mississippi and Memphis, Tennessee offices. My first appearance in Jackson brought forth a front page column of welcome in the *Jackson Daily News*, written by the colorful and able editor, Major Fred Sullens. He and his lovely blond daughter, Anne, frequently entertained me in their lovely ante-bellum home. Anne was married to a former Army officer, Scott Dickson. She owned a pack of hairless Mexican chihuahua dogs. One night after they gave a dinner party for me,the whole group escorted me to the late plane and went on board for fun. Major Sullens decided to accompany me to New Orleans. Another time I arrived in Jackson to find they had arranged for me—a bachelor—to deliver the dedicatory speech for a new foundlings' home.

Memphis was another way-station where I had some gay and exciting times. Memphis was politically dry: the spacious cocktail lounge in the aristocratic Hotel Peabody offered only orange juice and Coca-Cola. One evening I invited Phoebe Omlie, widow of the late popular aviator, Vernon Omlie (and herself a pilot who later ran a training school for fliers during WWII) down to have a bit of refreshment as I had arrived with a quart of good Scotch. On her way, she invited (quite casually) 37 friends to join us. I telephoned the management in haste and shortly was transferred to a two-story studio suite. Servants arrived with plenty of liquor and large plates of hors d'ouvres. A talented young colored man came to sing and dance for my guests. The hotel manager and his wife joined the party which lasted well into the night. Where could one find better hotel service?

I found a great friend in 'Jack' Carley, polished and affable editor of the *Memphis Commercial Appeal*, a former Canadian and fellow veteran of World War One. He and his beauteous Louise (who had a statuesque figure, large blue eyes and a maze of golden hair) took me into their circle of friends which included everyone worth knowing in Memphis. I persuaded Louise to join our office staff in Memphis as both she and Jack were very aviation-minded.

They asked me to join them for a trip to Baton Rouge for an editors' meeting. While we were there, we were guests at the governor's mansion at a reception for 800 guests. Governor Richard W. Leche and his lady were most cordial. Later, when I was leaving, they remembered my name and urged me to come again. I thought this was a remarkable display of Southern hospitality, combined with political sagacity. We were also entertained at dinner by the president of Louisiana State University, Dr. James Monroe Smith. About a fortnight later, a scandal broke over the heads of the two officials. Both were sentenced to penitentiary terms.

Two days before Christmas, I planned to leave New Orleans to spend the holidays with my mother and sister in Washington. In early evening, I was enjoying black beans and rice with the McIntyre's in their Bourbon House Bar when the pilots called from the airport to say that if I were going to Memphis with them, I should get to the field quickly as it was close to time for take- off. I grabbed a taxi, but we were stopped at a grade crossing for several minutes. When we drove to the airport, the airplane was soaring over the terminal on its way. The pilots, Stewart Hopkins and Reed Knight, were my friends. They hated to leave witthout me, but the flight was carrying mail and had to get through on time.

I took the first plane the next morning—in miserable weather! When we got to Memphis, it was snowing hard. I found my connection to the East was not scheduled to fly.

In the Peabody Hotel lobby, I encountered Mrs. Willis Campbell, the wife of the nationally-known bone specialist. She seemed overjoyed to see me and cried out, "I'm so glad you're in town. We didn't know where to send your invitation for our daughter's debut party tonight. We will expect you to be there."

I explained my situation and told her I had no evening clothes with me. I knew it would be an elegant party, but she insisted I would be welcome in business clothes. She said she'd have the first dance with me and the debutante the second one to show the gathering that I was a special guest. In the face of all this, I could not refuse. So, I called Louise Carley who agreed to go with me to the party.

The Peabody Ballroom was a bower of flowers: everyone was in floor length gowns or white tie and tails. But, I waded in, danced with the three most important ladies in the room, and had a wonderful time with the help of several toasts in champagne. My plane left at 2 A.M.: since the storm had abated somewhat, we were able to take off, flew all over the sky, and landed about 4 A.M. at the Louisville, Kentucky airport. After a few hours rest at the Brown Hotel, we tried again. At Tri-Cities airport in eastern Tennessee, the pilot came in and said, "Folks, this is the end of the line!" All eastern airports were closed down by the storm.

We were an odd lot: several Europeans, two forest rangers with baskets of freshly-killed pheasants for someone's Christmas dinner, and other assorted types. We were taken by taxi to Bristol where we had a Christmas Eve dinner, courtesy of American Airlines. We men scrounged around and found some boxes of candy for the stewardesses. They, in turn, found some good wine. So, we tried to make the best of our predicament. A lower berth was found for me on a train which brought me to Washington late the next morning. So it was Christmas, in spite of everything.

St. Louis was not such an interesting place to be: but, I enjoyed guest privileges at the Athletic Club which had outstanding food service as well as friendly and luxurious surroundings. The famous 'Jimmy' Doolittle and his delightful wife, Jo, lived in St. Louis. While dining with them on Thanksgiving Day, I was invited to sign the most celebrated tablecloth in the world. (See clipping at end of Chapter X.) Every noted figure in the early days of aviation, both in America and abroad, had dined and signed. Afterward, Jo would embroider the signatures. The cloth had been around the world and had crossed the ocean countless times.

Jimmy was noted for many things, such as his habit of reading a magazine when flying alone. One afternoon during the Cleveland Air Races, I was passing beside a country field when an airman parachuted down nearby, having lost a wing from his plane. When he landed, we were astonished to see Jimmy hurrying across the field toward us, smiling and undisturbed. Some years later, he became an Air Force General and led a bombing raid over Tokyo that shook the world.

Toward spring, a spell of zero degree weather, with lots of snow and ice, brought on a financial crisis in the airline. Passengers are naturally the life blood of aviation: there were few willing to risk air travel in those days under such conditions. A board meeting was called in Chicago. I offered to take a three months leave of absence without pay so as to save furloughing or dismissing the excellent staff which I had built up. I felt that a several months lapse in the promotional program we had underway would result in decreased business in the future. The board thanked me for my 'generous' offer and accepted it. However, the board also furloughed all my promotional people for three months! I resigned in a fury over what I considered a betrayal of faith as well as a very short-sighted policy.

I flew back to Washington, picked up my mother and sister, and took a cottage on the beach in Fort Lauderdale for one month. This was most enjoyable, with warm sunshine and surf, trips to Miami and Hialea horse racing, and a complete rest which I needed. We drove across Florida, around the gulf to Pensacola and Mobile, and on to New Orleans for the Mardi Gras, and a sad farewell to my cherished apartment.

The Mardi Gras, a festival which every American should see at least once, was fascinating. My mother, then 80 years of age, stood on Canal Street in the hot sun for four hours while one parade passed in front of us, another to our backs (we were in the neutral ground in the center.) After a cup of tea and a brief rest, Mother was ready for the Mardi Gras Rex Ball that evening. She was less willing to leave the brilliant and spectacular party at 2 A.M. than we younger people.

The morning after, there were plenty of aching heads. Mother and I drove to the Bourbon House for a last meal with the McIntyres, who had not been to bed all night. They were sipping absinthe at the bar. It is a milky, pearl-like liquid: Avis said cheerily, "Mother B, won't you join us for a melted toilet seat cocktail?" Mother thought not, so Avis clapped her hands and ordered the largest glass in the place filled with orange juice and brought to Mother. While we breakfasted, busy hands were at work outside: when we went to our car to start the long journey to Washington, dozens of bright balloons were floating above it, tied to every part. Thus decorated, we said good-bye to the festive and hospitable Crescent City.

****

I forgot to mention that the *U.S.S. New York* was in harbor for the Mardi Gras. At a tea dance on board given by the officers, I invited several of them to cocktails at my apartment the day before they were to sail away. I had asked them, and many local friends, for six o'clock. I reached the apartment just before that hour. In a few minutes, the doorbell rang and there stood the Navy—I believe every officer on board—dressed to Navy perfection and on split second timing. They enjoyed themselves until the witching hour of midnight, and waved farewell to us as their ship moved, sadly it seemed, downstream next morning.

Laura and Mother reluctantly gave up the lovely apartment I had secured for them in the Pontalba and told their excellent colored maid good-bye. She wanted to go to Washington with them, but it was not possible. Laura departed by train, hurrying back to her government desk. Mother and I made a memorable journey through Pass Christian, along the Gulf Coast to Mobile, stopping along the way at a seafood restaurant where the next table was occupied by eight big men, fastened together by handcuffs. We tried to ignore them and enjoy our platters of fresh flounder, caught in the Gulf that morning. We drove on through Alabama for an overnight stopover with our cousins, the Herbert Garges' who lived in beautiful Druid Hills in Atlanta. On through the Carolinas and up the Shenandoah Valley—after 1200 miles altogether, we finally arrived home.

Back in Washington, I joined the social whirl. At a private dinner with Georgetown friends, I was honored to be escort and dinner partner with the second Mrs. Woodrow Wilson. She was stimulating company: we chatted like old friends, mostly about aviation in which I knew she was much interested.

At another time, I had the pleasure of escorting the Vice- President's daughter, Miss Margaret Truman, to her box at the Tennessee State Society Ball. Other key figures of this affair were my dear friends, Colonel and Mrs. McCormick of Memphis and Marine Corps Commandant and Mrs. Cates.

I was offered a post as advertising manager of *American Aviation Magazine*, which I accepted. I was soon on my way to California with a group of news writers on a Paramount-TWA sponsored visit to the filming and premiere of "Men with Wings." We met movie stars by the dozens. I was photographed with actor Randolph Scott because everyone said we looked like brothers. We toured the aviation factories and were taken on a flight to Boulder Dam, the Grand Canyon and the Painted Desert. A press agent wanted to show me the Twentieth Century studios. As we seated ourselves for lunch in the cafeteria, a man came up with a loaded tray, asked politely if he might sit beside me and then held out his hand, saying "Crosby is the name."

Old Bing, himself! We had a delightful conversation while we ate. While lunching at the Brown Derby one day, there was a small panic as many persons rushed for the entrance doors. My companion and i joined the same rush and found the cause: the opportunity to gaze upon Elaine, the current favorite of the great idol, John Barrymore. She was walking by with a grubby little dog on a leash. Such is fame!

Home again, and to breakfast with Thornton Wilder, author of many bestsellers, especially *The Bridge of San Luis Rey*. He was in town to speak before some women's club, but complained that the unfortunate side of his fame was the need to waste time with such appearances, when he'd much rather be having a few martinis with me or some other friend. Oh well, one can't have everything, I reminded him.

It was my great good fortune to be present at the last public address by General 'Black Jack' Pershing, who shared the stage with Bishop James Freeman in the gardens of the National Cathedral one Sunday afternoon as part of a ceremony of massing of the colors of hundreds of patriotic organizations. Two of the greatest men of that day—and on the same program! Mother and I were shown to front-row seats.

When I left the aviation magazine the following spring (due to some executive jealousy), I was prepared for a period of job- seeking—something I'd never had occasion to do before—when, as a long-time member of the Arts Club of Washington, I was asked to be chairman of its annual Bal Bohme. This meant three months arduous work with committees, designers, decorators, musicians, actors, conflicting personalities,etc. No reward was to be expected except applause and credit if the ball were a success, blame and criticism if it were not.

The ball was held in the Willard Hotel where we had decorated the long ballroom with opposite rows of live trees reaching the ceiling. Representing a boulevarde in Paris, the trees were chestnut trees in bloom. There were sheltered canvas awnings and cafe chairs where one could sit and watch the world go by. The scheme was 'Paris au Printemps': the pageant of 300 players represented a day in Paris from cockcrow at dawn (recorded) until the opera ball at midnight, ending with the 'Rosencavalier Waltz'. The French Ambassador and his retinue graced the affair with their patronage. We had nearly 2,000 guests. It was a costume ball and I was done up in a gray silk tailcoat with much rose-colored braid, a powdered wig, black knee breeches and patent leather pumps with silver buckles (presumably a French nobleman, or something.)

The 1939 Ball was voted a brilliant success. When I had filed away all the pictures and newspaper clippings, I was free again to look for a job. The idea didn't appeal to me, however: I spent most of that summer at swimming pools. My coat of tan was the envy of my friends, but they were increasingly concerned over my indifference to 'gainful employment.' Autumn approached: I had a phone call from my close friend, Chester Wright, who said, "I want you to come to work tomorrow morning."

He had a public relations firm and published a letter of labor information for private clients. Soon, I was made a member of Chester M. Wright and Associates. My duties were to help industrial clients to get government orders for defense materials. Two of the firms I aided substantially in converting to war production, Electromaster Corporation of Detroit and the Murray Company of Dallas (makers of cotton ginning machinery) earned Defense Department "E" flags and invited me to be present for the awards ceremonies. I was on active duty by that time: the Air Force sent me on orders for Detroit, but turned me down for Dallas.

When the war came, my associates generously voted to furnish me with a fine outfit of uniforms and put me on half-pay status during my military service. When I came back after the war, the Wrights had retired to their lovely home in Miami. Another partner, their son-in-law, Charles Handy, had divorced and married again, this time to a Texan divorcee and heiress, and had joined her in the South. Our corporation set-up was unwieldy for the only two partners left, so we soon disbanded.

About the time I first joined the Wright organizaation, Katherine Hepburn and Burgess Meredith came to town to present a radio drama, "Suffer Little Children," a benefit for German refugee children. I handled the publicity for the affair. It was a network broadcast in the Mayflower Hotel ballroom with a local audience of society, diplomats, and other V.I.P.'s. Katherine's arrival was a big secret: but, I learned through airline friends that she and her current heartthrob, Van Heflin, were booked incognito on a flight from New York. I engaged a limousine and chauffeur and met the plane.

The plane landed and the great actress emerged, followed by Van and a female assistant. When I stepped up and introduced myself, Katherine scowled, swore, and demanded, "Who told you I was coming on this plane?" When I ignored the question and quietly said I thought it would be nice to have a car to take them to their hotel, she at first refused the offer. But, after Van quieted her down with a few words, they accompanied me to the limousine.

As we drove away from the terminal, a Goodyear blimp arose across the field. Katherine leaned out to see it, and exclaimed, "Look at that God-damned thing!" Her costume seemed well suited to her language: with her hair streaming in the wind, she wore a rough-knit sweater, dark slacks, and tan brogues. With my charges safely delivered, I went off somewhere to thaw out. Later, accompanied by my old friend, Jay Carmody, drama critic of *The Star,* I went to meet Burgess Meredith who had notified us of his train's arrival time.

Burgess was cordial and seemed pleased, almost flattered, to be met by committee, car and chauffeur. We had an interesting talk on the way. When I ushered him into his hotel suite, he exclaimed, "All this for me!" He walked around the rooms, borrowed my comb and straightened his locks. As I left him, I pondered on the differences among people—in all walks of life.

Katherine staged a few tantrums during rehearsal, I was told. But, both she and Burgess gave an enchanting performance before a well-packed audience. When the broadcast was finished, the younger, movie-mad element rushed the stage and seemed about to tear her clothing from her. She fled in panic, followed by Van, her assistant and me. She outdistanced us in the corridors and disappeared. Some minutes later, I heard she was leaving. I rushed to a side door in time to see their taxi driving off. She espied me, leaned from the window, saying, "Thank you so much for everything," and flashed me a smile that would melt a heart of stone.

Another encounter with the theater world at this time was when Luise Rainier came to star in "Saint Joan" with the Washington Civic Theater of which I was a board member. We had offered some brilliant successes (with amateur theater limitations) and decided to try a star play. It was understood the reason Luise accepted the part was because she wanted to appear in Washington as she was trying to get her aged parents out of hock in Europe. She felt some Washington contacts might help.

Her first demand that we hire one of her pet directors, Ervin Piscator, pupil of the great German, Max Reinhardt, was met by our board with some misgivings due to his fee. Rehearsals progressed: we thought it would benefit Luise and the show, also, for her to make an appearance at a National Press Club dance before the play opened. I was elected to escort her: at the appointed hour, I went to the Shoreham Hotel and phoned from the lobby. I was answered by a torrent of abuse.

"You newspaper men have no mercy," she cried. "Here I've been rehearsing all day and I'm exhausted. Now you want me to go and meet a lot of people who don't interest me and help put your party over. Don't you ever think of an actress as a human being?"

When the tirade stopped for a moment, I reminded her that she had AGREED to go. If she wished to rebuff the Washington press before her play opened, it was up to her.

"I'll be down in 10 minutes," was her response.

For the 20 minute taxi ride to the club, she sulked and smouldered in a corner of the cab. I was delighted to hand her over to the committee for tthe evening. She was ungracious to those who tried to please her, even in response to the spotlight after her introduction. Soon after, I asked her if she wished to go. When she indicated her preference was to travel alone, I refused, telling her I was going to take her back to her hotel. We had another charming 20 minutes of silence on the way back. When I said "good-night" to her at the elevator, she managed to mumble a reply.

The next morning, she wildly telephoned people she knew, asking how she could make amends. She knew how much a theater personality needs the appreciation of the press. At least, she gave a stellar performance for the week's run of the play. But, the director we had hired was not anxious to leave the Civic Theater. We couldn't afford him, so he then maneuvered his wife into a coaching position. She began casting her New York pupils in the best roles in our plays. Soon afterwards, the Civic Theater died a catastrophic death.

Another time, I escorted movie star, Hedy Lamarr to a Press Club dance. That evening, Senator Arthur Vandenberg, who was a widower and quite a ladies' man, upon meeting the actress, relieved me of any further responsibility of looking after her or of taking her home.

A happy incident occured one time while I was visiting in New York and had stopped at the New Weston Hotel. As I approached the elevator, Miss Jane Cowl entered it. We rode up several floors together. She spoke pleasantly: I later gathered up courage and telephoned her room. I was not a 'masher.' I simply wanted to tell her that she was my favorite actress: I had enjoyed immensely every play in which I had seen her, the most recent being "The Jealous Moon." She was not in, but she called me back and we had a most delightful chat about the theater. (When Mrs. Grace Coolidge, the former First Lady, rode up with me another time, I was not able to think of any reason to ring her room!)

My life's path seems to have been crossed by an extraordinary number of unusual women, some of them glamorous, some famous for beauty or talents, some young, some old, some rich, some poor—even a few who were of passing notoriety due to circumstances beyond their control. I can assure you that all were interesting. The inability to set one apart has kept me always a bachelor.

Women named Hildegarde seemed to have a special attraction for me, as I have four whom I have known as friends, all of them beautiful, clever, outgoing and worthy of any man's pursuit. There was Hildegarde Knef, renowned German actress of film, stage and television. She is also the author of two world-wide best sellers: *The Gift Horse* especially was translated and published in many lands. Then there was the famous Hildegarde, the 'French' chanteuse from Michigan whose songs have delighted unnumbered thousands in theaters and nightclubs everywhere.

Third was Hildegarde Lyons, society editor of the *New Orleans Times-Picayune,* mentioned elsewhere. When I brought up the question of marriage, she surprised me by saying, "I have another offer. What should I do?" Since the other guy was handsome, very well-educated, owned a large plantation (and presumably an income which surpassed mine), I advised her to take him—which she did!

Last, but certainly not least, there was Hildegarde Bathhurst, society hostess in Washington and New York. She was the wife and mother of two West Pointers and had a quick wit and sense of humor.

Another long-standing and very dear friendship is that of Avis Hughes McIntyre, whose name leapt out of the headlines in my morning paper telling me she had been left many millions in the controversial will of Howard Hughes. I sent a note of congratulations: her quick reply, "I wish I had got this fortune a little sooner, for I could have saved the *Evening Star* (a favorite Washington newspaper which folded some time ago.)"

There was also Mrs. Randolph Huntington Miner (a woman who proudly traced her ancestry to the officers of the King of Spain who once ruled over California), whose wit, wealth and style made her, at slightly past middle age, one of the grande dames and leading hostesses of Washington. She was the widow of a Naval commander who had served in the Phillipines with Admiral Dewey. She was dubbed 'Queen of the Pacific Fleet' by Naval officers in California: ever after, she basked in the glory of that nickname.

She told many fascinating tales of early frontier days: I especially remember one about the menace to the Spanish colonials by the Russians on the north and the Mexicans on the south. Baron Rozanoff, an envoy of Catherine the Great, had failed in his mission to make a treaty with Japan. Not wishing to return home empty-handed, he went to Alaska and then decided to found a new Russian empire in California.

Arrival of the Russians threw Monteray into a panic. 'Tuleta' Miner's great-grandfather, Jose Dario Arguello, then governor of Spanish California, sent for the Baron and invited him to the governor's residence in the Presidio. Here the Baron fell madly in love with the beautiful daughter of the house, Concepcion Arguello. Soon, all danger of an enemy invasion was over!

The later Mexican invasion was settled by a duel between the commanders of the two armies, which the Mexicans won. The haughty Spanish aristocrats were then subjected to Mexican rule for many years until California was admitted to the Union.

Tuleta Miner's admirers were legion. She was an expert bridge player, a warm-hearted human being, and she presented an absolutely regal appearance as she moved about in Washington society. She maintained a large apartment here, staffed by Spanish servants, and another residence in Pasedena where she spent part of each year.

Nothing titilates Americans quite so much as a title. So, there was quite a flurry when Lady Gertrude Ethel Leslie, big game hunter and widow of a British baronet, established an apartment in Washington which was open to the corridors but guarded by large wrought iron gates. She began a series of parties to which she invited both those of high and low estate, as she had come to know them here. Her buffet suppers for 100 people were notable in that each person served himself: one might be waiting in line between the German Ambassador and a Cabinet member—or between somebody's private secretary and a clerk on Capitol hill. When she entertained, she sometimes shocked her guests by displaying pictures of her African safaris where the retinue of blacks in substantial numbers were all without any clothes whatsoever, except for an occasional ring in nose or ears. It was whispered about that the late Baron, reputed to be worth millions, had passed away just as he was at the point of divorcing the lady. She managed to survive the bereavement with the back-log of a great romantic affair in Paris. One day as we drove in from luncheon at a Virginia estate, she told me of her great passion for the Frenchman and of his expiring in her arms. The memories awakened by this telling sent her into such a torrent of lamentation and weeping that I feared almost to leave her alone in her apartment after we reached there.

To get back to more prosaic people and events, I 'went to the dogs' quite literally in 1940 by handling the publicity for the National Kennel Club Show. This brought me in touch with an unusual group of people just like those I had met at the Cleveland Dog Show a decade before. Dog lovers, kennel owners and other doggie types are not crazier than other people: they are just specialized in their dementia. The different breeds of dogs have quite varied personalities and qualities: I love them all and view their devotion to mankind as one of the enduring facts of life. A mean dog, with a sour disposition, is like a mean man—little can be said or done for him.

The *Washington Evening Star* published at this time a classic cartoon by Jim Berryman entitled "The Best Dog in the Show." Jim presented me with the autographed original drawing which is a cherished decoration on my apartment wall.

This was followed by a several weeks' stay in Chicago on duty with the American Retail Convention at its annual convention. The top retailers of the nation were assembled: we lived and met under the roof of the Stevens Hotel, one of the world's largest. In one of the lighter escapes from the ponderous sessions, I visited the 'Gay Nineties' caberet one evening and entered a dancing contest with one of the chorus girls as my partner. We failed to win the magnum of champagne (the winners had a large party of friends who supported them with vociferous applause.) When the contest ended, the mistress of ceremonies announced that she would now take the floor with the best waltzer in the room, approached our table and, to my astonishment, held out her hands to me!

Several months before this, Hitler's legions had invaded Poland: now they were sweeping across the Low Countries, nearing the site of the historic Battle of Dunkirk. The news from Europe each day seemed of more interest to the delegates than convention matters. Occasionally, the sessions would be interrupted by the chair to read war news bulletins. The morning the war began with the invasion of Poland and I brought in the morning paper with big black headlines, my mother (then 82) declared, "I wish I could shoulder a gun!" With millions of others, she was envisioning the devastation that would be wreaked by the mad paperhanger before the war was ended.

Soon a call came from my friend, Ruth Nichols, a Quaker and pioneer aviatrix, who wanted me to handle public relations for Relief Wings, an air group she was forming to carry food, medicines and other help to the world's ill, destitute, homeless refugee adults and children. Her pacifist beliefs would not permit Ruth to do anything to help the war effort; but, she was a great humanitarian and wanted to help the needy. She had acquired a couple airplanes and started to accumulate funds and personnel to carry out her plans.

Ruth and I had been together at the Cleveland Air Races when Jackie Cochran won the Bendix trophy in the trans-continental air race. With Jackie's husband, Floyd Odlum, we met Cochran at the airport and spent the evening at their suite at the Cleveland Hotel, celebrating and receiving an endless flow of guests, flowers, telegrams and telephone calls. Jackie was flushed with victory and tired and nervous from the grueling flight. But, she was certainly 'down to earth' in her demeanor: I have always

71

found her to be a very realistic, kind and sensible person. She never denied her less privileged childhood: she had always known what she wanted, went after it and got it, thus becoming a world- famous person in aviation.

Now Ruth and I teamed up to use the new science of aviation to carry relief to the world's suffering, instead of delivering air raids and shattering bombs to make them suffer more. I was skeptical of the success of this effort, but quite sympathetic to its aims. Since I was a Reserve Officer, I was not too far from being called up for military service. Ruth asked me a direct question one day: "Do you believe in killing people?"

"Certainly not!" I replied.

"Then why don't you resign your Army Commission?"

Ruth's pacifistic inclinations made this seem quite a logical move to her. But, with the war going on in Europe which would soon involve our country, it would have been quite impossible for me to do this. Call it contradictory if you will, but I'd rather say that patriotic instincts made me willing to sign up, if called to duty, and go to the battlefields, gun in hand, for whatever fate awaited me there.

I could see there was no reconciling our beliefs, so I did not argue. I simply said, "Ruth, since you are wiling to die rather than serve in any capacity connected with making war, and I am ready to go to war and participate in any way I'm needed, let's not ever discuss these matters again. Our friendship is too great to be lost by endless discussion."

She agreed and we never mentioned the subject again.

From my studies as a reserve officer, I had had experience in writing war games. I prepared two simulated plans that would publicize the aims of Relief Wings. One was the massing of all elements of relief from a *Great Disaster, Military or Otherwise.* We used 'ham'radio operators to send out the call for help. They cooperated extremely well.

The massing point was Greenport, Long Island. At dawn on a Sunday morning, the call went out. Before noon, literally dozens of private planes had arrived, plus dozens of doctors, nurses, firemen, police, legionaires, press and radio representatives. After an informal and bountiful luncheon, all departed declaring the demonstration was a brilliant success.

The other plan involved a shipload of refugees stranded outside a harbor. Our planes were to fly out and drop blankets and food, also personnel to land on board and quiet their fears until the Navy and Coast Guard could organize their rescue and get them ashore.

As if by pre-arrangement, at this moment came word that we had been invited to stage this demonstration at Gloucester, Massachusetts as part of a huge 'Gloucester Day' extravaganza organized by Natalie Hays Hammond, a daughter of the wealthy and prominent John Hays Hammond family (he was a former Ambassador to France) who was organizing Massachusetts women for home front service if war came. She had great organizing ability and the publicity this occasion would attract made it an excellent setting for our project.

There was an abandoned schooner in Gloucester Harbor which would be the refugee ship. The Navy, Coast Guard, Boy Scouts, Women's Motor Corps and other agencies were willing to take part. The Boston newspapers, film and other photographic services would cover. When the day arrived, the *New York Times* and *Life* magazine were there.

Arriving the night before, Ruth and I were invited to a large buffet supper at Natalie's mansion on a hill overlooking the harbor. Here we found the Governor of Massachusetts, admirals, generals, senators, socialites from New York and Boston plus scores of celebrities of music and theater. Canadian bagpipers played their stirring tunes on a slope above the crowded garden. Dancing to music by a leading orchestra from New York followed dinner. A midnight swim attracted many to the spacious pool, surrounded by flowers, overlooking the sea.

The next morning, thousands converged on the scene. I tried to be everywhere, one moment explaining to wealthy Mrs. Jacob Leander-Loose (who owned Sunshine Biscuits) what was going on; the next seeking in vain for the chauffeur who'd been assigned to me by the Motor Corps. I helped the press, got citizens out to the stricken ship, arranged for expert swimmers to dive overboard for the cameras, and generally wondered how I'd ever got mixed up in such an uproar!

Ruth and I and the press went out to the ship in a motor launch while rescue planes soared overhead, and smoke poured from smudge pots which lined the rails. The camera men had a field day, climaxing when Ruth staggered ashore, carrying a hefty sailor of the U.S. Navy piggy-back over her shoulders.

Then it was time for lunch: we turned our attention from relief and rescue to another delightful social occasion at the Hammond mansion, highlighted by the presence of Bert Lytell and Helen Menken from Broadway, Margaret Namara of the Chicago Opera, John Davis Lodge (later Governor of Massachusetts and Ambassador to Spain) and his famous wife, the dancer Francesca Braggioti. After lunch, Ruth and the other celebrities joined in a radio broadcast describing the day's activities. Ruth, for sure, got in a vigorous plug for Relief Wings. That evening, all of us went to dinner at Magnolia Casino, followed by a benefit program in which all of our famous artists appeared.

Frequently those days, I saw my old friend, Danton Walker, who had acquired considerable eclat as the 'Broadway Columnist' for the *New York Daily News*. Dan formerly lived in Washington and for some time did research at the Library of Congress for Alexander Wollcott, the drama critic. One day he told me he wondered how he could get on the staff of some New York paper. I suggested walking in and asking for a job: I further advised trying the *Daily News.*

He was taken on as an assistant movie critic and, for quite a time, covered openings of second-rate movies and such news. One day it happened that Burns Mantle, the *News'* drama critic, was ill. An opera starring Lily Pons needed to be covered at the Metropolitan Opera House. Dan knew a lot about opera: when the search for a substitute was made, he volunteered to go. His write-up properly covered the music: he also dealt enthusiastically with the star's costume which exposed her attractive midriff.

Captain Patterson, the *News'* publisher, was delighted with this innovation. He called Dan into his office to ask him what he would like to be doing for the paper. Dan was tired of his job and seized the moment to unveil his secret desire to do a Broadway column. He got the chance, and did it so well that the next time I went to see him, I had to go through identification and a wall of secretaries to get to his desk!

Danton's beat was every place where the lights were shining on Broadway. A line of praise in his column was worth a small fortune to aspiring entertainers and musicians. I was with him one evening for a whirl through cocktails, dinner and visits to several cabarets. Each place we were given red-carpet treatment and greeted by everyone of importance. Along toward dawn, we breakfasted on fried chicken and had a pleasant visit with Robert Montgomery of Hollywood.

Hugo Inden, an outstanding German artist teaching in one of Washington's art schools came to me one day, complaining that at a party the night before, as the talk turned to the approaching war, one of the guests declared, "All Germans are swine!" Hugo, who was a naturalized American but still loved his Fatherland, asked me, "Do you think I am going to be persecuted all during this war just because I was born a German?"

I assured him there were stupid Americans who would make such remarks, but he should always consider the source, brush off such incidents and forget them. Ten days later, he was operated on for a perforated ulcer and died shortly thereafter, while his niece and dearest relative was crossing the Atlantic to be near him. I felt that Hugo was not only extremely talented, but had one of the greatest spirits of any human being I'd ever known. His family had been rich and prominent in Germany, summering in the Black Forest and wintering on the Mediterranean. Two brothers were lost in World War One: the family fortune was also lost and the parents died. Hugo finished his art education in Dusseldorf and embarked for this country with little money and no knowledge of English. But, he persevered and was just beginning to get wide recognition when he passed away, at 40, and escaped the lashes of thoughtless tongues in wartime.

The National Gallery of Art, made possible by Andrew Mellon's millions, was completed and dedicated in 1941. Of the many thousands invited for this auspicious event, some 8,000 came. It was zero degree weather: hundreds of cars carrying formally dressed and celebrated guests were halted in a gigantic traffic jam. Many left their limousines and walked the rest of the way. President Roosevelt and the First Lady headed the list of those present; the red-coated Marine Band played; and art patrons from throughout the world were awed by the newest addition to Washington culture.

Another exciting event was the arrival of the Duke and Duchess of Windsor for their first visit since their marriage. Having met the Duke years before at Wembley, I was anxious to see what changes had been wrought by his romance and abdication, and the intervening time. The famous pair stopped traffic wherever they went. Thousands gathered in the streets outside the National Press Club when we gave them a reception. (See press clipping at end of chapter.)

As we passed down the receiving line, both the Duke and his Wally were warm and friendly. As one reporter wrote the following day, "It is difficult to say what Wally has, but whatever it is, every woman who met her would give a great deal to possess it." She was elegantly attired and had a most engaging face and figure. But, the outstanding thing about her is a sort of personal magnetism that cannot be captured in words. The Duke's remarks were brief, but very much to the point and well- received. He also was smartly dressed and seemed to have withstood the passing years with little concern over the loss of an imperial throne.

THE WASHINGTON DAILY NEWS, TUESDAY, JANUARY 4, 1944

Tablecloth Autographed by Many Notables Prized Possession of Doolittles

By EVELYN PEYTON GORDON

"It is a story book in itself. Many of the things it recalls are stranger than any fiction. Once it was fascinating to reminisce about those truths. But today, in view of all that has happened, it is sometimes terrifying."

Mrs. James Doolittle was talking about a tablecloth. The wife of the new commander of the U. S. Eighth Air Force has a soft, musical voice. Her white hair is cut short and dressed smoothly around her fine-shaped head. And when she spoke of the tablecloth there was something nostalgic in her voice.

Yes, she spoke of a tablecloth. But certainly no ordinary one. In fact, the particular tablecloth was discussed is one of the proudest possessions of Maj. Gen. James Doolittle. It is a tablecloth on which the Doolittle guests have signed their names for more than 10 years. Later Mrs. Doolittle embroidered the written signatures.

Jo Doolittle is an adaptable wife. In fact, she believes adaptability to be a first requisite for an aviator's wife. But that is an understatement when you remember that she once picked up the telephone to hear a friend tell her that Jimmy Doolittle had bailed out of his plane at 300 feet. And again when the War Department called her to Washington, where she found Jimmy just back from his bombing of Tokio.

PUTS NAPKINS AWAY, TOO

"And yet, since Jimmy has been away so much, I just haven't had the spirit to work on the tablecloth. I started it back in February, 1926, and I worked on it for 10 years. Then I somehow felt that anything which had gone on that long might as well be stopped. It's not finished, but I haven't done much since February, 1939. Once I did start some napkins. But I've put those away, too."

The signatures on the tablecloth—and there are thousands of them—are of those who have actually broken bread with the Doolittles. The cloth is of heavy damask, 2½ by 3½ yards, and the signatures are finely embroidered in black. Guests have often commented on its beauty and wondered how Jo Doolittle got the India ink to take so well on fabric!

"As a matter of fact, toward the end it was so difficult to find a newly written signature that I'd have to search for hours before I could embroider it. In the beginning the names were in little groups and easy to find. Now it is almost solid with names."

HAS TRAVELED FAR

It is probably the most traveled tablecloth in the world. Mrs. Doolittle used to take it on airplane trips to occupy her spare time. It has been around the world and has crossed the Atlantic countless times. It didn't start out to be a celebrity piece. It just became one.

"After it became so well known, my friends used to say I was silly to risk it on those trips. They insisted it had actually become valuable from a collector's point.

"Yes, once I did start a card index of the signatures. I divided the cloth into squares—on a chart of course—and started cataloguing the squares. I've never finished that, so I really don't know how many names there are on it," Mrs. Doolittle sighed.

"Yes, it is a fascinating thing to mull over. But sometimes now it is not so pleasant. Too many of those people are gone. The most famous signatures? Oh, it would be hard to say. There are so many from all over this country, from nearly every nation of the world, from every walk of life.

"Just our friends and the people who came to break bread with us. There's Frank Hawks—he's gone now; and Lon Yancey, also gone. There's Lawrence Tibbett and Charles Francis Coe. Nearly all of the first around-the-world fliers have signed it, and"—this with a giggle—"even Laura Ingalls."

SAFER IN AIR

In all of Jimmy Doolittle's career, Jo Doolittle has never nagged to keep him on the ground. She thinks he's safer in the air than in an auto. So she could understand his business, she took flying lessons herself back in 1919, but gave them up because they were too expensive!

As the world knows Jimmy Doolittle, famed as one of the smoothest, most nearly flawless handlers of an airplane in the United States, so Mrs. Doolittle knows him not as the unpredictable man of the air, but as a home-loving, punctual, hospitable and sentimental husband. It is those qualities that Jo Doolittle knows best, which led in February, 1929, to the beginning of the famous tablecloth. It was in 1930 that Jimmy Doolittle gave up a job which was the highest service a pilot could give the Air Corps—scientific stunting.

And it was in 1940, when the tablecloth had been laid away, that Maj. Doolittle returned to active service, soon to become a hero of World War II. The signatures piled up during those 10 years that the Doolittles were not "Army."

Doolittle Tablecloth and Its Travels

*Hans Kindler, Conductor, National
Symphony*

Giovanni Martinelli of the Met

*Mrs. Randolph Huntington
Miner*

*Ruth Nichols in an Air Force
Jet*

76

An Admiral on Land

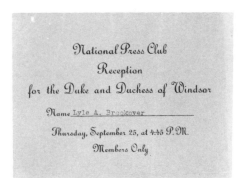

Invitation to National Press Club Reception

CHAPTER XI: 1939
BUYING A HOUSE

Lacking other excitement at this time, I bought a house. For someone who has never owned a house, this can be a traumatic experience. My mother, sister and I had been living in apartments for ten years. Mother, especially, was very tired of living where she could not walk out the door and tend her flowers or weed her garden. I was very proud of the adjustment she had made, at the age of 70, from a Midwestern country home to an apartment in the downtown area of Washington.

We started the search for a house that would have every advantage we wanted, yet was one we could afford. There was really no such place. After looking at the Sunday ads, we'd start out and cover a dozen places in the afternoon—with no luck. One happy day, we came to the end of the pavement on a street in a section just being built up. Beyond the paving was the 'dream house' waiting for us. A downstairs bedroom and sitting room with connecting bath was just right for Mother who was not able to be climbing stairs. The two upstairs bedrooms with bath were perfect for Laura and me. It also had a very nice dining room and kitchen, a den with lots of bookshelves, a story and a half living room with a beamed and peaked roof and a fireplace at the end, and a large and attractive recreation room in the basement.

The house, near American University, wasn't finished. The builder's sign was on it. Just after daylight on Monday morning, I called his number and breathlessly asked the price of the house. It was within my reach! "I'll take it!" I said. I startled the poor man, but clinched the deal in his office about an hour and a half later by putting down 'cool cash' as a down payment.

We had lots of happy times in the house; but, we did get off to a fiery start. We moved in about the first of September and could hardly wait for a cool night to initiate the fireplace. Mother's sister visited us in early October. One evening after dinner, as we gathered in the living room, I gave a shout of joy: "It's cold enough for a fire!" Everyone agreed, so I gathered a big bunch of papers: I'd already laid in a cord of firewood.

A big blaze was soon underway: fifteen minutes later, we heard the scream of fire engines. I looked out the window and saw a crowd in the street in front of our house. Rushing out, I found sparks and flames shooting up from our chimney. By the time the firemen had their hoses up to the roof and were about to send a torrent of water down the chimney (which would have ruined our furniture, rugs, and would have doused Mother and Aunt Alice, still sitting in front of that lovely fire) the fire was dying down. It was simply a bird's nest or some trash which had lodged in the chimney: the bricks were not about to burn.

I shouted to the firemen not to turn the hose down the chimney and got a sarcastic, "Oh, you want your house to burn down, do you?" Possibly, after waiting many days for a fire to fight, they were not about to be cheated out of this one! My earnest pleas finally prevailed and the fire died out of its own accord. My quick offer of free beer in the recreation room saved the day. The whole company came in and were having a wonderful time until a serious thought struck the chief.

He decided someone must crawl under the house to see if any sparks had got down to the timbers below. The man chosen for this job was undoubtedly the newest man on the force; but, he was really roly-poly. As he wiggled through the small window and disappeared into the crawl space, I wondered if we'd ever see him again. Sure enough, he got stuck and it took some ingenuity and pulling to get him out!

CHAPTER XII: 1942
AGAIN TO WAR

As World War II swept across the world, many individual disasters befell friends of ours. One of the worst reached the family of Dr. Karel Brejska, counsellor of the Czechoslovakian Embassy in Washington. When Germany overran that country, the mission in Washington ceased to receive money to pay the staff. Dr. Brejska and the ambassador were not on good terms: no help could be expected from that source. Although the family had property and resources in Prague, no financial aid could get through from there.

Dr. Brejska and his beautiful and elegant blonde wife were favorites of the diplomatic set: they had friends by the score. They entertained frequently and charmingly: at one of their bridge evenings, my partner was the widow of a former U.S. ambassador to Brazil, endowed with a sarcastic tongue. I played rather badly and lost. When the last trick was taken, she at once said to me, "You owe me (so many dollars!)" Concealing my anger, I replied quietly, "I'll pay you as soon as I can get out my wallet." The dear lady left soon after and my hosts brought forth a bottle of choice liqueur which all presentt drank to my health!

Dr. Brejska was a very distinguished man, a former military officer with degrees from several European universities. He tried to locate a teaching position, but the ambassador had him 'black-listed' everywhere. Brejska was well-known as an opponent of the mad Hitler and his campaign of terror. In despair, he decided that the family, with their two little girls, must try to get home to Prague. Swallowing his pride, he secured German passports to travel by way of Japan, Russia, and Germany. Enroute, they lost all their luggage and many valuable possessions.

Upon their return to their fine home in Prague, Communist families soon moved in with them—without their consent, of course. Going to their country place, the same thing occured. The last straw, it would seem, was that after the war, Dr. Brejska was accused of collaborating with Hitler. He wrote me and asked for a statement to help clear him, which I sent by cable. He told me later that it had been very helpful: he was finally cleared and released, but could not leave the country.

Their oldest daughter, Mia, escaped across the border in disguise and came to America. Her sister Blanca was married to a young American attache and went with him to Brazil when he was posted there. She later divorced him and came to live in Washington where we helped her gain American citizenship. Both girls are still very dear friends.

The daughters never ceased in their efforts to get their parents freed from detention in Prague. Years later, they were able to escape and to come to Washington. They later moved to San Francisco where Dr. Brejska had served as Consul-General. Not long after, he passed away, a broken man. His widow still resides there.

****

On December 6, 1941, I was a guest at the Romanian Legation where the Charge d'Affaires and Madame Brutus Costa were giving a musicale. They were a charming couple, very popular with old Washington as well as the diplomatic circle. The evening passed pleasantly, but there seemed to be an electrical current of concern and anxiety. The war was coming so close and the diplomats were uneasy.

The next day came the news of Pearl Harbor, followed by the declaration of War. The Romanian Legation was closed for the duration. I have never seen nor heard of the Costas again. I was with a Marine Corps friend from Quantico when the news of the Japs' bombing raid was flashed over the radio. We held our breaths as we listened: his next words were, "I guess I'd better be getting back to camp."

My call to duty was delayed until the following spring: I was ordered to report for duty on my birthday, March 30th, to a refresher course at Fort Washington. There, with 300 other reserve officers, I began to 'shake down' from civilian life into military uniform. General William Rose, the Assistant Adjutant General of the Army, had called me in and asked me if I would like assignment to 'dangerous' military duty as an armed officer courier. He said I would be carrying top secret papers between embassies and military commands anywhere in the world. I would be expected to give my life rather than let my papers fall into enemy hands.

"I have never thought active duty during war time would be a picnic," was my answer. It apparantly satisfied him as my orders were cut. But, my reporting day was marked by a tremendous end-of-winter blizzard: I could not get to my post on time. I sent a telegram and reported the following day.

The first thing that impressed me at camp was the Officers' Mess. The tables would be loaded with good food, family style. When the mess call sounded, we formed into line and marched to the dining hall. After breaking ranks, we raced into the hall and seated ourselves at the first available place. Fifteen minutes later, there was not a scrap of food in sight: the meal was over.

This showed, I thought, what 300 men with a single-mindedness of purpose can accomplish in a short time. Somehow, this seemed to me the philosophy of winning battles, strange as the analogy may seem.

It was late spring and very warm. Most of us had been away from classroom days a very long time: our Army officer instructors were, to put it mildly, not all gifted in the teaching profession. Some read monotonously from army regulations and then asked for questions. We dozed after lunch while flies buzzed around and the green outdoors was calling—if we dared look out of the windows.

Written examinations were held each Friday: my first one was a disaster! My papers came back marked with a big 'U' meaning unsatisfactory. I was summoned to the commanding general's office. Fortunately, I had previously met him socially. He was most sympathetic to my problem of adjustment to school routine and asked me to try harder the next week. The following papers bore a satisfactory 'S' and I graduated with my class, despite a slight discrepancy in the results of my tests on the firing range.

I can still hear the ringing command, "Ready on the right, redy on the left—ready on the firing line." My trouble seemed to be in finding the target, which was NOT the paste pot which attendants used in pasting up the targets. It really was fun to see the paste fly! My stance was good, my grasp of the '45' was steady, my eye sight was perfect. But it seemed as if the target moved just as I fired. Oh, Well!

When I got back to Washington and General Rose, I found he had lined me up for a trip to every American embassy in Latin America. I was to travel in civilian clothes: I was given a State Department passport and an airline ticket three feet long to cover the entire journey.

This was too good to be true! I'd always wanted to travel to South America. Suddenly, I was summoned from my dream. General Rose asked me if I could leave for New York at once. Naturally, I said "Yes." What else does a first Lieutenant say to a Brigadier General? I mean, "Yes, Sir!" He told me not to go home for clothes, but to leave at once by motor to report to Morgan Annex (the foreign mail building of the New York Post

Office) and await orders. As I drove rapidly north, I could not see how this was going to get me to South America!

The next day, a group of officers, headed by Gen. Rose, arrived: with the aid of postal officials, they installed me as the Office-in-Charge of the first Army-Navy V-Mail station in the United States. Soon I had a score of soldiers and the same number of sailors attached to my command. Officers began reporting for training; but, none of us knew what it was all about. One soon learns in the Army, however; when a group of Eastman Kodak Company technicians arrived who knew all about the process of filming V-Mail, my troubles began to be over.

Complying with Army regulations, I had issued the Officer-in-Charge's 'Order No. 1' establishing the station and my authority. I had need of many supplies which were available at Army Headquarters on Governor's Island; so, I acquired a truck from the motor pool and set forth with some enlisted men to get typewriters, paper, etc. for our needs. Upon arrival, I was met with a blast from a starchy colonel who had read my order. "What in the hell is the Army doing, setting up a new command right under our noses without consulting us!?" he wanted to know. I was floored, but kept my cool. When he recovered his, I got my supplies.

We handled the first exchange of film greetings between the King of England and the President of the United States, and then got down to business establishing fast communications between hordes of servicemen all over the world, and the home folks. We received letters outward bound with $20 bills enclosed, candy bars and chewing gum, photographs, etc. I was prepared any day to open a package with a roast chicken or a candied ham sent by a loving mother to her patriot son!

Since we could not film these extraneous objects, we took scrupulous care to return them with a careful explanation of V- Mail limitations. We spot-checked 10 percent of the letters for security reasons. Some correspondence was incredible: some of it, unbelievably sad.

There came a day when V-Mail and I were stars of the Sunday afternoon Army Hour on world-wide radio: I got lots of fan mail. I was interviewed and pictured in the New York newspapers, national magazines and wire services. Just as I was becoming resigned to a career in V-Mail, the Adjutant General's office discovered I had been in New York 90 days on per diem pay: per diem was limited to 10 days on temporary assignment. I was hurriedly called back to Washington.

Not a word about good performance, or even bad! Not a reason why they couldn't have changed my orders and eliminated per diem! Just a grave concern over a few dollars which, of course, I had already spent for the necessities of living. At least, they didn't ask for the per diem back!

The New York assignment had had its brighter side. I was living in the Hotel Pennsylvania, near my office, owned by the Statler chain. Mrs. Ellsworth M. Statler, widow of the founder of that great corporation, was ensconced in a luxurious suite on the top floor. A mutual friend gave me a note of introduction and asked me to call on the great lady.

When I rang up, she invited me to come by for a cocktail and I met one of the most gracious and charming women I've ever known. She was most kind and generous with her hospitality during my stay. One night, she mentioned that she had tickets for "This is the Army", the great Irving Berlin show just opening on Broadway, and asked if I would accompany her. As I'd been wishing I could afford to attend the opening, I jumped at the chance. Off we went for a delightful evening I shall never forget. There is so much that is amusing in Army life, along with the hardships: the skits and songs of this show brought out most of the hilarious fun. We nearly fell out of our seats with laughter. Later as we strolled, at Mrs. Statler's suggestion, back to the hotel, we recounted merrily the enjoyment we'd had during the play.

In a moment free from V-Mail concerns, I rang up my friend, Marjorie Starr, then living at the London Terrace, to let her know I was in New York—and available. Soon after, she called to ask me to escort her to a dinner at the Waldorf-Astoria for the King and Queen of Greece who were on a state visit to this country. Since I'd been on duty such a short while, I had not acquired a dress uniform; thus, I had to decline a golden opportunity.

Marjorie was one of those persons not just accident-prone, but crisis-prone. She was always immersed in some critical adventure: life with her would have been difficult, but never dull. We were quite fond of each other and had gone around together a lot in Washington. I had a threatening rival, a distinguished attache from one of the Middle Eastern embassies who played the violin brilliantly and was gradually playing his way into Marjorie's heart. He wanted to marry her, but his country's laws banned marriages of its diplomats to nationals of countries where they were assigned.

I was interested in marrying her, too; but, an instinct of caution made me hesitate to declare myself. She was tall and had a regal bearing: when she was dressed for a formal occasion, I was always proud to be her escort, knowing her arrival would be noticed by every gentleman in the room. Things drifted along until the diplomatic suitor figured out a way to achieve his desires.

He managed to get posted to the Netherlands where the ban would not apply, since he was not marrying a Dutch national. Then, he urged Marjorie to come over and marry him, which she agreed to do. There was the usual flurry of farewell parties, to all of which I escorted her. The final night, we just couldn't seem to say farewell. I took her home by taxi; then she called another taxi and took me home; then I took her home again;

and we kept this up until dawn was breaking in the east.

The next day, I was one of a large group which gathered at Union Station for a last look at Marjorie who, accompanied by her mother, was leaving by train for Baltimore where she was to embark by ship for the Hague. Three days later came word that her ship was stuck on a sand bar in Chesapeake Bay. She finally arrived, married her diplomat, and was presented at court. After curtseying three times before Queen Wilhelmina, she was retiring backward from the royal presence when she managed to upset a large rubber plant on the throne room floor. Such were the crises!

The groom being of alien background and customs (and also much older than Marjorie), misunderstandings arose. The marriage did not fare well. Before long, they were again in the United States, the husband having left the foreign service and taken a post as tourist representative of his country in Washington. They took a second floor apartment in Georgetown, but their troubles continued. The husband was drinking heavily and had acquired the unpleasant habit of kicking Marjorie down the stairs occasionally! She left him at last, was divorced, and re-established herself in Florida.

A couple years passed: one night she telephoned in her usual breathless fashion from the Union Station in Washington, asking me to come there immediately. I replied that I would be down, in an hour or so, to take a train to New York, and would see her then.

"You mustn't go to New York," she wailed. "I've got my husband's body here and you must stay and help me arrange his burial!"

It seems the poor guy was living alone in New York, in quite destitute circumstances, and had passed away suddenly. Police who investigated could find no identification—nothing but Marjorie's name and address in his pockets. So, they telegraphed her and she came on to do what she could for the father of her little girl.

I politely bowed out of participation in the last rites for the deceased, and heard no more until I learned that Marjorie was living in New York. But, I was forewarned when she called to ask me to be the groom's attendant at a wedding where whe was to serve as matron of honor. The bride was an old friend of hers who was marrying a Dutch diplomat who, it appeared, had no close male friends in this country to call upon to serve as his best man.

With some misgivings, I agreed. On the appointed day, I met Marjorie and went to the uptown apartment where we'd meet the happy couple. I'd never met the prospective groom, but I was almost overcome by the lady who proved to be the divorced wife of a close friend of mine! We met in the groom-to-be's apartment: presently, he brought forth a large pitcher of strong martinis, which was soon followed by another.

When it began to grow late, I inquired where they planned to be married, and by whom. The groom said he had understood I would make those arrangements. I picked up the telephone directory and, in the yellow pages, I found the nearest church. I phoned the minister and, since it was wartime, explained this was an unusual marriage without time for planning. He was most understanding and agreed to perform the ceremony.

The bride wished to be married, this time, as the clock hands were rising to the hour. So, we set the time at a quarter to eight. The sun's dying rays were flooding the church with golden light as we entered: I, being in uniform, presented the other three. We practically crawled to the altar, but the minister appeared not to notice. The ceremony was solemn and beautiful; the bridal couple received the clergyman's blessing; and we signed the register and were off to Chambord, one of the city's finest restaurants for the wedding dinner.

The groom, in an expansive mood, told the captain who seated us we wanted the "best in the house." Just as the expensive gourmet repast was brought to the table, he passed out cold. We three went on with our dinner as though he were not present. Afterward, I paid the enormous check and kind attendants helped us get our comatose groom into a taxi. With considerable effort, we managed to get him up to his apartment, said good-night to his bride, and departed. One more crisis met!

Not too long afterward, without Marjorie's help, I got involved in another history-making wedding in Washington. A vivacious divorcee, auburn-haired with green eyes and ivory complexion, had come from artistic and social circles where I had met her in Connecticut and settled here after her divorce. She was beautiful and provocative: I took her out occasionally. She had a magnificently decorated apartment in an exclusive building, a custom-built car, and lots of money. But, she was very unhappy.

I lost the inside track with her when she encountered a handsome widower one day in her apartment elevator: romance exploded into bloom. When she called to tell me she'd agreed to marry this gentleman— only if I would be best man at the wedding, what could I say?

We had reckoned, however, without another suitor, a Texas millionaire who had been seeing Lucretia frequently after I introduced them. He no doubt would have been the lucky man except that he already had one wife. He arrived on one of his frequent business trips a couple days before the wedding and was immediately asked also to be one of the attendants.

The Texan had a large suite at Wardman Park and insisted that the wedding be held there. He called in the leading florists and asked them to spare no expense in decorating the suite. They created a bower of beauty complete down to the last detail of a white altar and prie-dieu in a bay window. I was present when the florists finished their work: my friend handed each man a $20 bill. One said, "Oh, no don't pay us. The office will send a bill." They went away happy when assured the twenties were just a small gratuity.

Cases of liquor and champagne were brought in. Expensive individual gifts were presented to the bride and groom. As we assembled for the nuptial rites, our host guided the minister into an inner room from which they emerged somewhat later, much the worse for the detour! The minister declared loudly, "If there's to be a wedding here, let's get on with it."

So we knelt, the bride and groom, two male attendants, and a matron of honor provided by the groom from among his friends. The couple were united in marriage with the ring ceremony. Toasts were drunk and the groom, by this time doubtless wondering who was in charge, announced that he was giving the wedding dinner at the Carlton Hotel, noted for excellent food and superior service.

The wedding party, with a few guests, assembled there shortly at a long table, smothered in flowers, in the main dining room. The menu featured well-chosen and expensive delicacies. But, nobody wanted any food. Cocktails were served; but, no one needed anymore. The waiters were mystified as they found the plates untouched and carried them back to the kitchen.

Two evenings later, I encountered the new bride and groom on the street at the dinner hour: they literally carried me off with them to the Occidental Restaurant. The groom began to drink heavily: the bride sat in silence before her untasted food throughout the meal. "Oh to be happily married," I said to myself!

****

Getting back to the war, after the V-Mail episode there came a period of waiting and non-assignment, lost in the incredible shuffle of wartime Washington. One day at lunch, a fellow officer asked me how I liked the Air Force. I thought he was joking, but he said, "I saw your orders to duty in the Air Force several days ago." I checked at the orders department and found it was true. So, I scurried over to Air Force Headquarters and reported, just under the wire. If I hadn't had lunch with that guy—

I was assigned to the cable office in commanding General 'Hap' Arnold's headquarters. I took an immediate aversion to the Captain who was to be my superior—and the feeling was obviously mutual! Due to this and the fact that I would be unable there to use any of my wealth of experience in press and public relations, I asked for re-assignment after the first day.

This earned me the undying enmity of the good Captain who was heard to say, "that guy will stay here and rot before he gets a promotion!"

He made good on that threat for many weary months until one day, I told my sad story to my old friend, Thornton Wilder, now an Air Force Major. He discussed it with his Colonel. I got quick action: two promotions came through in rapid succession.

My work brought me in touch with all the top generals in the Air force who were lined up in offices that we called the 'Gold Coast.' I saw most of them every day. I also saw hundreds of cables each day from the theaters of war and was in a front-row seat to watch the war. But, I was unhappy and wanted to get overseas. When a cable request for me, by name, came from an overseas commander, but was refused by General Arnold, I realized I was compelled to serve as best I could where I was ordered. I would stay and make the most of it.

Two of my great friends of those days were Colonel Malcolm 'Mike' Moore and Colonel Bruce Holloway (who later became a full general and Vice Chief of the Air Force staff.) I greatly admired Generals Wedemeyer and Stratemeyer. Colonel Arthur T. Rogers, who earned great glory as bombardment commander in the Pacific Theater, was also one of my close friends. He had chosen an Air Force career after asking my advice years before when he was finishing college.

The war years ground on and on without much change of pace for me. I was living at home and my sister was a secretary to a Navy Admiral who was engrossed in the preparations for D-Day. We came home in the evenings, but were unable to talk about the war for we were both loaded with military secrets.

While we were far from the theaters of war, we were devoting ourselves to helping win the war. I worked days, nights, seven days a week, Thanksgiving, Christmas Day and other holidays for so long, it became routine. With millions of others, I longed for an end of it. When the end came, I celebrated 'til dawn after VE Day; yet, I 'delivered the body' to the Pentagon at 8:00 a.m. sharp. Then came VJ Day and a repeat of this crazy performance; but, I was not formally released from duty until February, 1946.

Two incidents stand out in my mind during this time. I had formed an intense admiration for General Omar Bradley, the U.S. Army commander beloved by a million soldiers. On New Year's Eve 1945, I escorted a charming WAC officer to a dance at Fort Meyer. In the course of the evening I looked up, astonished to find General Bradley bowing and asking me for the pleasure of a dance with my lady. I hastened over and took the delightful Mrs. Bradley for a whirl about the floor: when I returned to my table, I had a very pleasant chat with the good general. He showed excellent judgment in choosing my girl as a partner!

The other incident was the speech of General Douglas McArthur to Congress when he was recalled from Japan by President Truman. All military men were deeply stirred by this event: we turned out by the thousands for his welcome back to Washington. I was in the Army and Navy Club when he appeared before the joint session of Congress and uttered the famous words, "Old soldiers never die—they just fade away." I can safely say there wasn't a dry eye among the veteran soldiers in the room where we were listening to the speech.

A few years later, I was among the thousands who stood in unpleasant weather for hours to pay their last respects to General McArthur as his body lay in state in the Seventh Armoury in New York. That tribute showed how little a President's rebuke could dim the luster of McArthur's past.

Back in civilian clothes now, there shortly came a call from my old colleagues at the American Road Builders' Association for me to accompany a State Department-sponsored tour of highway engineers from 20 countries to handle the public relations. The party traveled throughout the Mid-West in a big, comfortable bus, stopping at industrial centers of Pittsburgh, Akron, Canton, Columbus, Middletown, Dayton, Minneapolis, Cedar Rapids, Peoria, Chicago, Clintonville and Milwaukee.

It was most interesting to see how the great leaders of Westinghouse, Firestone, Caterpillar, International Harvester and others received their guests from China, India, Egypt and many South American countries.

They wanted to show the visiting engineers everything and tired them to death walking miles through large plants, showing things they had seen before to the engineers who politely tried to show enthusiasm even when dead-tired. Then came the well- intentioned hospitality, with long bars set up for men who drank little, if anything. Good dinners were spoiled by long-winded speeches. One which capped the climax was the speaker who reminded the engineers that their expenses were being paid, while in his town, by his company. The Latins particularly were insulted by these tactics and threatened to leave the party.

Highlight of the hospitality was in Milwaukee where we were put up at the elegant Athletic Club and were royally entertained there, and at the Milwaukee Club. Enroute to Clintonville and the Four Wheel Drive Company, we passed through Oshkosh and learned the name was not a vaudeville joke. Our Clintonville hosts took us to a Chippewa Indian reservation on a lovely lake where we were treated to freshly-caught fish broiled in banana oil. Afterwards, the Latins provided musical records and showed the Indians the Latin tango, samba, and rhumba which contrasted amusingly with the Indian dances which our hosts presented in costumes with many feathers.

The tour broke up on our return to Chicago: the visiting engineers went on to working assignments for a year at various industrial plants. The bus driver, Harold Thompson, and I celebrated the finish at the Palmer

House. We started back to Washington in the big red bus the next morning, stopping on the way at Notre Dame University to buy ripe cherries by the roadside.

Another public relations client for several years was the National Rivers and Harbors Congress which held a convocation each year of city and state officials, Chamber of Commerce leaders and many other types who came with plans and programs for water projects, dams, harbors, dredging, relocating—anything you might think of—making their plans in hopes our congress would back them in seeking tax-payer funds from the U.S. Congress. My friend William Herbert Webb, the salaried head of this group, led them through two or three days of speeches and conferences, ending with a final banquet and more speeches.

A convention of the Canadian Good roads Association offered my next travel opportunity. Flying from Boston airport on a bright August afternoon, I headed for adventure in Nova Scotia, a land I had never seen.

At Saint John, New Brunswick (after passing over the seemingly endless forests of Maine), I boarded the little overnight steamer across the Bay of Fundy to Digby-by-the-Sea.

The Bay of Fundy tide changes are the greatest in the world with a 40 feet difference between high and low tide levels. This gives rise to Reversing Falls Rapids at the mouth of the Saint John River. When the tide comes in, the water falls upstream: as the tide ebbs, the fall is naturally downstream.

Passing through a narrow waterway between towering green hills, we came into the cozy little port of Digby in early morning. high on the hill above nestles the resort hotel named Digby-by-the-Sea, operated by the Canadian National Railways. It is old-fashioned, but charming, in a style reminiscent of England. The spacious gardens were aflame with autumn flowers. At high tide, ocean waters lap the base of the hill: when the tide changes, great flocks of sea gulls search acres of mud flats for a seafood lunch.

The convention was held here. The Canadian hosts and delegates were charming: the program was well-planned. The final banquet was stimulating, and the Lieutenant-General of Canada was quite impressive in colorful regalia, attended by several aides. Toasts in champagne were ceremonially offered to the King of England and the President of the United States. I was at the head table, the only representative of the U.S.

The final day, we toured by bus past rich valley farm land to visit Annapolis Royal, the ancient seat of government. I learned of the many changes of colonial rule, beginning with the discovery and settlement of Port Royal in 1604. I questioned a Canadian companion about this date. "If it is true," I said, "the English colony at Jamestown was not really the first settlement in the New World."

"We know that," was his answer, "but we do not choose to make a fuss about it."

Annapolis holds much lure for the tourist. At Fort Anne, I was given a copy of "The Theatre of Neptune," the first dramatic production in the New World, staged in 1606 on the waters opposite the fort. Much careful restoration of Port Royal Habitation, the colonial scene over 300 years ago, adds to the visitor's pleasure.

During World War II, Annapolis was a busy repair center for crippled British Navy shipping which played such an important role in conveying war supplies.

Unfortunately, time did not permit a visit to the historic ports of Yarmouth and Halifax, nor further examination of the scenic beauty of Nova Scotia and the neighboring islands. However, I saw enough to vow that I would return some day, for Nova Scotia is unquestionably a vacationer's paradise.

Soon after my return, I undertook the chairmanship of a United Service to China benefit at the vast Archbold estate in Georgetown (built by Standard Oil millions and noted for having a stuffed giraffe and other animals in one of the reception rooms.) The occupant, Anne Archbold, and others of her family were big game hunters and had brought back these trophies from their hunts.

We were all trying at this time to help China stay out of Communist hands. This benefit was much publicized and well-attended. All in all, it was a great success. I secured the U.S. Marine Band for concerts afternoon and evening: Hildegarde, the French chanteuse, sang and helped me with the auction. Among the guests were the Secretary of State and Mrs. George Marshall; the Chinese Ambassador, Wellington Koo, and his wife (who donated precious treasures for the auction); the future First Lady, Mrs. Dwight Eisenhower; the director of the U.S. Mint, Mrs. Nellie Tayloe Ross, and Washington social leader, Mrs. John Allen Dougherty.

Later that year, I made a trip down the East Coast to Kill Devil Hill (where the Wright Brothers had made aviation history), and to Manteo to see the brilliant symphonic drama by Paul Green, "The Lost Colony" which had played there each summer for forty years and more. I was happy to greet my old friend, Foster Fitz-Simons, who was the leader of the Indian dancers in the pageant. He had originally appeared with the Ted Shawn dance group.

The finalle, as the lights slowly dim, the music fades and the colonists march into the dim forest and to oblivion, is an unparalled moment of theater.

Returning, I paused in Williamsburg to see the reconstruction of this colonial town and to visit Paul Green's other dramatic triumph, "The

Common Glory ", which depicts pre- Revolutionary history, Christmas at Mount Vernon, the Constitutional Convention, and the writing of the Constitution with most telling music, audio, speech, and sound effects. It is history visualized in a play that everyone should see. The scratching quill pen with which Thomas Jefferson was writing tthe Constitution gave me goose pimples.

The following year I again returned to the Road Builders to handle the international part of their great convention in Chicago. The world's greatest road show completely filled the Soldier's Field and overflowed into exhibits in the Stevens hotel which housed the convention.

There were representatives from 60 foreign countries: I had the responsibility for their registration, housing, and entertainment. My sister, Laura, and Harold Thompson were with me. We hired several college students and secretarial help in Chicago.

The entertainment included a symphony concert at Ravinia Park, a formal banquet and various dinners and luncheons. But, the highlight for me was an international reception which I arranged in the vast Stevens Hotel ballroom. On very short notice, I secured from the Great Lakes Training Station, a group of 60 U.S. Marines. From the hotel, I secured uniformed ushers, music and a loud speaker system. From a commercial house, I got 60 flags, one for each country represented.

When the 1,800 guests had assembled and the lights were lowered in the ballroom, 'Tommy' Thompson manned the speaker and, in a loud and clear voice, began reciting the list of nations represented. As the name of each nation was called, a spotlight played on a far door through which a Marine entered carrying the flag of that country, marched to the center of the vast room, dipped the flag in salute. He then carried it to a place in front of the stage, placed it in a standard and stood at attention beside it, until the entire complement of flags were placed and the ceremony was over.

I had a host of compliments on this affair which was my debut and farewell as a producer. Since I was the only one present who had a concrete idea of what was supposed to happen—and there had been no opportunity for the various elements to rehearse—I was quite pleased. The ceremony was most impressive and went off without a hitch. There were tears in the eyes of some of the foreign visitors when their country's flag was honored. You can always count on the U.S. Marines!

Back in Washington, I was invited to what seemed to be a peaceful testimonial dinner to Maj. Gen. Harry H. Vaughn, President Truman's pal, who had been getting quite a going-over from the press for his alleged favoritism and other questionable acts, using the White House as a most excellent background for his operations.

These attacks had made the President mad: he wanted to show some special mark of approval for his war-time buddy. The Reserve Officers' Association, to which both men belonged, offered to arrange the show. The dinner was given at Fort Meyer Officers Club. It was formal attire with the ladies present, and most convivial. When the President began his address, it was evident that he was 'fightin' mad.

When, in the course of his remarks, the President referred to the late Drew Pearson as a 'son-of-a-bitch' who had been writing lies about his friend, General Vaughn, I knew the story would appear on the front pages of the Nation's press the next morning. And, it did! While Pearson was not always popular with all his colleagues, such a public attack by the President upon a newswriter was unprecedented. It brought many of the newspapers to Pearson's defense. (Perhaps it brought him some additional subscribers, too.)

It has been said that Washington's chief industry is society; if so, the Trumans did not contribute much to the social scene while they were the First Family of the Capital.

Mrs. Truman (generally referred to by her husband and the press as 'Bess') seemed, in public appearances, to be longing for the neighbors and garden fences of her small hometown of Independence, Missouri. It was easy to understand, as one met her in receiving lines, why a columnist wrote that she "looked like her feet hurt." She was undoubtedly a worthy wife and mother. The Trumans' only child, Margaret, was a wholesome, unspoiled example of young American womanhood. It was a pity that, while her hopes for a musical career were boosted high by ambitious agents, her voice could never reach operatic stature.

Off To World War II

Officer in Charge   First Army-Navy V-Mail Station, New York

CHAPTER XIII: 1949
GENERAL "PETE" QUESADA
AND THE AIR FORCE RESERVES

Three years after World War II ended, there were some 800,000 former members of the Air Force who had elected to remain in the Reserves—warm bodies with no training program, no planes to fly, nothing to do but bitch to their congressmen who passed the letters right along to the White House. Mr. Truman was so disturbed by their plight that he called in Lt. Gen. 'Pete' Quesada (my friend for 20 years) to formulate a program to get the Reserves organized and happy. I wrote Pete a note of congratulations and good wishes. A few days later, I was back on active duty—on his staff!

Here I was working with Brig. Gen. John McConnell (who later became Air Force Chief of Staff), Brig. Gen. Harding, and finally, with Maj. Gen. Earl Hoag who succeeded Quesada when Pete, becoming impatient with the results of his efforts, resigned. My assignment was to write speeches for the 'brass' and to create and supervise the publication of a newspaper for the Reserves. I had the assistance of a civilian, an excellent former newsman, Tom Conner. An Irishman from Scranton, Pennsylvania, his wit and humor lightened our task. We had a number of junior officers and secretaries—perhaps 15 in all.

Conner and I made a memorable trip to Fort Benjamin Harrison in Indiana in connection with the magazine's records. When the day's work was done, we were invited by a young captain, Ray Bartholomew, to come home with him for some refreshments. He lived in a trailor with his

97

charming wife, a former Austrian countess. The cocktail party they staged that evening was an all-time record! There were only five of us, but the amount of room was much more limited than the booze. The party waxed merry!

Someone suggested that we try an idea which had lately been brought out: many conversations, particularly in the Pentagon, were merely a series of grunts. You would never believe how long we carried on a general communication with grunts in various keys, some with rising inflections, others with with negative shakes of the head. We finally became so hysterical, we had to abandon the experiment. but, I suggest that any group can make considerable headway in this manner—but not if they are stone sober. It works much better 'the other way.'

When an Air Force show was scheduled for Chicago, our office was asked to have a booth to publicize the Air Force Reserve program. WAF Major 'Dixie' Ryland and Major Leonard Smith accompanied me and assisted in setting up a very inviting space with fake green grass rugs, wicker furniture, floor lamps and a water fountain.

The booth proved to be a magnet for all kinds of happenings. Picnic lunches were spread out there by our guests. Water melons were carried in, carved and eaten. One female visitor arrived, so evidently pregnant that we feared, even if we called an ambulance, it might arrive too late! There was practically no other place in the great exhibition hall in which one could be so comfortable. "The Booth" made history of sorts and probably helped the Reserves. We handed out scads of literature and talked seriously to every young man or woman who stopped by.

Home again and Col. Davidson and I attended a testimonial dinner at the Hotel Astor in New York honoring Robert F. Wagner (who later became mayor) organized by a group of his friends to recognize his great service to the City of New York. The drinks, food and speeches were endless and the compliments to Wagner getting a bit boring when General Walter Bedell Smith rose to make a presentation to the guest of honor. It was the most perfect and polished speech of that sort I'd ever heard.

Later in the evening, the dinner ended and several hundred guests went home. The rest of us adjourned upstairs to continue the party. A quarrel arose over some girl. Two men began fighting, finally rolling under a bed where one of them came within an ace of choking the life out of the other. Meanwhile, we stood around, unaware of the near tragedy which could easily have turned a festive occasion into a horror.

One of my genial Air Force colleagues, Col. Dan Yielding, had never been to a race track. When the Preakness was to be run at Pimlico, I prevailed upon him to accompany me and to learn how to make money betting on a good horse. Our luck was casual in the earlier races. When the Preakness came on, we chose our horse and took our places down in front of the grandstand to await our fate. When our horse walked away from the others at the finish line, we two colonels jumped up and down like two maniacs! When we had collected our winnings, we went to a Maryland inn for a wonderful dinner.

Colonel Yielding also went with me to the Army-Navy football game that year in Philadelphia. After the game, we went in to the Bellevue-Stratford hotel where we encountered Senator 'Joe' McCarthy who invited us for a drink. I knew and admired the Senator, never dreaming then what the future held in store for him, and the tragic ending of his promising career.

In the final weeks of my Air Force activity, with General McConnell's permission, I assumed the chairmanship of the Bal Boheme for the second time. The Arts Club Board of Governors voted to resume giving the ball (which had been suspended throughout the war and for the 11 years since I had held the chairmanship in 1939) IF I would again be chairman—which I considered quite a compliment.

We chose as the theme, "The Year 2001." Those invited were asked to wear costumes in accordance with this theme. There was an imaginative variety of visitors from other planets, space suits and vehicles, nearly-nudes, balloon wearers, etc. I was rigged out in a space suit with high silver boots, a large silver eagle on my chest and headgear with an electrically lighted antenna. Mrs. Mary G. Roebling came down from Trenton, New Jersey in a magnificent space creation by Brooks Brothers and led the Grand March with me. Good old friend Ted Shawn lent his dancing talents in a special number written for the occasion. We had, I'm happy to say, a beautiful dancing group in the "Dance of the Moon Maidens"— which indicates that we were the 'advance guard' of the future walks on the moon!

I gave a large cocktail party before the ball which included military and social celebrities and many old friends. I was pleased by the spectacular attire of all of those coming. Mrs. Roebling was the judges' choice for the best costume; but, she declined as she was the chairman's guest. The prize winners were amazingly costumed and well-publicized. The affair was considered a high point of achievement in the many years the Ball had been given. But, it did not make a profit, so the chairman was roundly criticized by some of the Arts Club members. C'est la vie!

When the Air Force decided to put a senior colonel (who admitted he knew nothing about our work) above me, despite the successful results in our office, I returned to civilian life. Shortly afterward, I went into the real estate business in Washington.

I soon found out that the world of real estate was one in which you could hardly trust your best friend. Since the 'pocketbook nerve', the most sensitive one in the human body, was so directly involved, everybody was out to get the best of the other guy—whether it be the buyer, the seller, or one of your competitors.

The seller wants top price; the buyer wants to pay the least he possibly can; and your **FRIENDS** engaged in real estate are trying to swipe your prospects, sell them a property you've shown them, and collect the commission which, by rights, should have come to you.

It is a world full of disappointments and an occasional thrill when a sale literally falls into your lap. I recall one happy incident when I attended a dinner party where my good friends, Col. Bruce Holloway and his Frances, were guests. The conversation turned to real estate: I maintained with vigor that any military officer stationed in Washington should buy a home instead of amassing a handful of rent receipts.

"In four years of station here, it is possible to acquire considerable equity in a home." I said. "Then, when you are transferred, you can sell at a good profit or rent the house and have a nice income from it. If you should choose to retire here, you already have a home, by then, almost paid for."

The colonel was listening intently. The next day, Frances telephoned me to say, "Your arguments have convinced Bruce. When can you show us some houses?" We made an appointment for the next Saturday. I showed them four properties (while suffering from a hangover) but they didn't like any of them. In the late afternoon, I was ready to quit for the day when Bruce reminded me of another one I had mentioned on the far side of town from where we were. I was sure they wouldn't like it either, but off we went.

They showed more interest and went through this house very carefully. We went back to the car and Bruce said, "Do you mind if I go through the house again?" Of course I didn't: when he came out and asked the price, I saw a sale looming up. It was a new home and I knew there was little opportunity for bargaining on the price. Bruce asked me if I thought it was worth what they were asking. I assured him that I felt the price was fair: he said, "We'll take it!"

The sale went through without hitch and I was a guest for dinner as soon as they moved in. They spent some happy years there and sold, I believe, at a profit.

****

During this period, my dear mother (who had taken bravely to a wheel chair a few months before) began to decline rapidly, healthwise. Despite the care of a good doctor and nurses around the clock, she passed away in her 92nd year in the spring of 1952.

****

Eventually, my former associate, Harold Thompson, joined me in opening an office in Arlington where we managed to pay the rent for several months.

At Christmas time, we drove to Florida for a respite from real estate and basked in the sun at Fort Lauderdale. On Christmas morning, we swam and sunned on the beach for several hours; then, we motored to Coral Gables for an old-fashioned turkey dinner with friends.

We enjoyed the marvelous Orange Bowl Parade on New Year's Eve and the Orange Bowl Game between Baylor University and Georgia Tech the following day. At half-time, there was a spectacular show: we were sprayed from the air with orange blossom perfume.

Soon after our return, a man walked into the office who was looking for investors in a Florida project. I was full of enthusiasm for Florida just then and listened to his story very carefully. But, I did not happen to be loaded with idle money to invest. The project was to develop, under franchise from the city, the Ravine Gardens at Palatka, a natural beauty spot with the deepest ravine in all Florida which had previously been planted with tropical growth of many kinds, especially hundreds of azaleas.

The town had tried to operate the Gardens as a tropical resort and had failed financially; but, it was willing to give a contract to a private group. It would cost about $35,000 to get the Gardens in shape to make money, the agent said: from then on, we could "sit back and count tourist dollars pouring in." It sounded great: the agent was impressed with my reaction to his proposal.

So much so that, a week later, he came back and offered me a job as manager of the resort with a salary which was enough to live on plus the same amount more to be held as my share of the investment he had originally sought from me. I was to have a one-fourth interest. I fell for this plan: Thompson agreed to go with me. A month later, we sallied forth to a new adventure.

It was quite exciting at first. The *Palatka Daily News* gave its front page over to my picture and an interview in which I painted a rosy picture of the future of Ravine Gardens, under my management. We put a maintenance crew to work, reclaiming the Gardens from the jungle growth of recent years, and had a gala opening in November, 1953, featured by the presence of Neva Jane Langley of Lakeland, "Miss America of 1952." Also in attendance was my friend, Mrs. Jane Fisher of Miami, the widow of Carl Fisher, famous builder of Indianapolis Speedway and Miami Beach.

The crowds came: the Christmas holidays were beautiful. My sister came down from Washington: we drove on to Cypress Gardens, to Fort Meyers for a New Year's Eve party on the beach and an unforgettable dinner the next day at Gondola Inn. We crossed the moat and entered the castle where we were warmly welcomed. As we dined, in a huge room with vaulted ceilings and tall windows facing west, we watched a colorful sunset across the Gulf of Mexico.

In the ensuing weeks, I visited almost every resort in Florida to study their operations and to get ideas. Orchid and parrot jungles, rainbow falls, underwater ballets, the "Fountain of Youth," horse and dog racing tracks—I visited them all. I especially enjoyed the fabulous Columbia restaurant in Tampa, unquestionably the best Spanish eating place in the United States.

One of the unusual and interesting places I visited was the Homer Rodehaver Boys' Ranch on the St. Johns River, some 25 miles from Palatka. Rodehaver (who was the famed evangelist Billy Sunday's choir leader) then retired and living in Florida, visited Ravine Gardens. While I was showing him around, he told me of the ranch home he had founded for unfortunate boys and invited me to come out and look it over.

I spent a day there and was much impressed with the ranch, the management and the happy environment provided for the under-privileged and homeless boys. There were gardens for them to work in, animals to care for, classrooms and school hours, swimming, boating, baseball—all the things which help boys grow into men.

At dinner, one of the boys asked the blessing and especialy mentioned me as deserving of God's consideration, which I was told was the regular custom when they had guests. A few weeks later, I was made an 'Honorary Rancher' and invited to come again to the ranch when Billy Graham, the evangelist, and his wife would be there to present a fine speedboat for the boys' pleasure boating on the river.

The ceremonies were brief; then, the launching took place. For the first trip, Graham invited me aboard: he, Mrs. Graham, Rodehaver and I roared off down the St. Johns to the cheers from all present. I found Billy Graham a delightful, hearty, serious and sincere individual and have maintained that feeling about him during the years since, amidst frequent criticism of his methods, sincerity and his money-raising successes. He is obviously trying to bring faith, help and happiness into a troubled world which is more than many of his critics are doing.

The tourists kept coming to the Gardens and my partners were delighted. However, they seemed reticent about putting their share of the investment into the till. I had completed my obligation. Warm weather came; the tourist flow stopped suddenly; and we were pressed for cash. No one seemed to have any. I stayed on without pay for several weeks, finally getting into my car and driving rapidly back to Washington, sadder and wiser—but sick at heart. I remembered Mrs. Mabel White, a Florida 'cracker' and one of the partners having said, "In summer, we skin alligators; and in winter, we skin the tourists." I had been 'taken' like a tourist by these psalm-singing sharpies and an unscrupulous Washington lawyer. I also learned a lot about many things at a very costly price!

My sister welcomed me home, with no questioning and no retribution. When I was notified of the next board meeting, I drove back to Palatka, arrving at noon, only to learn that my associates had held the meeting before I arrived and voted me out of my office and the company. It is good to learn what wretched people there are in the world: some of them go to church every Sunday, especially in Palatka, Florida!

Col. Brookover, Mary Roebling, and Ted Shawn

CHAPTER XIV:1953
LIFE IN TRENTON

Soon after I was summoned to Trenton by my friend, Mrs. Mary Roebling, nationally-known banker, art and charity patron and hostess extraordinary, to help organize a rally in support of the United Nations. We filled the War Memorial, Trenton's largest auditorium, for three inspiring meetings—morning, afternoon and evening—addressed by Eleanor Roosevelt, Dr. Charles Mayo, Ralph Bunche, several UN ambassadors and other important guests. Marines in dress uniforms were detailed to the celebrities as personal escorts. The eminent Dr. Mayo won the undying admiration of his escort when, weary of the oratory, he suggested that they make a walking tour of the sights which included a stop at a local bar.

When the rally was over, I stayed on as a public relations officer with the Trenton Trust Company which Mrs. Roebling headed. The ensuing ten years were filled with action—and that's the understatement of the decade!

Discovering that Trenton's relations with its military neighbors were at low ebb, I helped found that chamber of commerce's military liaison committee to cooperate with the Army at Fort Dix, the Air force at McGuire AFB and the Navy Testing Laboratory and Lakehurst Naval Base. We held monthly dinner meetings wich rotated between the city and the military officers' clubs. For ten years, we staged a military ball each Christmas for thousands of airmen, soldiers, sailors and marines. I was chairman twice and took an active part in all ten balls. Ilona Massey Dawson, adorable former movie star, entertained the troops at one ball; Martha Scott of "South Pacific" fame, Danton Walker (the 'Broadway' columnist) and

Ruth Nichols, the pioneer aviatrix, lent glamor another year. Governor and Mrs. Robert B. Meyner, Trenton Mayor Donal Connelly and a batch of generals and admirals were always welcome and helpful guests.

In connection with various projects at this time, interesting visits were made to Mrs. Wendell Wilkie and to Gloria Swanson. Miss Swanson received us in her upper East Side residence in New York which was colorfully banked with red roses. She explained she'd been interviewed on TV the evening before. After listening politely to our story, she plunged vigorously into enlisting our support for her earnest campaign for pure foods. I was sitting drowsily on a sofa when she interrupted her plea to say, "I think the Colonel must have had a late night." My face was red, but she smoothed over the incident by ringing for a servant to bring us drinks. A cute little French maid came in, bearing a tray with glasses of apple juice.

The famed Elsa Maxwell and Salvador Dali were fellow guests at a brilliant dinner Mrs. Roebling gave at Carlton House for Prince and Princess Ernst August of Hannover. It was one of those evenings when the big question was, "Who outshone whom?"

Mrs. Roebling is a Leo and interested in astrology. At another time, she gathered stars of the New York stage, arts and society for a reception to honor another Leo, Mrs. Perle Mesta, the Washington 'hostess with the mostest.' to make this occasion memorable, a real lion was added to the guest list—much to Perle's dismay and some of the other cats.

When you serve on one civic board or committee, you're a natural target for others. My list included the Trenton Symphony, Heart of Trenton (for which I judged the "Miss Heart of Trenton" contest), United Givers' Fund, Citizens Action Council, the Mayor's Citizens' Committee, Elks Crippled children, Executive Health Club of the YMCA, History of Trenton (which published a book), Invest in America, America-Israel Society, Trent House (one of the best examples of Colonial architecture), and both the Trenton and Mercer County Committees for the New Jersey Tercentennary in 1964.

I served continually on the Board and as chairman of the Trenton USO (also on the state and national USO boards)and was president of the National Defense Transportation Association. I was master of ceremonies for a radio series, "This Is Advertising" on station WTTM for which I got a Merit Award. I was M.C. also for the 25th Anniversary of the Visiting Nurses Association and the 50th Anniversary dinner of the Trenton Rotary Club with International President Pettingill as the honor guest and speaker and at a swearing-in ceremony of the U.S. Marine Corps Reserve.

Each year I spoke in the public schools on Memorial Day for the American Legion. On occasion, I dispensed a few well-chosen words (I hope!) to the Optimist, Kiwanis, Exchange, Rotary, Soroptimist, Zonta and Business and Professional Women's Clubs as well as to Rider College, the

Valley Forge Foundation and the Bank Women of Massachusetts. In the latter two appearances, I was pinch-hitting for Mrs. Roebling. After all this, I took the Dale Carnegie speaking course and was elected president of my class!

I received the "Good Neighbor" award in 1961; also, the I.V. award for Outstanding Humanitarian Service. I was an honor guest at McGuire AFB for the 2,500th crossing of the Atlantic by the Military Air Transport Service (MATS) and was named, for the second time, an 'honorary Admiral' by American Airlines. The Department of the Army bestowed on me that year a Certificate of Appreciation for Patriotic Civilian Service. This honor was ceremonially given me by Maj. Gen. Earl C. Bergquist at a dinner at Fort Dix Officers Club when I retired as chairman of the Trenton USO.

Mrs. Roebling was a delegate to the Republican National Convention in 1956 and I accompanied her to San Francisco. The most vivid memories of that hectic week are the stirring sessions in the Cow Palace, the scores of parties, notably those of Frances Diehl (State Department hostess to foreign notables arriving in San Francisco) and Elizabeth Arden, the beauty specialist. We had dinner with Walter and Lee Annenberg at Trader Vic's, lunch with 'Mr. San Francisco' Lurie at the big round table at Jacques, went shopping in Chinatown, heard the wonderful convention songs by the late Nat 'King' Cole and the magnificent ovation given Ike and Mamie at the final session.

Staying on a couple days, I had a chance encounter at the Top of the Mark restaurant with a young and handsome Iraqian prince who introduced himself and asked me if I knew the city well enough to show him the principal points of interest from that spectacular height.

We engaged in conversation and ended up by dining and doing all the night spots together. He was a gifted painter and, being somewhat low in funds, was displaying his pictures for sale in a first class saloon. He claimed he was in the United States incognito to avoid a marriage of convenience which his family was insisting upon. As a parting gift, he presented me with my first and second choices of his paintings. I was quite delighted to have them.

When Harold Stassen tried to "stop Nixon" from the vice presidential nomination in 1956, he asked Mrs. Roebling to head the activities of women for this cause. She asked me to go to Washington to see what it was all about. I spent the most of an afternoon with Mr. Stassen who explained that it was a crusade, on his part, to save the country.

He described how he'd walked the floor for many nights, trying to decide whether he should risk political suicide by the move; how he'd prayed to God and consulted with Mrs. Stassen; and finally come to a firm decision (which, in the final analysis didn't matter much, when he seconded Mr. Nixon's nomination at the Cow Palace.)

Leaving Stassen's room, I walked across to the Army and Navy Club and ran into an old friend, Col. Tom Weed, who said, "Where are you going? Come with me." and hustled me into a taxicab without further explanation. When we arrived at the Capitol, we were ushered into a party the California delegation was giving for Mr. And Mrs. Nixon. I nearly passed out, but managed to see the hour through! The guests of honor could not have been more charming to everybody, even me. I shook hands firmly with Mr. Nixon and wished him all success!

I had the pleasure of meeting Mr. Nixon again in 1960 when he gave a fine address at the annual dinner of the International Chamber of Commerce at the Hotel Pierre in New York. Also that year, I heard him at a Republican ralley in Camden, New Jersey. Here he remembered me, flashing that delightful Nixon grin as he said, "I guess Mary keeps you hopping, doesn't she?" He came to Trenton in 1965 to speak at the dedication of the Boys Club: he was national president of the Boys Clubs of America at the time. He greeted me with a warm handshake after his address and then was on his busy way.

****

Early in 1957, I came to Washington for the Eisenhower Inauguration. I encountered Tilghman Bunch, of the Washington 'cave dweller' crowd, who invited me to come by for a cocktail that evening. At his apartment, I met many old acquaintances whose first comment was, "What brings you to Washington? Oh, yes, the inauguration is tomorrow."

At the Inaugural Ball in the Shaoreham Hotel, Ike and Mamie were radiant; the room was jammed; Lawrence Welk was playing and said, as a special favor, he'd let me dance with one of his songbirds (whose name, I fear, has slipped my mind.) I had nice chats with actress Helen Hayes, the Clifford Hoods from Pittsburg (he was president of United States Steel) and many other VIP's.

Another inauguration came along shortly—that of the new President Lopez Mateos of Mexico. Mrs. Roebling was invited as a special guest by the Mexican government. Also invited from Trenton was Mr. Leslie Brown, the leading figure in Lenox China Company, makers of fine china seen on the best dinner tables around the world. Mr. Brown planned to take along a 24-place setting of Lenox for the President and First Lady: he had negotiated through the Mexican Embassy in Washington as to the details of style and decoration.

I was to accompany the two to Mexico. We had reservations on the Mexican airline, Aeronavas; but, when the time came to depart, formal invitations had not yet arrived for either guest. After two days of hectic conversations, telegraphed invitations came from the Mexican Embassy.

We took an evening non-stop from New York and dined practically all the way to Mexico City. Never have I had such a dinner aloft! It was served in many courses with abundant cocktails, wines and champagne. We'd hardly settled back in our seats—in a stupor—when the landing announcement came over the intercom.

David Rockefeller, the Drew Pearsons and many other dignitaries were on our flight. They were officially met and escorted through customs; but, our party received no courtesies at all. Our rooms were ready at the Del Prado, but the desk had no official recognition of our arrival nor any invitations to the inaugural affairs. The next morning early, I set forth to the Foreign Office to try to straighten things out. I found one kind gentleman who provided us with a car and chauffeur for our entire stay; but, he could do no more. That was the kindest thing that happened to us during our visit!

Many inquiries finally brought the necessary invitations to the large party at the American Embassy. I hastened out to the flower market, one of Mexico City's great attractions, and brought back enough flowers (for about $11) to transform Mrs. Roebling's suite into a bower. She promptly arranged a cocktail party by telephone for that evening. Earlier, we had lunched at the Jockey Club and attended a bull fight. There were six bulls waiting to enter the arena: after two events, Mrs. Roebling returned to the hotel and sent the car back for us. The chauffeur was delighted to slide into the vacant seat: we watched until the fifth bull bit the dust. Then I suggested that, since it was so warm, we should get away and have a cold beer.

As luck would have it, the sixth bull refused to die—which happens about once in a century in the bull ring! Repeated sword thrusts from the matador brought the bull to his knees, but his brave resistance brought thousands of handkerchiefs fluttering in the stands. Responding to this appeal, authorities released the bull alive and free to roam pleasant pastures for life. When I read the accounts of this thrilling event the next morning, I was provoked that I had left the ring so soon.

We approached the American Embassy with regard to presentation of the gift of china to the President: it was suggested that we should wait until he was inaugurated. Afterward, clever diplomats seemed unable to do anything about it. Mr. Brown finally found a young lady, far down the totem pole in the Embassy ranks, who realized what a run-around he had been getting. She said if he would leave the china under her care, she would see that it got presented.

While it was a disgrace that the gift could not have been presented in person, Mr. Brown agreed to this and left for home. A few weeks later, he got a printed—not even a PERSONALIZED—card of thanks from President and Mrs. Matteos. Our ambassador at that time was Mr. Robert Hill.

He never so much as recognized our presence in Mexico, let alone doing anything for us. Yet, he was eventually rewarded for his 'great service' in Mexico by being appointed the American Ambassador to Spain. I was nauseated when I read newspaper accounts glorifying his record.

We attended the Inaugural Ball at the Palace in Zocalo. Our driver, who was a real expert, managed to penetrate the jam of cars and thousands of pedestrians and get us to the palace doors. We made our way through the throng; but, before we reached the receiving line where the President and First Lady stood, they tired of shaking hands and went to their private quarters. The crush was caused by 5,000 guests having been expected while 8,000 actually came. Every little political dignitary from the provinces had felt that he would be expected even if he hadn't received an invitation!

Our chauffeur stuck with us throughout our stay and, after both Mrs. Roebling and Mr. Brown had left, he drove me to the floating gardens at Xochimilco, teaching me Spanish on the way. He helped me to bargain with the shops and saw me off at the airport when I finally left for home. He was always prompt, always courteous and added a lot of pleasure to offset the floundering of our own and Mexican bureuacracy.

Astrologist and Two Leos
Mary Roebling and Perle Mesta

Judge of Beauty Queens,
Heart of Trenton

Style Show,
Heart of Trenton

111

Fred L. Bohn, Grand Exalted Ruler, F.B.O.E., Robert B. Meyner, Governor of New Jersey, Lyle A. Brookover

Army Award of Achievement

CHAPTER XV: 1958
NATIONAL PRESS CLUB FLIGHT

The National Press Club announced a charter flight to Europe in September, 1958: I signed up for it. I asked my travel bureau friends in Trenton, Bill and Ollie Moore, to work up a flying itinerary for 30 days in Europe in which I would visit ten countries. The ticket they handed me was complex; but, the plans were perfect and every plane was on time.

The flight over on Pan American Airways was very crowded; the dinner made several ill, including myself; and my colleagues frolicked up and down the aisle, patronizing the free bar, the whole night through. We were due to land in London at 8:00 a.m.; but, dawn comes early when one is flying eastward. I was awake at 5:00 a.m. A request for coffee was met with the astonishing answer that there was none aboard. Over London, we encountered a severe thunderstorm and circled the airport for two hours. After five hours without coffee or breakfast, I downed several glasses of champagne in desperation. This brightened my outlook and dulled my headache, for the moment.

After settling in at London's newest hotel, the Carlton, and unaware that I was suffering from 'time lag', I decided to take a walk to Hyde Park. Here I encountered a vast column of silent and sad-looking paraders who were protesting the atomic bomb, as much as I could discern. I stood at the curbside watching the faces and reading the banners, unaware that my colorful sports jacket was directing a lot of attention to me in return. Their comments were quite personal, but friendly. It was clear that they all were aware that I was an American.

I was frightfully tired when I returned to the hotel; but, I telephoned the

Clarence Chafey's of Tenton who were returning home from a round of Europe and were staying at the Grosvenor Square. They invited me to dine with them and meet some new, interesting and wealthy friends they had made. I accepted, then lay down to take a nap. I slept for 16 hours, never waking at dinnertime, nor until the next morning when apologies had to be made.

Two or three days of London sightseeing, lunch at the Cheshire Cheese, shopping at Selfridge's, dinner at the Strand Palace and I was off to Stockholm where I arrived to find every hotel crowded to the guards because of the annual St. Erik's Fair.

I hadn't made a reservation, for I was to be met by old friends, Tore and Gurli Kögemann of Kristenehamn, whom I'd met in Washington years before and with whom I had corresponded ever since. A message at the airport said they would meet me for dinner that evening. The SAS girls at the desk were most helpful and telephoned at least 25 places to find me a room in a small hotel halfway to town.

My friends presented me with a lovely vase of Swedish crystal saying it was a Swedish custom to greet an arriving guest with a gift. I told them of my experience that afternoon when I took the subway into town and got off at the central square and found myself unable to talk to anyone, for no one could speak English. I managed, however, to see a great deal and still get back to the motel on time.

We dined that evening at the Strands Terrace, 32 stories above the street, with a delightful view out over the harbor and waterways and with an excellent menu which featured seafoods. Our meal began with Crepe Romaine, a delicate pancake stuffed with fish and cream sauce. The main course was Falserade Fikvals Filet Nantua, again fish and sauce. The beverages were Campari, an Italian apertif; Swedish Aquavit; a Skane Birnel Konig Mosel; and coffee with Strega liquer.

Next day, we went to the other extreme in location, lunching at Den Gyldene Freden (The Golden Peace), several flights of stairs below the street. This restaurant was founded in 1705 and is quite picturesque. It also has fine food and their own beer which they brew underground. I enjoyed Briksil, an appetizer, and Kebale Orientale.

Another day Tore took me to lunch at the Rotary Club to which he belonged, and of which I was a member in Trenton. Fortunately, I'd taken with me a few of the Trenton club's flags. I was introduced to the president who placed me on his right at table. I wasn't prepared to speak, but I was in for it. After a brief business session, the president introduced me with a flourish. I stood up, talked about "hands across the sea," and finally presented the flag. I was thrilled when the whole assembly rose, cheering loudly, and I had my second standing ovation within one year. When the applause died down, I was presented with a lithograph of an old Swedish palace where the club had formerly met. And they didn't even know I was coming!

Tore's Mercedes whirled me around the city, to the zoo where an Alg 12 feet high, with a great spread of horns, was calmly eating shrubbery and small trees and looking like an American moose; to Millesgarten, which displays the world-famed works of the Swedish sculptor, Carl Milles; to the Stadhus, the City Hall where celebrities arrive ceremonially by yacht. The hall has a golden chamber with gold-leaf walls and ceiling, so vast that I was told that 2,000 guests can be accomodated there at official dinners. There was an extraordinary public park, on a high plateau, with a quaint chapel in which my friends had been married.

I was charmingly entertained also in private homes: one host proudly showed me his new $1,000 desk trimmed with pink leather. I at last left Sweden with real regret that I could not stay for weeks. Enroute to the airport, we drove to the docks for a look at the Swedish warship VASA which had been sunk, with all hands on board, in 1528. It had recently been floated again and was being restored as a historic museum. On the way, we stopped in Copenhagen, Denmark.

My friend Mrs. Fan Louwers was waiting in her Jaguar at Brussells airport: we dashed across the country to Vondelgem, near Ghent, where her husband and delightful children were waiting to greet me. Shown to my quarters, I found a bathroom with fixtures I never could understand. The choice between being frozen or scalded by the shower was limited, so I decided to postpone bathing as long as possible.

The next day my hosts drove me from Vondelgen, a charming small village with much greenery and old, homey-looking houses, to Ghent which was much larger but with a rather stark and ancient look. We also went to Ostend where hundreds of summer houses line the coast-front, looking forlorn at the off-season. At last, we arrived in Bruges, a story-book town with canals lined by many centuries-old palatial mansions. Red geraniums bloom in window boxes, giving signs of life within. White and black swans float gracefully on the canals, while painters are busy at their easels under majestic trees along the banks. At some houses, elderly ladies wearing white bonnets and shawls cluster around the steps in the sunshine, tatting the lace for which Belgium is world-famous. Carved in stone on the canal wall are the words, "No one who travels the canals of Bruges will ever be happy until he returns." I believe it!

After we'd had an unbelievable, dreamy boat ride, I insisted on being host for dinner. We went into a large public square with a handsome cathedral on one side, topped by a tower from which the bells sang out every quarter hour. Outdoor restaurants lined the other sides of the square: we chose one where we settled down to a feast of excellent soup and roast partridge. When we came to dessert, I ordered the most expensive one, Peche Ninon, for all of us. What a creation! A great half-slice of peach, nested in ice cream, piled high with small, tangy strawberries and yet higher still with thick whipped cream and thinly-sliced toasted almonds. I can taste it, even now. Dusk came down; the bells formed a backdrop to muted conversation from passers-by; and, it seemed as if all time had ceased.

The next day, Sunday, the Louwers (Fan, Leiva and the four 'kids') piled into a big car and set off for the River Scheldt to sail all day on the 33-foot yacht, with a 36 foot mast—truly a dream boat. Fan said, as I admired the paneling, "The woodwork is the same as that in the royal yacht of Princess Beatrix. It was done by the same man."

The young Louwers spoke no English whatsoever: my French is very poor. So, we got along with gestures and smiles and many small courtesies on their part for they were very well-mannered. They loved the yacht, the river and everything about the day. So did I. The Scheldt is very wide and we glided along near the center watching the blue sky overhead, the river stretching endlessly, ruffled with small waves, land vistas of farms, roads, bridges and small villages. The land was absolutely flat in every direction. We passed into Holland and began occasionally to see windmills beside the farm houses.

My knowledge of yachting is quite limited: the youngsters outshone me completely in handling the tiller, the sails and masts, and in the knowledge of how to catch a breeze and sail in the direction you wish. I learned a lot that day, however. When evening came, we put in at a small Dutch town, Ternheuzen, where Fan said he knew a restaurant owner where we'd get a good meal. Leiva had packed a bountiful lunch, but it had vanished hours before.

We docked and walked up the village street. We came upon an excited crowd made up mostly of young people. Fan explained that they were surrounding a drunken man which was such a rarity there as to cause a commotion. We found our restaurant. The door was closed and locked. Fan stepped to the bell and rang it. In a moment, the proprietor came down, all apologies for having been closed when good friends had come to town. Within an hour, we were served an excellent meal of tiny shrimps, steak, green salad—complete even to waiters. How they were summoned, I'll never know.

Vondelgem has a Rotary Club, too—or maybe it was Ghent's. Since I would not be there for a meeting, the officers called upon me and we exchanged flags. Then, I was off to Geneva, by Caravelle on the Swiss Air Lines.

The Mrs. Adrian Davids', junior and senior, snatched me from the Geneva airport and rushed me off to High Genthod, an attractive suburb overlooking Lake Leman. Adrian was my 'British problem'; we'd met during

World War II when Col. David was stationed in Washington and we became great friends. On a week-end leave, we flew to Miami. As we sat talking in the evening on a park bench beside Biscayne Bay, we noticed a sailor and a girl quarreling nearby. Suddenly, the girl dashed to the seawall and jumped over. The sailor went to the railing and looked down. When we asked him if he were going to do anything about saving her, he shrugged his shoulders and said he couldn't swim.

Adrian quickly stripped to his shorts and dove into the water. By this time, the girl had surfaced as the water was very shallow. Adrian picked her up and was able to wade to shore at the end of the seawall. He had cut his foot badly on a rock. So, when the ambulance came, accompanied by a rescue squad, fire engines and shrieking sirens, I boarded the fire engine in which they had placed Adrian for a wild ride to the hospital. The girl was put in an 'iron lung' by the rescue squad: they came along. The sailor disappeared.

After Adrian's wounds were treated, the police asked him to go to see the girl who wanted to thank him for having saved her life. He was somewhat embarassed by the whole affair. But, his act was truly heroic.

The David's hospitality in Geneva was superb. One evening we dined out at a place they particularly liked: I had a most unusual experience. After finishing my plate of tournedo (filet mignon) and several deliciously cooked vegetables, the waiter removed my plate and then set down another exactly like it. At first, I suspected my friend Adrian of playing a joke; but, he insisted it was the custom of that place to make sure no one went away hungry. You may be sure I did not.

Tom Aldridge, a young American student from Duke University whom I met at an outdoor bar, invited me to drive with him the 120 miles around Lake Geneva (Leman). We had a glorious day and a glorious trip with a thousand marvelous views on every side. We passed Lausanne, Vevy, Evian and other picturesque towns; we passed Lord Byron's castle; at Montreux, we climbed high into the mountains where we lunched in a vineyard amidst ripening grapes. We ordered wine, of course; but, the air was like wine also. We were at the head of the lake: we feasted our eyes as well as our stomachs for we could see down the lake for perhaps 50 miles.

Another day, Adrian's wife, Anne, and his mother, a dear old girl who was visiting them from Wales, drove with me to Chamonix in the Alps at the base of Mont Blanc. We selected an elegant place for lunch, the Hotel des Alps, and ate on an outdoor gallery where the huge glacier hung just above us, sparkling in the sun. Afterward, I almost got cold feet about going up in the teleferique (cable car) for an airplane had cut the cables only a week before, leaving the passengers stranded in mid-air for hours.

Mother David urged me not to go, but Anne said I'd never forgive myself if I passed up the chance. So, away I went to the starting place. We climbed twelve thousand feet to the very top of the Aiguille (needle). I stepped out in freezing air to enjoy a sight I could never have imagined—nothing but snow and ice all around, electrical air, deep blue sky and the valley below appearing to be many, many miles away. I made a snowball and threw it a mile or more down the mountain. Fortunately, I had brought a sweater so did not suffer as much as others less wise. I found the descent on that slender cable just as heart-stirring as the ascent. But, we made it. I'd love to go up again some day.

Another wondrous trip Adrian and I made was crossing the frontier into France and driving some 50 miles amid spectacular scenery to Lake d'Annecy, an almost circular lake surrounded entirely by high green hills, actually mountains. The blue sky is reflected in the lake's surface. I was told it was very deep and cold. Plump white fish live at 200 feet depths and provide luscious meals for the elegant Inn Abbeye (converted from an abbey built in the 12th century) which stands on the shore. The inn had smartly uniformed pages, spacious and attractive public rooms, and doubtless charming private rooms as well. Outdoors offered water sports of all kinds, colorful gardens and a never-tiring view. A composite vacation spot, it offered all one could need to really get away from it all. Here also are the noted restaurants, Pere Bis and another just beside it owned by the son of Pere Bis.

Adrian and I lunched also at the Palais des Nations, former seat of the ill-fated League of Nations, a magnificent building with a majestic view from the eighth floor dining terrace. Here world statesmen labored nearly five decades ago to preserve the peace and failed. Now the UN carries the torch: the United States, which had stayed aloof before, is much involved in its present position of world leadership.

Time came to say good-bye. Adrian rushed me to the airport and I flew across miles of snow-capped Alps to Nice. Here, I engaged a taxi for the day and toured the Riviera for many miles. There were several large yachts to be seen and quite a few sun bathers and swimmers. However, it was off-season: most of the great mansions of the rich were unoccupied. It was easy to imagine what an exciting place it must be at the height of the season.

Off again by air for Venice. I sat with a serious, good-looking young man who boarded at Milan. (I had time there only to buy a few picture post-cards.) He was dark complexioned and I guessed him to be an Asian student in Europe. He scarcely spoke during the trip. When we boarded the bus at Venice to take us to the gondola landing, I found the only vacant place to be, again, beside my fellow-traveler from the plane. When the conductor came through, he seemed enraged because I had no lire to pay my fare, only Swiss, French and American money. My companion insisted upon paying my fare: but, I said I would repay him when we got to where I could get money changed.

We took the same gondola: he told me he had not made a hotel reservation. I was booked at the Gritti Palace which modestly advertises itself in slick European magazines as "the most beautiful hotel in the world." Arriving there, my room was waiting; but, there was none for my new friend. The concierge, noticing that we had arrived together, discreetly suggested that my room had two beds. I offered to share it, rather reluctantly. My offer was immediately, but politely accepted.

My 'roomie' proved to be the nephew of the president of an Asian country—a student at Oxford University, a polo player, flamenco dancer, painter, traveler, and all-round interesting and charming companion. We spent three delightful days together, dining each night at 10:00 p.m. on the hotel balcony while an aquatic parade passed by on the Grand Canal below us. A large boat would lead, strung with lights and flags and loaded with singers. Never was "O Sole Mio" offered to better effect. Then followed scores of gondolas—lantern-lit, decorated with flags and flowers, with costumed oarsmen and blissful occupants. It is quite an unforgettable pageant.

The food and drinks, also the services of Gritti Palace were of the finest. One's every wish seemed to be anticipated and supplied. Everyone was polite and helpful in our efforts to cope with the lira. A 10-lira coin was worth about 1.6 cents American. My friend and I shopped, saw an art exhibit in the doge's Palace, strolled everywhere, spent hours in the Plaza of St. Marks where there were concerts every evening and pigeons all day and evening. They lit on heads and shoulders, begging for peanuts. The shops were enchanting with their hand-made gifts of glass, silver, leather, lace and textiles. Venice may be sinking, but may it never sink entirely! It is more than just a city: it is an experience.

On to Florence and the Grand Hotel, another wonderful home for the way-worn traveler. It was expensive, but worth every lira. The staff there was the very best I've ever seen, even to the elevator boys and wine stewards who treated me like I was a personal guest. Shopping on the Ponte Vecchio bridge across the Arno kept me busy for almost one day. The handicrafts again were hard to resist: solid silver hand-carved cuff links for $2 a pair; beautifully tooled leather belts for $1.50! And, the leather merchant actually tried to sell me his whole shop, assuming that I was a 'rich Americaine.' Little did he know, but we had fun.

Visiting the museums was a joy in Florence. I was enchanted with every glimpse of Michelangelo's grandeur. I don't think anyone can visit Florence without becoming aware of this man's many-sided greatness. In the vast hall of the Academy of Fine Arts, his heroic, naked glistening white sculpture of "David" stands under spotlights. The path leading to it is lined with "The Prisoners," figures of men seeming to burst from huge blocks of marble—but never getting free since the statues were never finished. This is a place to which I think I could go one hundred times and never tire of it. Those whose sensibilities are offended by nude sculpture would certainly have to admit that the magnificent anatomy of David could never have been so well-displayed with his clothing on. It is unquestionably the world's finest marble male figure.

Other equally great Michelangelo figures are displayed in the Medici Chapels, notably "Day and Night" and "Dawn and Twilight."

Florence is one of the wonder cities. Along with its wealth of ancient palaces, museums, churches and works of art, it has impressive modern villas on the surrounding hills. Streets in center-city are thronged with expensive cars—a host of Rolls-Royces—while the shops are a-glitter with expensive clothes, jewelry, and objects d'art. The great cathedral of Sante Maria Del Fiore, its huge doors with ten scenes depicting the life of Christ, embellished in gold, was so beautiful it made me want to cry. This cathedral with its immense dome by Brunelleschi (said to mark the beginning of the Renaissance) is nearly 700 years old. It is the third largest cathedral in the world. St. Peters in Rome is first: St. Pauls in London is second. I have seen all three.

I hated to move on, but the evening express to Rome (Mussolini's crack streamliner, the "Bella Citte") was waiting. Due to a mix-up with the concierge, I missed the man with my first-class ticket at the station. I asked at the ticket window for another. I was given a second-class ticket and got into the first-class compartment with it.

When the conductor came by, what a scene! With his arms waving, his cheeks crimson, he shouted at me in Italian until a pleasant young lady passenger asked if she could be of help. She translated the trainman's lament and also said that, if I wished to stay there, I'd have to pay more lira—a dollar or two in American money. I paid and all was well. It seemed only courteous to ask my rescuer if she would have dinner with me. She would. We passed through the first-class car which, with overstuffed furniture placed casually around, low tables and floor lamps, looked like a mansion drawing room. We made our way to the dining car which was equally decorated and ornate.

The train streaked its way down the Arno River valley, rounding curves at 90 miles an hour: dining on it is an experience. Apples, oranges and anything round, like rolls, fly into the aisle on curves and roll away. This creates merriment: a bottle of good wine adds still more, so this trip with dinner enroute is highly recommended. So is the young lady from Trieste, a Yugoslavian who spoke her native tongue, fluent Italian and English, and various other languages. She was a model on her way to a job in Rome. I truly meant to call her later, but you know how busy one gets in Rome. Or if you don't, it would be nice to find out.

The Grand Hotel in Rome could only put me up for one night. The next day I moved to the Quirinale, an old, but fine hotel where visiting Italians stay. There were no tourists from the States and I was happy. My distinguished Italian friend, Dr. Umberto de Martini, had suggested this hotel: he soon came to call. He took me to the American Hospital where he was on the staff, showing me many of the great attractions of the Eternal City on the way. He invited me to dine at his home where his aristocratic mother and aunt greeted me with smiles and words of welcome in Italian since they spoke no English.

It was a luxurious Roman apartment, just off the Vio Veneto: the dinner was a delight. I was pressed to have more of each dish. the final touch was a large epergne proudly carried in by the maid, bearing 12 kinds of grapes, all grown on Umberto's farm in the country outside Rome. Never have I tasted finer grapes! I was offered many varieties of wine, also homemade. Walking back to my hotel, I was in such a glowing mood that, when a taxi driver slowed to insist on showing me "Rome at Night," I argued with him that it was too late. He finally drove me home without charge. I'll venture that doesn't happen very often in Rome.

Two things in Rome are an enigma: one is the traffic circles which Roman drivers enter without slowing down a particle so that the question is one of survival (but I never saw an accident); the other is the Expresso cafes where the beverage comes from something like a soda fountain, only much more complicated, with flashing lights, roaring steam and levers to push and pull. The young Romans operate them with fiendish delight.

I climbed the famed steps of the Piazza Espagna; visited the Fontana Trevi (Three Coins in a Fountain); the Forum and other crumbling ruins across the Tiber; and, the four Roman Catholic basilicas—St. Peters, St. Mary the Major, St. John Lateran and St. Pauls Outside the Walls.

These four visits insured that I would be blessed, according to legend. St. Mary's, with pure gold ceilings, is said to be the richest church in Christendom. St. John Lateran is known as the Pope's church. I spent a half day at the Vatican as part of a tourist group. When the guide said all ladies must have head coverings when entering St. Peters, my neighbor, an elderly man from South Carolina, hauled out his red bandana and offered it to his wife. But, she chose her small white kerchief instead.

The Library and Sistine Chapel in the Vatican are awe-inspiring, especially the Chapel ceiling by Michelangelo. The Swiss guards are garbed in traditional colors and plumes. St. Peters' Square is like ten football fields combined into one and paved all over. This world center of Catholicism is a place to give Protestant, Jew or Muslim pause, and to inspire reverentt thoughts.

I'd been asked to look up a Catholic priest from Trenton who was studying in Rome at the International College. His name was Father Seraphim: when I called, he came at once to my hotel, joined me in a Scotch-and-soda and asked if he could take me sight-seeing the next day. He borrowed the school's only car, a beat-up Volkswagen. We drove about until lunch time when he suggested sausages, sauerkraut and beer at an interesting Austrian restaurant as a respite from the inevitable Italian pasta.

Later we drove out to Villa d'Este, stopping at Villa Hadriana on the way. This ancient ruin was built by the Emperor Hadrian centuries ago: it is a walled city with everything needed for a full life in those times right inside the walls. It was said hundreds of people lived there: many hundreds more were frequent guests. There were pools to swim in, theaters for entertainment, luxurious baths with aqueducts furnishing water, all the comforts of life. There is a light and sound performance at night there: we stopped to see it on our return. One hears the Emperor's footsteps as the commentator describes him stalking through wide halls. As we walked among the ruins in the moonlight, we found ourselves speaking in whispers.

Villa d'Este, the country seat of a noble Italian family, is a palace notable for its spacious terraced gardens, alive with flowers and birds, and fountains flowing over ancient walls as they have for hundreds of years. We drove in to the nearby village of Tivoli and shopped in open-air booths; then, we enjoyed a bottle of wine on the esplanade in a lovely park. At this scene of beauty, Father Seraphim asked if I would like to see the other side of Italian life. We drove through a slum area where the one-room houses opened to the street all across the front. Pigs and chickens were roaming freely about.

The next day, my spiritual guide drove me several miles to see St. Pauls Outside the Walls, thus completing my blessing. It is a very old church with architecture and works of art that leave one breathless, as do most of Rome's churches. Upon parting, I asked Father Seraphim what I could send him from home as a mark of my appreciation. He reminded me of the Franciscan vows of chastity and poverty which he had taken. He had only a robe for work, a suit for the street, a cell with a table, lamp and bed. That was all. I arranged for a liqeur to be sent him for Christmas dinner and received a cordial note of thanks for the gift which he had shared with all his associates.

I then joined friends from home, Dr. and Mrs. John Finley of Haddonfield, New Jersey and Dr. and Mrs. Chester Allbright of Harleysville, Pennsylvania who were touring the area in the Finley's new Mercedes. I traveled with them down the Appian Way, visited the Catacombs, enjoyed several exciting visits to St. Ignacio's and other fine restaurants, climaxed by our final evening together when we went to Hostario dell Orso. After a sumptuous repast, we joined in singing "Arrivederci, Roma" which was our farewell to Rome.

I had notified our Ambassador to Spain, General J. Anthony Drexel Biddle (at his request) of my impending arrival in Madrid. A message awaited me at my hotel stating that the Ambassador was ill and confined to his room. However, Mrs. Biddle was receiving that evening and would be pleased to have me come in if I were not too tired. Tired from a two hours flight from Rome? Never! I hastened to the Embassy where Margaret Biddle gave me a warm welcome. She introduced me to her other guests, including the producer and stars of "El Cid" the story of Spain's legendary hero then being filmed. Charleton Heston had the leading role.

My stay in Madrid and Spain passed all too quickly. I spent a day in Toledo, the walled city high above a bend in the Tagus River which is approached by crossing a narrow ancient bridge and entering through arched gates. It is a fascinating city, with the factory where we watched the famous gold and silver Damascene jewelry and artifacts being made. I purchased a number of gifts. I visited the home of El Greco and the old church where one of his most famous works is hung and saw the unusual shops and street scenes. After a typical Spanish lunch at a *cigarral* (inn) on a high hill nearby, we left with happy memories.

We traveled by bus: I sat with an interesting German student, Volker Blumel from Cologne, who was traveling through Europe with his parents. they invited me to dinner that evening at their hotel in Madrid. I have corresponded with Volker very many times since.

Another day, we visited the Valley of the Fallen, a great memorial to those who lost their lives in the Spanish civil War in the mid-Thirties. On top of a bleak mountain, a huge cross marks the spot where a great cathedral was built, all underground. Some distance from the entrance are wrought iron gates which admit one to the cathedral proper. I was told that, as originally designed, it would have been larger than St. Peters in Rome which is not permitted by the Catholic hierarchy. The Mother Church is always to be the greatest church of all; hence, the iron gates and shorter distance lengthwise, although it seems a quarter mile to the altar. This was the highlight of my whole European tour. We went on to the Escorial, the tomb of the Spanish kings and the royal families—a most impressive sight.

The evening at the Embassy was followed by dinner at one of Madrid's fine restaurants, Bermejas, the favorite of the diplomatic corps. I spent quite a bit of time with an attache and his wife. When they sugggcstcd driving me to my hotel, I countered with an invitation to dine at any place they chose. We feasted on gazpacho (a cold soup with diced vegetables), roast suckling pig, excellent wine and the inevitable flan, a caramel pudding found on all Spanish tables. When the check came, I was embarrased to remember I had no Spanish money; but, the check was quickly taken care of by my guest. When I went to the chancery the next day to repay him, I was shocked to find that our fine dinner for three had cost less than $6 American. Everything in Spain was quite inexpensive according to our standards, even my hotel, the Castellana Hilton.

I spent some delightful hours in the Prado, Madrid's famous art museum, where Grecos, Goyas and many priceless works of other famous artists are hung on every wall. I lunched afterward on top of the highest building in Madrid where, from the balcony, I could look out over miles of brown countryside.

One evening in a cafe, I met a bull-fighter. We spent some time together. In hot-blooded Spanish fashion, he proffered vows of eternal friendship on short acquaintance, followed by the suggestion that, if I would advance him $1,200—the cost of a fine and proper costume for a famous toreador—he would dedicate the next bull he fought to me. With the proceeds of his winnings, he'd repay the loan. I resisted this chance to participate indirectly in Spain's national sport: I'm afraid that decision chilled our new friendship somewhat.

The newspapers carried bulletins each day about Ambassador Biddle's condition which did not improve. The night before I was to leave, I telephoned the Embassy and talked with his Margaret. She said he was still quite sick, but she added that he wished to speak with me. He expressed great regret that he had not been able to show me around and entertain me. But his doctors had forbidden him to leave his room. He sounded strong and we parted with an enthusiastic hope for a future meeting soon.

Three weeks later, he was rushed home and entered Walter Reed Hospital where he died a few days afterward of a malignant infection of the throat. Thus passed one of this country's most distinguished men, a man as simple and kind as he was great, one who had served as an ambassador to exile governments in London during World War II who was a great military leader and splendid gentleman as well.

I'd planned to fly home from Spain, but Mrs. Roebling and her daughter Betty had arrived in Europe. They called me in Rome from London and asked me to meet them in Paris. We first met in Rome, however, at Fiumicino airport where Umberto had driven me for the take-off to Madrid. They arrived just in time for Umberto to give us a scrumptious luncheon at a seaside inn before taking them into town.

My departure from Madrid was the only moment in my whole 30-day, 10-country trip where I got off schedule: this was because of mechanical trouble with the aircraft. We were delayed an hour and a half. While I was wandering around the terminal, one of the gate guards smiled and spoke to me: I stopped to chat. He spoke little English, but said at once he would love to learn the language and to come to America. Whereupon I spent all of my waiting time giving him an English lesson. Our conversation in my halting Spanish and his halting English would have made an amusing record. But, we parted with a warm handshake and a mutual hope to meet again. There is 'something special' about the Spanish race, a mixture of ancient culture, gentility and humility which results in very warm, likable people.

In Paris I met Mrs. Roebling and Betty at the Hotel Meurice: preparations were underway for a dinner party that night, although they'd just arrived. This was nothing out of the ordinary for Mary, for she'd always been able to gather an interesting group quickly in any port. Among the number of distinguished guests were Air Force General Leon W. Johnson and his wife Lucille. Their daughter, Sally Abbott, has an exciting art gallery in McLean, Virginia where I now live.

The next day, Betty and I started explorations of Paris that included an evening in Montmartre where we sat at an outdoor cafe and watched the amazing throng while an artist drew caricatures of us; luncheon at La Vert Galant, across the Seine from Tour d'Argent and said by many to have better food at a much lower price; another luncheon on the balcony halfway up the Eiffel Tower; and a night club visit to a smoky, dingy place suggested by our cabbie where we were charged $8 apiece for a scotch-and-soda.

With other American friends, our whole group drove to one of the old courtyards, Place des Vosges, far from the center of Paris, to dine at Marc Annibal De Coconnas, a supurb restaurant where white fish broiled in wine was a 'poem', no less.

The flight home on Air France was a delight compared with the journey on Pan Am going over. The next few months were quite hectic. By midsummer, I was needing a rest and change when a kind friend pressed upon me a round-trip ticket by air to Puerto Rico. I passed through San Juan and rested for several days at the luxurious Riviera Hotel on Dorado Beach. It was very warm there and the hotel had few interesting guests. Life would have been dull if it were not for the sea beach and large swimming pool where I spent much of each day.

The pool manager, a young college student in Puerto Rico, took pity on me and drove me in to San Juan one evening for a royal seafood feast at his favorite restaurant. Afterwards, we strolled to the Hotel Hilton and found a wonderful group of Spanish singers, "Los Cavalles", appearing in the floor show. My guide knew the head captain: we slipped in and enjoyed the stirring and artistic performance.

The El Covente Hotel in San Juan was my next stop. This is one of the most unusual hotels I know about, an old Spanish convent converted to a hotel with each floor having wide inside galleries above a patio garden with swimming pool and casino. Authentic Spanish furniture is in all the rooms. From here I wandered on foot through the old city, its interesting cathedrals, colorful shops, the Governor's Palace and the old fort. I made a one-day flying trip to St. Thomas of the Virgin Islands with a motor trip to the mountain top hotel which features banana daiquiris at the bar. A visit to Bluebeard's Castle, shopping in a variety of fabulous tax-free stores in Charlotte Amalie, and a surprising gourmet lunch at a French restaurant (the Left Bank) kept me very busy on a frightfully hot day.

Soon after my return from Puerto Rico, I added to my worldly possessions a diamond ring especially designed and created for me by a jeweler friend, David Samel. As he and I drove to a countryside inn for dinner one evening, we were philosophizing on the unrest of the young.

"They want too much and are so impatient," I said. "Not like me, for I don't know of anything I want—not a single thing."

Dave thought this interesting; but, after a while, I amended my statement and said that for years I'd thought a successful male, be he banker, journalist, lawyer or politician, ought to have a diamond ring. I had looked at them in stores of other jeweler friends: I had one friend, a diamond merchant, who offered to help me find a fine stone at a discount. But, until that moment, I had never crystallized my desire for such a ring.

Three or four weeks later, Dave called me in to show me the design he was creating for me. Home from my trip, I couldn't wait and telephoned in mid-evening to see if the ring were finished. Dave and his charming wife Florence drove in from their country home in Pennsylvania, unlocked the store and handed me the ring. It was so beautiful, we joined hands like children and danced around the shop as we admired it. And, the price was right—expensive, but right.

****

The art exhibits at the Trenton Trust were under my management. A request came, by way of an Episcopal rector in Trenton, for the display of a number of paintings by an 80-years old Scottish painter, J. Torrington Bell. I was a bit wary about presenting a show by an unknown painter from another country; but, the clergyman assured me he'd known Mr. Bell a long time and had seen most of his paintings. He guaranteed they would please our audience. He also guaranteed all costs in connection with securing the exhibit.

The paintings came and were delightful. They were misty Scottish marinescapes, landscapes, forests and gardens in subdued, but artistic, colors. The artist was delighted to realize his life-long ambition to have an exhibit in America. He asked me to price the paintings as he was not aware of American standards. I priced them from $200 to $500 and sold several.

126

When I forwarded the money to Mr. Bell, he wrote at once with many thanks. He also requested that I choose one of the remaining pictures as my reward. When I did so, and wrote him my thanks, he responded, "It is a gret source of pleasure and gratification to me to have one of my paintings given a place in your American home."

Leaving a Trenton hotel one evening after dinner, I observed a knot of people gathered down the street, apparently excited over something. So, I wandered down to see and found David McDonald, president of the powerful United Steelworkers Union answering questions into a microphone held by a newsman. A camera was taking shots of the occasion. Steel workers were on strike at the time: the giant Fairless Works near Trenton was the cause of Mr. McDonald's presence to attend a meeting.

Then the commentator, who was obviously asking questions that provoked McDonald, inquired if his future leadership of the union was not at stake in the strike. This made McDonald furious and he turned and hastened into the hotel. (The interview was taking place on the sidewalk.) At the same time, one of his associates stepped forward and assaulted the newsman, knocked the photographer's camera into the street and smashed it.

I knew this would be a 'page one' feature in the morning newspapers: I thought of my friends on the morning *Trentonian* who were missing the story. I picked up a telephone and called for the city editor. A sleepy voice assured me he had gone home. I then asked for **anyone** in the city room; but, the man (who said he was from the composing room) again said there was no one there who could take a story. I couldn't believe my ears! A big story breaks at 11 0'clock at night and the staff had already gone home to bed!

The thought occured to me to call my friend, the publisher, but I thought better of that. The next morning, the *Trentonian* was scooped all over the nation on a story that was in its own front yard.

There were many other highlights of the year 1960. One was the visit to Trenton of Governor and Mrs. Lindsay Almond of Virginia. As they were collectors of the famous Boehm porcelain, they came to visit the sculptor, Edward Marshall Boehm, and his wife Helen. They were lavishly entertained: one of the outstanding parties was a dinner-dance at the luxurious Bath and Tennis Club at Spring Lake. Everyone they met was pleasantly impressed: all of us received cordial invitations to visit the Governor's Mansion in Richmond.

When the Boehms first came to Trenton, Ed had been working for some time in a small shop in northern New Jersey: he was turning out beautiful work which was little known at the time. The move to Trenton was the beginning of fabulous success. He had been sculpting horses and bulls, but now turned his talent to flowers and birds. His artistic creations eventually would become known around the world.

Helen invited me to lunch on day to discuss publicizing the sculpture. Her appreciation was expressed in a gift of a beautiful "Pieta Madonna." I later arranged a showing for them at the Arts Club of Washington.

The Boehms later gave me another madonna and several birds, including the famous "Canadian Geese," the originals of which were presented to the Prime Minister of Canada. These gifts increased in value as the Boehm works acquired international fame: the prices skyrocketed.

****

I had become very much interested in the Episcopalian faith, due to my friendship and admiration for Dean Frederic M. Adams of Trinity Cathedral, a warm human being who was also a great clergyman with a host of friends of every faith and in every walk of life. I also admired very much his successor, Dean Lloyd G. Chattin, a former GI in World War II and a handsome, youngish priest with strong religious convictions and a cheerful personality.

While I had been reared in the Methodist faith, I felt that Methodist services subject the individual who goes to worship God to long, and sometimes tiring, sermons by the minister. In the Episcopal service, the worshiper takes a continuous, active part in the liturgy with only brief remarks by the priest. Jokes are heard about the frequent rising and kneeling of Episcopalians; but, to me, the ritual of the Book of Common Prayer is full of meaning. I took instructions from Dean Chattin and, on the Sunday after Easter, 1964 I was confirmed by the Bishop of New Jersey, The Right Reverend Alfred L. Banyard. I love the Episcopal Church so much that I wish everyone I know belonged to it. But, I still do no proselytizing. I feel that all roads lead to Heaven if they are followed straight enough.

The Church has honored me very much, for I was named a delegate to the Diocesan Conference my first year. At that meeting, I was elected a trustee of the Diocesan Investment Trust: at the first meeting of these trustees, I was elected treasurer. I served five, four year terms before retiring in 1984. Bishop Banyard was chairman: it was an honor and a pleasure to serve with him for he was a stalwart, straight-thinking churchman who had no patience with many Episcopal leaders who sought to change everything, be the change good or bad, and who stirred so much controversy within the Church. At retirement, he was succeeded by Bishop Albert W. Van Duzer, an inspiring churchman and my good friend.

I had been taking no part in church affairs for many years; but, I suddenly realized my obligation as an adult of considerable intelligence, in fact as a person looked to for leadership in the community, to have a definite part in church work which is so vital to human health and happiness. Now that

128

I am a regualar church goer, I feel the question that each of us must answer is not "Why should I go to church?," but "Why don't I go?" The latter is harder to answer, I believe.

At the Scottish-American Games that year (an annual event in Trenton), I greatly enjoyed the soccer game, the Highland Fling and other dances and the competition between several bagpipe bands. As a special guest, I was given the honor by Mayor Arthur Holland of presenting the trophy to the winning County Tyrone Irish Pipe Band of New York City.

I was scheduled to go with Mrs. Roebling to the Republican National Convention in Chicago in August, but the Saturday before, I attended a large party given for Devey Simko and her fiance, Clarence Chafey, at the country estate of the Richard Pistells. Late in the evening, I was crossing a rustic bridge on the grounds: I lost my footing and fell headlong, knocking myself out and breaking my nose. When I became conscious, I was in St. Francis Hospital with a nursing sister bending over me to ask how I felt. I cancelled my flight to Chicago, my reservation at the Chicago Athletic club and all my invitations, including one for the following week-end at the Fred Walkers' home near Cleveland.

****

An exciting invitation had come my way during those Trenton years to dine with Mr. and Mrs. John B. Kelly in Philadelphia who were the parents of Grace Kelly who would later become Her Serene Highness, Princess Grace of Monaco. The dinner occasion was the premiere at a Philadelphia theater of the film "To Catch A Thief" starring Grace Kelly and Cary Grant. The dinner was a brilliant affair with both stars present. Mrs. Kelly was a most gracious hostess: her husband, a big, bluff and successful millionaire, presided with dignity and friendliness. The Kelleys are a large and friendly family, ardent Catholics and all distinguished: son John is a star in the world of sports.

After dinner, we all trooped off to the theater to enjoy the film. It was highly entertaining and a great tribute to the acting abilities of Cary and Grace. Dancing until the early hours followed at the Bellevue-Stratford: here again, Cary and Grace's friendliness and charm provided everyone with a real thrill, following so closely after having seen them in the film.

I remembered this incident some 20 years later when I read, along with the rest of the world, of Princess Grace's tragic death in an auto accident.

CHAPTER XVI: 1960
ICC CONGRESS IN WASHINGTON

The next big event on the calendar was the Congress of the International Chamber of Commerce in Washington. Mr. Philip Cortney, head of the United States delegation and American representative of the famous Coty perfume house in Paris, asked Mrs. Roebling to undertake the giant task as chairman of the 'ladies' committee to plan the entertainment of thousands of women from around the world. He left the details to her. Her secretaries, Devey Simko and Irene Frost and I came down early to set up a committee of prominent Washington women as hostesses for the Congress. The group included Perle Mesta, Mrs. Robert Low Bacon, Ilona Massey Dawson, military and political leaders' wives, socialites—a total of 75 women that comprised one of the most distinguished ladies' committees ever set up for a Washington affair.

Two or three sumptuous luncheons were arranged at the exclusive 1925 F Street Club to plan the program. Irene and 'Devey' helped make the arrangements for registering the visiting ladies, inviting them to the various functions and planning details of the functions themselves.

There were many brilliant occasions: the opening receptions for both men and women; a dinner and reception for both by the Secretary of State and Mrs. C. Douglas Dillon; a reception at the famous National Gallery of Art; a speech by President Eisenhower; dances and movies every evening; and receptions at most embassies for their own nationals. Events exclusively for the ladies were a visit to Mount Vernon and a country picnic in rural Virginia; a reception by the First Lady, Mrs. Dwight Eisenhower, at the White House; small teas at embassies and private homes; and a colorful fashion show and luncheon at the Pan American Union.

When the Congress was over, I was personally and cordially thanked by Mr. Courtney for my assistance. Later, when the U.S. Committee met at luncheon in New York, I was presented with a Copenhagen china sculpture of the "Maid of Copenhagen" with the wish that I might be present when the next Congress was scheduled to meet in Denmark two years later. Mrs. Roebling was presented with a gorgeous silver bowl and the Committee's gratitude.

In 1962, the International Chamber of Commerce scheduled a meeting in Paris. Mrs. Roebling suggested I accompany her to help with the details. One of the immediate things we did was to plan a luncheon for all members of her committee at the exclusive Cercle Interallie. On a previous sashay in Paris, I'd met a kindly Frenchman from whom I purchased Christmas cards. Now, I went to him asking for a rush job on invitations: he certainly cooperated to the fullest. When the invitations were received by the delegates at their hotels a short few days after the conference began, they were amazed that such a thing could happen. The day of the luncheon was bright: cocktails were offered in a lovely garden. the affair was voted a success by the many nations represented in the list of guests.

Our friends, General and Mrs. Cornelius Ryan, gave a charming dinner party for us in their interesting town house across the Seine. Other friends took us to an exciting night club, Franc Pinot, where the tables were set on several floors with a circular stairway and an open well where musicians played and the floor show went on. I stayed this time at St. James d'Albany hotel, across from the Tuilleries Gardens. It was a small, old, very French establishment where I was both happy and comfortable at half the price of popular tourist hotels.

With nostalgic remembrance of my first visit to Paris 38 years before, I enjoyed the Folies Bergere, a spectacular musical review, and the Lido, a supper club with a fabulous floor show. both shows are typically French, glorifying the female, the beautiful and the unusual. The final event of our stay was an official banquet at the hotel, King George V.

Joined by astrologer Carroll Righter, we were off for Rome. Our plane was met by Frank Folsom, RCA executive from New York, and David Cameron, the husband of the great German movie star, Hildegarde Knef. We were whisked off to the Cameron apartment for drinks. They had leased a very old and exciting palazzo for their home while Hildegarde was filming the story of the Russian Empress Catherine at studios outside Rome.

The palace was being restored: we had to climb stairs, avoiding piles of lumber, bricks and plaster barrels—but the climb was worth it. Hildegard's welcome was gracious and warm: the apartment was luxurious and gave a commanding view of Rome. We had dinner that evening and brunch the next day at excellent restaurants nearby. the following morning, I went with David out to the film studio to see Hildegarde at work. She is a most engaging person, high-strung, but kind and a very talented actress.

We watched the throne room scene where dancers presented a classical ballet before Catherine (Hildegarde)moved slowly down the room to the throne to receive the imperial crown from her predecessor. It was quite a thrilling sight. Afterward, we visited with the star in her dressing room; then, we three lunched in the commissary where our party was the focus of all attention. That night I dined alone with this charming couple in their palace apartment. the meal consisted mostly of a huge pot of nutritious soup of which we had two or three servings, cheese and dessert. Hildegarde was excused early, for she had to be up at dawn to meet the studio's demands.

On this visit to Rome, I stayed at the Bernini-Bristol, a very pleasant hotel just down the hill from the famous Via Veneto and the Excelsior Hotel where all tourist paths converge. I telephoned Father Seraphim who came by: we had a pleasant reunion. Mrs. Roebling soon left for home; but, I stayed on, dined at the Hostario dell'Orso with Carroll, shopped for gifts, buying a black bag for Laura at Gucci's and some unusual haberdashery in a smart shop across the way called Son and Man.

When a cablegram summoned me home, I was able to get space on the Italian airline, Alitalia. I left for New York with a stop in London where I purchased a fine woolen muffler at the airport. Upon arrival in New York, I dashed to a train for Philadelphia where Mrs. Roebling was giving a reception for her actor son, Paul, and his lovely bride, Olga. Paul had been playing in Tennessee William's play, "The Milk Train Doesn't Stop Here Any More." Mr. Williams was a featured guest. When that party was over, I had put in about a 22 hour day—and was I tired!

At this time, I was chairman of the executive committee of the Trenton Symphony. Hoping to find new ways to progress, we summoned the inventor of the idea of 'brainstorming,' one of the executives of Batton, Barton, Durstine and Osborne, who showed us how to dredge up ideas from a group. We had 206 suggestions to improve the orchestra's future when the meeting was over. But, I'm sorry to say, very few were ever put into effect.

Dr. Nicholas Harsanyi, who had been conductor and my close friend for several years, decided to form a chamber orchestra and finally withdrew from the Trenton group. He was chairman of a music festival in Princeton that summer: I attended the opening night. Byron Janis was the guest artist, playing a piano concerto with enthusiasm and skill. Governor and Mrs. Richard Hughes had invited the patrons to a big reception later at

"Morven." There was a large marquee on the mansion lawn, much food and many beverages. I had a wonderful time.

CHAPTER XVII: 1960-63
A HANDSHAKE WITH CASTRO AND OTHER HIGHLIGHTS

One of my frequent weekend trips to Washington to visit my sister coincided with a visit there of the mysterious new leader of Cuba, Fidel Castro. The Cuban Embassy gave a huge reception for him and his entourage who looked like a band of gypsies with their long hair, weird costumes and swarthy skins. Castro at that time was courting our government, hoping to receive approval and aid for his regime. Denied this, he turned to the Soviet Union where his advances were warmly welcomed—with the natural result that Cuba is now a Communist satellite.

At another party, I encountered my friends, Mr. and Mrs. Roy St. Lewis, who were going on to the Cuban reception. They urged me to come along. Standing alone to receive the guests, Fidel was quite a figure. He welcomed the ladies with particular attention, but was reasonably cordial with all who passed. He stood tall, with bushy hair and beard, a firm handshake, dark eyes that bespoke a poet and dreamer, but seemed to pierce the visitor's mind. He wore a somewhat unkempt dark brown uniform. There was little evidence that day of the cruelty and arrogance that later marked his path. He was, of course, putting his best foot forward.

****

In the autumn, I was working very busily on behalf of the United Nations which I have believed from the beginning was a better way to 'keep talking' rather than to 'start fighting.' We were organizing a chapter of the

135

United Nations Association in Trenton: Mayor Holland asked me to be chairman of the event. I made many speeches on the UN at this time. One that I recall with particular pleasure was before the Men's Club of Adath Israel Congregation. When I finished, the half-hundred men present rose to their feet and applauded, the third such ovation I'd had. The president then volunteered to join our UN chapter and passed around a paper for others to sign. Eleven men signed up and paid their dues: then, a motion was offered and passed to make me an honorary member of their club, along with Mayor Holland who had also addressed their meeting.

When United Nations Day came along, Governor and Mrs. Robert S. Meyner gave a reception and buffet supper for dignitaries at "Morven," the executive mansion in Princeton. Then, we adjourned to the rally at the War Memorial in Trenton where Mrs. Eleanor Roosevelt presented me with the charter for our new chapter. I was called back to the podium to receive, from Mrs. Roosevelt, an autographed copy of her book, *You Learn By Living,* as an award for organizing the largest chapter in the state. We had signed up 140 members. Mrs. Meyner, sitting next to me, smilingly said, "What next?"

The Trenton Symphony prepared to open that season with a gala concert featuring Eleanor Steber, Metropolitan opera diva, as guest artist. The day arrived: so did Eleanor with her husband, Col. Gordon Andrews. There were parties at which La Steber enchanted all with her personality and charm. Snow was falling when we went to the concert hall. The orchestra played on and Eleanor sang like a bird. When the program ended, we found a thick blanket of snow outside: travel was very difficult.

A blizzard ensued that kept Eleanor and Gordon marooned in Mrs. Roebling's town house for three days, giving several of us a chance to know them well and to enjoy their prolonged stay. Eleanor returned to sing with the Trenton Symphony several times: she was a favorite of our audiences. She sang with the choir at Trinity Cathedral on Sunday, giving a rendition of the "Lord's Prayer" that was unbelievably touching and beautiful.

The next blizzard to come my way was early in the New Year when John F. Kennedy was inaugurated President. I came down by train; but, on arrival, I found traffic completely tied up. I walked, with luggage in hand, some 18 blocks to the Army and Navy Club. Here I was to meet my friend Kitty Lane of Los Angeles and go to the Inaugural Concert at Constitution Hall. After a long wait, she had not arrived: I slogged the few blocks to the hall to hear a fine concert by the National Symphony. The hall was reasonably well-filled despite the storm. When I got back to the club, Kitty had managed to get there by engaging a taxi driver as her personal chauffeur, for otherwise, taxis were not to be had. When we got her safely to her lodgings, she asked the driver to take me to Virginia. He demurred—and I didn't blame him! The drifts were so high that snow plows were stalled; but, he finally made it to my sister's aprtment in Arlington.

The next morning dawned freezingly cold. Street workers had, by some magic, cleared the inaugural parade route. Although I had a good seat for the ceremony, I chose, instead, my sister's TV in a warm room to watch the swearing-in and parade. No wonder Robert Frost forgot his lines! It was cold enough to put his brains in deep freeze.

In the evening, I ventured forth to the Inaugural Ball: Kitty and I had a happy evening there. The Kennedy's, with all their cohorts, were there in diamond-studded array. It was more fun to watch the antics of the celebrities than to dance; but, we did enjoy the refreshments. There were balls in several hotels: we chose the Mayflower which, for many years, has been the center of Washington's social life.

Some time later, in Washington for another weekend, I went to one of the 500 guest parties for which Washington is well known. Leaving the first port of call, glass in hand, I noticed a group of people gathered closely: I approached to find out who was the center of attention. I came up behind a well-built, well-tailored young man who suddenly turned toward me, held out his hand and said, "Hello there. Glad to see you." It was President John Fitzgerald Kennedy.

In 1963, the 75th Anniversary of the Trenton Trust Company was upon us: We went all out to celebrate. The first event was an all-day Sunday celebration of the launching of the communications satellite "Telstar" which honored the many New Jersey companies which played some part in its manufacture. The affair was held in an Atlantic City mansion, lent for the occasion. The luncheon featured the 'Omelette King' with his variety of succulent instant omelets. Most of the honorees were present, along with some 300 other guests.

Then came a fashion jubilee, "Styles from 75 Springtimes," held in the War Memorial with some 200 local participants. A special film was prepared, "Biography of a City," and shown in schools and at many local meetings. The crowning glory was something Mrs. Roebling called "The Birth of the Brotherhood for the Survival of Free Enterprise." Quite a mouthful! It was to honor American corporations which had been in business 75 years or more.

It took the form of an all-day extravaganza: forenoon speechifying; an elaborate luncheon for invited guests; afternoon, more speech-making; a huge cocktail party, a banquet, a symphony concert and more speeches, all in rapid succession, in the evening. Trenton was never more 'shook up.' Hundreds responded to the invitation to participate.

The distinguished panel of speakers included Governor William W. Scranton of Pennsylvania; the honorable James M. Saxon, Comptroller of the Currency; the Very Reverend Theodore M. Hesburgh, President of

Notre Dame University; Drew Pearson, the famous columnist; the afore-mentioned David J. Macdonald; also, several top corporation executives.

Sometime afterward, I went one day to the state capital with one of the ever-blooming beauty queens to have her photographed with Governor Hughes. As we waited in the antteroom, word came of the assasination of President Kennedy in Dallas. It was unbelievable at first, but only too true. Picture-taking was forgotten: the next three days are remembered by our constant presence before the TV screen, watching the sad events of the laying-in-state and the impressive funeral rites.

The Presidential campaign of 1964 loomed on the horizon: Senator Barry Goldwater of Arizona emerged as the Republican candidate. I'd heard him make a brilliant speech as the 'fall guy' at a Saints and Sinners' dinner in Miami Beach and had followed his Senate career with interest and approval. He and Mrs. Goldwater were guests of Mrs. Roebling at a small private luncheon in Philadelphia. This close-up contact caused me to admire him even more.

I have never, since I became of voting age, desired the election of any candidate for President so much as I did that of Barry Goldwater. As the campaign progressed, he was always on the defensive, the object of scurri-lous attacks by the opposition and unfair treatment by a hostile press and radio, poorly advised by his management and staff. I lost whatever belief I'd ever had in the process of democratic elections.

I attended his final campaign appearance at Madison Square Garden, an exultant, jam-packed meeting, reported by the New York press as a gath-ering of "a handful of partisan admirers." The man who won the election afterward did all the evil things, and more, that Goldwater's foes had warned that he would do. I was delighted when Arizona's voters wisely returned him to the United States Senate.

Eleanor Steber of the Met

Trenton Trust 75th Anniversary features the "Telstar"

139

Licia Albanese of the Met

CHAPTER XVIII: 1964
NEW YORK WORLD'S FAIR

I was asked by Mrs. Roebling to represent her at the Hall of Free Enterprise at the New York World's Fair. It was a pavilion set up by the American Economic Federation to extol the merits of the free enterprise system. Mrs. R. was a member of the board. After a time, when I was working in the Federation's New York office and commuting back and forth from Trenton, I transferred to the Federation payroll and moved to Tudor City, a high-rise complex on East 42nd Street, across from the United Nations.

Here I lived and worked very happily for the next year and a half. My public relations activity for the Hall of Free Enterprise started with arranging a big celebration for the formal opening. A lighted Olympic torch was to be carried by an Olympic runner from the Statue of Liberty in New York harbor to our fair pavilion, arriving as the spectacular gambit of the opening ceremonies. The U.S. Coast Guard was assisting with the ceremony. The party went out to the Statue, lit the torch and took pictures. The water was so choppy that the runner could not be carried across by boat in time. The wind blew out his torch; somehow, he arrived—breathless, but punctual.

I suspect the "Lady with the Torch" was smiling a little, although doubtless she has seen many amusing happenings—and tragedies as well—in nearly a century of watching over the harbor. I was reminded of the time many years before when, returning from Europe on the mighty *S.S. Leviathan*, we caught our first glimpse of the mist-wrapped statue from the liner's deck, shortly before dawn.

141

There was great excitement among steerage passengers over their first sight of the New World's far-famed, welcoming figure. But I must confess that those at cabin and first class rails—the more sophisticated on board— also felt a surge of emotion, patriotism or, call it what you will.

Visits of V.I.P.'s to the Hall of Free Enterprise were arranged by me. These included Lowell Thomas, Ann Harding, Eddie Richenbacker, Claude Kirk (later a governor of Florida), and prominent business leaders, educators and scientists by the score. During my frequent visits to the Fair, I took advantage of the opportunity to explore the many exhibits from large U.S. corporations and two-score other nations. When the Fair closed, I had visited every one: I think there were about 160 exhibits.

I attended church each Sunday at the Little Church Around the Corner and I made many friends during this period, about one of whom I wrote the following story:

"Will you have ice cream on your apple pie?" was answered in the affirmative as I faced the smiling countenance of Roberto Francis Xavier Nieves Ayala who stood patiently behind the counter of Schraftt's. I came to know this young man well, for I lunched at his counter almost daily and dined there frequently at night. I called him by his fourth name which means 'snow' in Spanish because of the 'snow job' he gave feminine customers (both old and young) who flocked to his regular station.

'Nieves' had just turned 25 and was a very arresting personality. Of medium height and magnificent build, he had dark curly hair, one lock always straying over his forehead, dark brown eyes, olive skin, a trim, smooth walk and deft hands to supply a rapid flow of food to the hungry and then remove soiled dishes to a conveyor belt.

"He would definitely stand out in any group of such employees because of his constant courtesy. He spoke in the soft, languorous tones of his native Spain, but many of his comments were in colorful terms generally known as 'New York-ese', a shade more understand- able than Brooklyn-ese. It was impossible to get him to sound the 'h' in 'with.' Any faults in diction, however, were offset by a flashing smile and very quick wit.

"He regarded no one as a stranger: outside such hours, he was always ready to exchange banter with a well-known patron or a per- son he'd never seen before. His outgoing way earned the familiar 'Bob' from regulars who followed him from one post to another as promotions came along. He was patient with the troublesome and adept at handling the 'lunatic fringe'.

"After hours, over a beer, I gained his confidence: Nieves told me about himself. Not surprisingly, he disliked his job: not only was it hard, but it offered very slow advancement to an ambitious young man. Spanish parents who had brought him to the States when he was three were now separated: he was loyal to both. Several brothers and sisters were married with annually increasing families. The whole family centered around the mother, a typical *duena* who spoke no English and resided with Nieves in a small uptown East Side apartment surrounded by Spanish and Puerto Rican neighbors. The family group leaned heavily upon the youngest member (who was single and earning more than any of the others) with the result that Nieves seldom had a dollar left to spend on himself.

"Hedged in by the Spanish tradition of 'togetherness' and by limited funds and opportunities, Nieves had, nevertheless, during service in the U.S. Navy, tasted of bright lights, luxury living and travel, and found them agreeable. Without the group obligation, he might have found a high road to success and won a measure of recognition. As things were, he seemed a very friendly squirrel—on a treadmill! But, he was not only devoted to his immediate family; affectionate with a host of friends; especially fond of a rabble of nieces and nephews—he also wanted to assume further burdens, to marry and have a family of his own. However, he was having trouble finding the right girl.

"Away from this family clutter, Nieves preferred not to be known as Spanish: yet, he took his mother regularly to mass at a Roman Catholic church with a Spanish priest to whom he confessed and talked over his problems (although he was not always inclined to accept the priest's advice.)

"Nieves had lots of style, excellent taste in clothes, and was most particular in his choice of girls, movies, restaurants, his favorite brand of cigarettes (Tareyton's), and Scotch (Chivas Regal). He chose intimate friends with especial care and deep understanding. When one of them asked what he wanted for an approaching birthday, Nieves answered, "A good dictionary." He meant it; after he got it, he pored over its pages studiously by the hour.

"While 'seeing the world' with the Navy, Nieves learned about things naughty as well as nautical, but on the whole seemed to have escaped basic damage to his character, while deriving the utmost benefit in discipline, health, travel and general knowledge incident to military life. He was now in the Naval Reserve and studying hard to earn an Ensign's commission and stripes. He spent a half day each Saturday in volunteer work with underprivileged boys from the city streets, teaching them games, good sportsmanship, physical fitness, and taking them on educational trips.

"There was very little evidence of bad qualities in this man, and much of good. Although he chose friends who'd help him to grow and learn, in his home neighborhood, he was surrounded by great temptation and many hard-bitten companions which must have affected his outlook. Among his in-laws, there were those who pursued the 'fast buck' method of getting along and who would far rather do that than work hard for a living, as Nieves did. His friends asked him for a quick loan to keep out of jail or to pay off some girl they'd got into trouble. He knew of labor union's shortcomings, of industrial rackets which preyed upon the public, of the ways of street gangs.

"He had seen so much of crime, he became interested in it and left his lunch counter to join the New York City police force (in the criminology and crime investigation section.) When I heard this, I wondered to myself—Will the new things he learns about crime, plus what he already knows, turn him away from wrongdoing? Or, will it have a tendency to give crime a familiarity that suppresses the feeling of wrong? Knowing Nieves' love for high living (the Metropolitan Opera and supper at the Chateau Madrid); knowing how small is the legitimate income of members of the police force, makes his future path a bit hard to forecast."

During my last year in New York, Father Carleton Sweetser of the Episcopal Church enlisted me as a chaplain's assistant at huge Lenox Hill Hospital where I had the help of several young men who were preparing for priesthood at General Seminary (Episcopal). Outstanding among them was Alan Houghton, son of the wealthy president of Corning Glass company who had given up a promising future with that company to enter upon religious concerns which he is presently serving with distinction.

My experience at Lenox Hill gave rise to another story:

"Pauline Stevens turned her head ever so slightly on the hospital pillow. Her pale blue eyes were bright with welcome as she said, "It's Thursday and I knew you'd be here."

"Each Thursday I called upon Protestant patients to let them know the church hadn't forgotten them and to remind them of Sunday morning services for all who were able to attend.   "Each week there was a large turnover in my 'clients' as new patients took the places of those discharged. Pauline had been there many weeks and I'd come to know her as a worthy person; but, as I teased her, not a good prospect for our prescription. She was always lying flat on her back, breathing through tubes inserted in her nostrils, unable to turn either way, altogether a most pitiable human being.

"Her spirits seemed never to falter, however: I was pleased that she had learned my schedule and awaited my visit each week. I always tried to spend a few extra minutes for she was able to talk and appeared to enjoy our conversations. I did, too, for she never complained: we purposely put aside the fact of her illness and talked of many things.

"Soon after I came on one particular night, I noticed her eyes were filled with tears. Fighting bravely for self- control, she questioned me:

"Do you think the chaplain might have time to come and talk with me? I feel that I'm drifting away from God and the church, lying here, and I need reassurance so badly."

"Of course, he'll find the time," I said, knowing that my chaplain never failed to answer a call for help such as this.

"When will he come?" She was very eager. "Will you let me know? Will you please ask him to make it as soon as he can? I'd like to have communion if he thinks I'm worthy."

"I promised to see to it at once and let her know. Father Sweetser said he'd come and give Pauline communion right after the Sunday morning service. I telephoned the floor nurse and asked her to deliver that message. The chaplain later told me he administered the sacraments and had a long talk with Pauline which seemed to give her much peace of mind. A woman volunteer called on her twice during the next few days. All agreed that she was a brave and remarkable woman.

"Making my rounds the next Thursday, I came to Pauline's room and found she was not there. The floor nurse said she'd been removed to another floor. I felt a sense of relief: meanwhile, the nurse continued checking her records.

"I'm wrong about Pauline Stevens," she said suddenly. "She passed away unexpectedly early this morning. She had seemed much improved lately, but something happened—we don't know exactly what, and she's gone."

"Now it was my turn to fight against the tears, but I felt that this dear woman's death in a state of grace justified all my weariness as I pressed on with my volunteer tasks."

****

About this time, an interesting cocktail group assembled one evening at the spacious mid-Manhattan studio of the world-renowned artist, Buell Mullen who paints with epoxy resin on stainless steel.

Her huge 'canvasses' light up the lobbies of several great buildings in New York City, particularly the Western Electric Building, Chase Manhattan Bank and the International Nickel Building.

She is most unassuming, despite her great gifts, and a charming hostess as well. A number of her guests were asked to remain for supper: among them was a priestess of ESP (extra sensory perception) who wore a large garden hat with huge flowers (I thought I saw some vegetables!) falling over the brim.

The ESP lady gathered us into a semi-circle after supper and told us some extraordinary things. The son-in-law of the President of Peru who sat next to me was fairly overcome with what she told him about his country, his wife and children, and his pending divorce. She told a prominent columnist that the lady with him soon would be his wife, when it was a state secret. She told me that I was a bachelor, but that I was dominated by a woman who pretended to be my friend but who was slowly ruining me. "Get away from her," she said. "As quickly as you can, if you value your own identity."

****

I was planning to return to Washington at the first of the year 1966; but, since the Fair closed in October, 1965, I was about to try for a holiday rush job in Macy's basement or some such place when my erudite and elegant associate, Patricia Goodstadt, declared flatly, "If you're going to do something like that, try Tiffany's. They're more your type."

I was astonished; but, since I knew Pat always had my best interests in mind, I sat down and wrote a note to Walter Hoving, the Chairman of the Board of Tiffany's. Three days later I had a job there, starting in the jewelry business at the very top, with no experience in selling jewelry, or any kind of retailing. Their personnel man asked me what I wanted to do there, and I told him, "Whatever you want me to do."

I was assigned to the sterling silver department: I made a record selling silver Paul Revere bowls. My first day, November 9, was a long-remembered day in New York for, at 5:30, just as I was preparing to leave the store, the lights went out all over the city. They did not come on again until nearly dawn—the night of the Great Blackout!

I crawled down five flights of stairs: out in the street, I managed to find my way to a little restaurant where I hoped to get some dinner. They were closed, so I joined hundreds of people walking down Fifth Avenue. At 42nd Street, I went into a steak joint where the grill flames gave some light. After I had collected my food, it was difficult to find a table and then to find my mouth. However, I finally made it to Tudor City, and, in my room, undressed in total darkness and went to bed. One great lesson learned from this event was to know how blind people feel and act and survive.

Tiffany's was a great experience. The difference between the sexes, which seems to be disappearing, is still marked when people approach the shopping counter. Women want to see the entire stock, price every piece, engage in conversation and ask their companion's advice. Then, they often leave without buying, but with a promise to come back later. Men know what they want and choose quickly, hardly ever haggle about the price, and go on their busy ways.

One gentleman I remember wanted a silver money box: one of our aggressive sales ladies, unable to hook him, suggested that he might try the gold department. He went off, but soon came back. He bought one of the silver boxes, placed four $100 bills in it and asked that it be Christmas-wrapped for his 'secretary.'

We had many strange requests. One lady asked for a cooking cross, which proved to be silver bars crossed to support a china dish. Another wanted napkin rings to match those stolen from her gold dinner service—bought in 1860! One of the most honest and forthright females I encountered there was a woman in a babushka, sweater and pants.

"This is the first time I was ever in Tiffany's," she said gleefully. "What is Vermeuil?" I told her it was gold overlay applied to sterling silver. One asked for a 'Wall and Tree' platter, "with a place for gravy in the middle."

An amusing incident happened when a male customer, accompanied by his wife, took a fancy to a star ruby ring I was wearing, (Mr. Hoving rules that his salesmen may **NOT** wear diamond rings) and commented as to its possible value. While I knew it to be a Linde (synthetic ruby), he was convinced it was genuine. He explained to his patient spouse the difference between a real ruby from Burma and a synthetic which tends to be cloudy—only he got it the other way round and left envying me for my very valuable 'real' star ruby.

When Christmas came, although exhausted, I was pleased to be asked if I would like to remain permanently at Tiffany's. But, I had made final plans to come down to Washington. I returned at midnight on New Year's Eve to Virginia where my sister and I settled down in an Alexandria garden apartment. Within a month we were visited by a howling blizzard which kept us indoors for five days. Otherwise, the change was made rather smoothly. I refused to retire, at least from action, so occupied myself with lessons in a writer's course. I soon became active,, also, in church work, a little theater, local politics and a community center.

The following autumn, Laura and I flew out to visit old friends in Phoenix, Arizona—Mrs. Elizabeth Folkerth, her daughter, Mary Lynn and son, Larry. They live in the shadow of Camelback Mountain, in an ultra-modern suburb which showed us a few things about progress in the East. Phoenix is flat as a floor, very modern, apparently has much wealth—it is surrounded by desert extending for miles until it reaches high mountains on the horizon. Camelback, Squaw Peak and South Mountain are three within the city limits.

Our hosts were most generous in showing us all the sights within driving distance. We drove to Tucson, on to Nogales and crossed into Mexico. On the way back, we spent a night in Tombstone, famous relic of gun fightin' days. Here we found the *Tombstone Epitaph*, Arizona's oldest newspaper still being published; Boothill Cemetary, with over 250 graves of ladies and gentlemen of interesting and unsavory reputations, many of whom met violent ends at the hands of the law or otherwise! The inscriptions on the gravestones are embarassingly frank about the details of departure of the deceased.

We descended into the earth and inspected a silver mine which has yielded millions of dollars worth of the precious ore. The town is named for the first rich mine discovered in 1877. The Crystal Palace, still serving drinks, and the Birdcage Theater are reminders of gay nights in earlier times; but, Tombstone resolutely refuses to be a ghost town. Tourists are shown the world's largest rose tree, a Lady Banksia about 80 years old which stretches its branches over an entire garden. Each spring it is covered with fragrant white flowers.

We took a bus tour over the Apache Trail to the new Roosevelt Dam and lake, over mountain trails where the bus rounded curves where the danger, as well as the view, left us breathless. We also toured up to Flagstaff and the Grand Canyon, passing Montezuma's Castle and the cliff dwellings, beautiful Sedona with its red cliffs, and the Oak Creek valley "where the deer and the antelope play."

Our overnight stay at the Canyon was fortunate in that it was a bright, moonlight night. The Canyon is fantastic in daytime, but its beauty under full moon is eerie and indescribable. We stayed in rough, but comfortable, cabins and had excellent meals at the Bright Angel Hotel. Returning, we saw the ghost town of Jerome, stopped at Prescott to see the wonderful Old West Museum and the former Governor's Palace. We skirted the twin snow-clad San Francisco peaks for many miles.

One day we drove 40 miles out across the desert to the aptly-named village of Carefree, which sits apart. In the distance you can glimpse the blue-misted Superstition Mountains where a legendary Dutchman found a gold mine; but, both he and the mine became lost to history. At Carefree there is an elegant resort hotel, the fine Elbow Bend restaurant and many little ranch houses that look as if they had been dropped by parachute upon the white sand and among the rocks.

The village square has an immense sun-dial: it is said that time is of so little consequence to the fortunate residents that those who wish to know the time, walk to the square. Here are artists and writers and people who want to pick desert flowers in the daytime and to walk at night under the stars which seem so close in the desert sky.

Moving on to Los Angeles, we stopped at the Biltmore Hotel—ancient, but with excellent service, beautiful lobby and public rooms, reminding one of an aristocratic old lady who revels in memories of the past. An old friend of WWII in Washington, Capt. Allan Davenport, came with his car to show us around: he did a perfect job! We toured the San Fernando Valley, Hollywood, Beverly Hills, the Bowl and the Strip, all the choice residential districts and ended up for lunch at the Brown Derby. On our own, we visited Marineland and the fabulous new music hall and opera house, a cultural center which is a source of pride to the city.

A short flight brought us to San Francisco. We were met by old friends, Mrs. Brejska and daughter Blanca from Czechoslovakia, mentioned earlier in this story. One daughter, Mia, is married to Col. Oscar Drake, an Army officer now retired. With their three children, they now make their home in Ocala, Florida. Blanca is now Mrs. John Boland and they live in Oklahoma. Our friendship with this wonderful family has survived and strengthened through all these years and vicissitudes.

Their hospitality made our San Francisco visit a delight. They drove us to the Muir Redwood Forest, to Mill Valley, Sausalito, and Tiburon where our New Orleans friends, Stewart and Elinor Hopkins have built their retirement home at the very highest point overlooking the whole city and San Francisco Bay. We drove to the beaches, through the parks and to Fisherman's Wharf where we dined heartily on seafood and watched ocean liners coming up the channel. We rode the cable cars, visited the new and thrilling Ghirardelli Square, with exotic gift shops and restaurants reminiscent of cities in Europe. In Chinatown, we had the most marvelous Chinese meal I ever tasted.

Other friends, Glenn and 'Skip' Carter entertained us with dinner and uproarious stories at the San Francisco Press Club; Mrs. Frances Diehl, formerly mentioned, entertained us at cocktails; and Ivy Baker Priest, former U.S. Treasurer and later treasurer of California in Governor Reagan's cabinet, came to our hotel for an hour's visit. We went by bus to see Leland Stanford University down the bay at Palo Alto: we were shown the fine campus and university buildings and the late President Hoover's home.

The time came to say farewell. We enjoyed a daytime, non-stop flight over the snowy Rockies, across the plains and the Mississippi river, arriving at nightfall at Dulles Airport where we were greeted by Laura's friend, Anne Callahan, who got completely lost in driving us home to Alexandria, although she also lives there!   As the holiday season approached, the postman brought a formal card of invitation from Mr. and Mrs. James Robb of Milwaukee to a reception to meet their son, Capt. Charles 'Chuck' Robb, USMC, and his bride-to-be, Miss Lynda Bird Johnson, eldest daughter of the President and First Lady. Just 30 years before, I had attended the wedding of 'Jim' Robb, whose name appeared earlier in this story, and Frances Wooley. It was a very fashionable affair; the bride was a Junior

Leaguer, her father was prominent in Democratic Party politics; and the groom's family was well connected with distinguished families in Washington, Maryland, Virginia and throughout the South. I presented the newlyweds with glass animals, hand-blown by my old friend, Baroness von Allesch, who grew up in Germany and played, as a child, with Kaiser Wilhelm's children.

Through the years, except for a brief time when Jim was running an Arizona dude ranch, he has been associated with American Airlines; but, he is now retired and living in Charlestown, West Virginia. I hadn't realized their son could possibly be grown up; so, when I read of the Johnson-Robb romance in the newspapers, it never occurred to me whom 'Chuck' might be. He is now the governor of Virginia.

I hastened to the reception and was warmly greeted by the hosts. Frances embraced me, saying "We still have the glass animals, except for one broken when Chuck's Marine Corps buddies were visiting us." The bride-to-be was radiant in pink costume: I thought she had the smallest waistline I'd seen except in old-fashioned magazines. The groom was tall, handsome and outgoing and looked every inch a fighting Marine. Both are of striking appearance, with dark hair and flashing dark eyes.

There were perhaps three hundred guests, with Secret Servicemen trying unsuccessfully to blend into the background: not a politician was to be seen. It was obviously a Robb party, not a Johnson party. Most of the guests were old friends of the Robb family. When the First Lady arrived, she was immediately surrounded by people who wished to be introduced. I was not in that category. I'd met the Johnsons socially at a party at Perle Mesta's.

As the crowd shifted, I suddenly found myself directly facing the First Lady, not more than three paces away. While I pondered whether to advance and greet her, she stepped forward, held out her hand and said, "I am Lady Bird Johnson." (As if I didn't know!) Not to be outdone, I responded, "How do you do? I am Lyle Brookover." We shook hands quite pleasantly.

My next remark was absolutely inspired. I said, "I'm sure you and President Johnson must be very happy to welcome such an attractive son-in-law into the family." I was still thinking it was a Robb party. Mrs. Johnson replied, with just a hint of pique in her voice, "We think the Robb's are getting a very wonderful daughter-in-law, also." I felt like saying, "Touche," but we both laughed at the repartee. She then turned and graciously presented me to several of the bridesmaids and groom's attendants before moving away.

President Lyndon, who had been sequestered in a private room, possibly for a snort or two, finally entered the ballroom in tow of the groom's father. He made a hand-shaking tour the length of the floor, hardly stopping for a word with anyone. Obviously the very select group were all strangers to him. He bestowed on me one of his wintry smiles as I said, "How do you do, Mr. President?"

CHAPTER XIX: 1965
HAWAII CALLS

Another spring, sister Laura and I flew from Dulles and on to Los Angeles to board a Pan American flight for Hilo, Hawaii. This was another black mark for Pan American, for we were enroute five hours without the stewardesses approaching us once to offer food, drink or service. Before landing, I told the chief stewardess I'd rather swim home than fly back Pan American—and I meant it!

At Hilo airport, we had our first Hawaiian meal, and a good one. We were paged by a military driver who'd come to take us up the mountain to the Kilauea Rest Camp in Volcanoes National Park. We were shown to a comfortable cabin with a fireplace; but, the night was so cold, we had to pile on all the blankets. In the morning, after a fine breakfast at the military mess, we boarded buses for one of the free tours provided each day for guests. We visited the volcano area where Halemaumau was erupting for our entertainment. We went several evenings after dinner to watch the white-hot lava flow, gradually filling up the crater which appeared to be a half mile across. The skies were lit for many miles by the eruption: it was truly an awe-inspiring sight.

The daily tours included tropical and orchid gardens, black sand beaches; the famous Volcano House, a swank hotel almost on Halemaumau's rim; a tree-fern jungle, bird forests, a majestic waterfall and other exciting scenes. Each day a nourishing lunch, such as terriyaki steaks and beer with salads and side dishes, was served by our military hosts at lovely parks or scenic spots.

I wanted to visit South Point, the southern tip of Hawaii, as I'd learned from space scientists in Washington that this spot was the perfect site for space blast-offs to the planets Mars and Venus sometime in the future. I talked over the trip with Sargeant Ira 'Butch' Walden, one of our tour guides, and he was eager to go with me. I asked the motor pool for a jeep, a request which was readily granted. Off we went on a fantastic journey. For 60 miles down the highway, we traversed the length of Mauna Loa, which is called 'Big Hill' and is an extinct volcano, 13,000 feet high. The other great volcano on Hawaii, Mauna Kea, is equally high, but not so long.

Arriving at Kaalehu, where a sign in the public square proudly proclaims it "The Southernmost Town in the United States," we stopped in a restaurant for a cold beer, it was such a hot day. As I passed through the garden, I was amazed to find double poinsettias as large as a cabbage, and a charming bonzai garden laid out with miniature plants and trees of all kinds, a waterway, a rustic bridge and a white bell tower. I remarked about this to the Japanese proprietor who admitted to a fondness for flowers. The poinsettias were "registered," he said quietly. On we went as the roads became more primitive, past a tracking station operated by the Air Force, and came at last to a lighthouse which is 34 miles further south than Key West, Florida.

The area is a great plateau formed many years ago by lava flow from the volcanoes which spread out to several miles width before it reached the sea. Here it formed a high palisade with waves lashing the rocks far below. The top soil is very rich and cattle graze peacefully on lush grass from which men may some day come and go to Mars! Advantages of this site for such a journey are its low latitude and uniform weather (I was told there had been only one bad storm there in 100 years, and that one was a hurricane that got 'off course.') Also, it would be an easterly launch, over water, with no traffic to worry about.

While there was plenty of black sand among the lava rocks which appeared to fold upon one another, within view, there were at least seven shades of green growth. Butch said there was a green sand beach nearby and he thought we ought to try to find it. I thought so, too, for it certainly would be something to tell about back home. We drove on over the lava flow, jumping from rock to rock at times, and proving that there are many places where only a jeep can operate. We finally had to abandon the jeep (I was sure my back was broken!) or be abandoned by it, and proceed on foot. We jumped, stumbled, fell and considered turning back; but still, we plunged on. Above us were low green hills and below, the open greenish sea with waves breaking in white foam at the edge.

We rounded one more hillock and at last, we saw it! A green drift of sand, like a waterfall, slanting about 200 feet from the lava edge to the water, too steep to be called a beach, nevertheless it was—green sand! We gathered up enough to prove our story and tramped, on lagging feet, back to our jeep. We knew the sand had come from olivine deposits in the lava which were ground up by the action of the waves. (Much olivine jewelry is found in Hawaiian shops.) Night was falling, and we found the jeep's lights were not working. We made the journey back to camp safely as we met no traffic, and there was a waning moon. The volcano's glow helped as we drew nearer home.

The remaining days on the Big Island passed quickly. We flew on to Maui, the Valley Island, and took a bus tour for the day through vast sugar cane and pineapple fields, up Mount Haleakala, an extinct volcano with a crater 20 miles across, and down again. We lunched at the Sheraton Maui, built on a cliff at the water's edge. You enter the lobby from your car and take an elevator 12 stories **DOWN** to the dining room at sea level. We helped ourselves from a magnificent orchid-graced buffet, meanwhile feasting our eyes as much as our stomachs. Later, we stopped at the exciting old whaling port of Lahaina, a still lively and colorful town.

We took to the air again for Kauai, the Garden Isle, and spent the night at the Sheraton-Kauai, then just 15 days old, but ideally located on the sea front and bound, eventually, to be an unbelievably beautiful spot. The service and food were supurb. We engaged a driver, Tony Texeira (a Portugese-American who spoke perfect English and knew every foot of the island) to tour the 'Grand Canyon of the Pacific' which has sheer green walls and very heavy rainfall. The rain and mist obscured our view to some extent, but our guide tried to point out and explain everything. High in the mountains in the midst of heavy forest, he took us to an inn which featured 'homemade pies.' At the museum nearby, he introduced us to an elderly retired missionary teacher who was engaged in writing a letter to President Johnson. The end of the day found us at the most unusual cathedral-like hotel, the Coco Palms, which piled more beauty on what we'd already seen.

We embarked in a downpour for Oahu. The trip was a bit rough. As we landed at Honolulu airport, the pretty stewardess spoke over the address system, saying, "We have landed . . . landed . . . landed at Honolulu, " suiting her words to three big leaps of the airplane. Everyone howled with laughter and we decided we liked Hawaiian Airlines.

U.S. Marine Colonel and Mrs. Edward Stansel, and their boy Eddie, hugged us and threw leis around our necks in the terminal, then carried us off to the Tropic Surf Motel on Waikiki Beach where we were to stay. Ed had thoughtfully provided a huge bag of groceries and a bottle of bourbon, so we were soon 'at home.'

The next day, Sunday, the Stansels took us to a delightful brunch at the huge Tripler Military Hospital Officers' Club. Then, we climbed a mountain to get a wonderful view of Pearl Harbor where the battleship *Arizona* lies half-submerged as a memorial to the Japanese raid which started World War II. Later, we stopped at the Pearl City Tavern (which has a bar with a background of live climbing monkeys) on our way to dine at the Stansels' attractive Marine quarters in Pearl City.

A visit to the International Shopping Center and to the beach at De Russey Military Recreation Center occupied us the next day. Staying much in the center of things, we made these jpourneys on foot. At the shopping center, we found a host of colorful shops, offering things not only from Hawaii, but also from the rest of the world. We came upon the Duke Kahanamoku Club: I went in to tell them how sorry I was that the 'Duke' had died suddenly on his yacht while we were enroute to Hawaii. I'd written to tell him we were coming, and that I hoped to renew the friendship we formed on the *Leviathan* forty years before.

His secretary, Alison Sanford, received us, and gave me clippings and pictures of the Duke. She urged us to visit the club which we did the following evening, taking Ed and Iris with us. We were shown to a floor-side table and hosted to drinks by the management. We had a glorious time: the girls drank Mai Ti's and I met Don Ho, the M.C. and singer who was still grieving for the Duke. The floor show lasted three hours and was terrific!

My old AF friend, 'Dixie' Ryland and her companion, Mabel Gilliam, turned up on the floor below us at Tropic Surf. We dined with them at De Russey Officers' Mess. They were enroute to Manila by 'space available' travel. The girls shopped the next morning and lunched at Le Ronde, a rooftop revolving restaurant at Ala Moana shopping center. I went Swimming at De Russey beach. My dear Washington friend and lawyer, Bob Klepinger, had suggested that I call a client of his, a wealthy German girl, Christel Guessfelt, which I did. She brought her new car to drive all of us to the Pali, where the winds nearly disrobe you; the upside-down fall nearby caused by those strong winds; up Mount Tantalus, to Round Top and the Punch Bowl National Military Cemetery where thousands of Americans who lost their lives in the Pacific area lie buried; and on to the Garden Court for lunch.

Then came 'Happy Hour' at H.M. Smith Marine Corps HQ with Karl and Joy Mueller and the Stansels; later, to the 'Top of the Eye' at Hotel Ilakai; still later, to De Russey for a Hawaiian floor show. The next day, we drove along the north coast to Laie and the Polynesian Cultural Center where we toured the native villages, enjoyed a real luau, and a marvelous floor show of native dances of the various Pacific Islands.

Sunday again and we had a luscious dinner at Cannon Officers Club on Diamond Head, with an unsurpassed view of all Honolulu, the surrounding maountains and the sea. Midge Carden and Mrs. Davies took me to lunch at Oahu Country Club the next day. In the afternoon, we left for

Barber's Point on the south shore for a three-day rest by the sounding surf. The Muellers and children joined us for a big feast and bonfire the last evening. In the morning, we left our comfortable cabin and drove along the shore westward to a spot where the waves are precipitous. The world's greatest surfers come to practice for competition. A stop for lunch at Y&I Officers Club (Waianae) and then across a mountain pass up among the clouds, down through Schofield Barracks and home. The dog, 'Big Red' was very happy to see us.

I shopped for olivine pins, Hawaii's only gem which resembles an emerald, for Laura and Iris and cuff links for Ed. We all lunched at Fisherman's Wharf and had a great meal, to be sure. On Saturday, March 30th, we dinner-danced at the Marine HQ Officers' Club. I received a kukui lei from Ed and Iris for my birthday. The Hawaiian royal family wore kukui leis made from big black glossy nuts, instead of flowers. I was proud and pleased to wear mine with my black and white sport coat. There was wine-tasting before dinner, much champagne in my honor. We met the Gen. Krulachs, Col. Goulds, Morans, James and many more. Then, to the Muellers for coffee afterwards. What a birthday!

On Sunday afternoon to Friedson's on Diamond Head to see my dear friend Helen Graham from Vancouver, B.C.—a vivid personality and a person of wealth and charm. Her daughter, son-in-law and their kids were a captivating family. Little Grant Freidson (Beverly Grant Burns, he said, explaining that his mother has married twice) ran beside our car for a long time as we left. We then went to the old, but distinguished, Hotel Halekulani on Waikiki for Mai Ti's, hulas and the sunset view. Sail boats crossing the sun as it hung just above the sea made an unforgettable picture. A farewell dinner at Fisherman's Wharf rounded out a perfect last day in Hawaii. The morning came with more leis and a few tears as we took off with Ed for California. Ed spilled his champagne at lunch and hugged us both twice at parting.

After a short flight to Phoenix, we were met by the Folkerths. In the days following, we drove to see the desert flowers, to Lake Suguaro, to Gene's Broiler in Scottsdale for an unusual hamburger buffet, to the 'Lulu Belle' for drinks and to Mag's Ham and Bun in Scottsdale for lunch. Lt. Steve Van De Car came from Williams Air Force Base to a picnic dinner at Pleasant Lake, and home for drinks and philosophy. I enjoyed his new yellow M.G.

We had an amazing trip across the desert and up into the hills to Castle Hot Springs, a millionaire's club and oasis that was hard to find, but beautiful. It has since burned down. We stopped to inspect a Gila monster along the way: road runners (prairie chickens) tried to outdistance the car. We had an interesting frontier dinner at the Golden Nugget in Wickenburg.

We sure hated to leave the Arizona sun, the stimulating desert air, the lucious fruits, and the cars which stop and wait for the pedestrians at intersections. Reluctantly, off we flew to Dulles Field where we were met by Helen Ray and Pat Abernathy who chauffeured us home. It seemed nice to be back!

Duke Kahanamoku of Hawaii

CHAPTER XX: 1968
THE OLYMPIC GAMES IN MEXICO

The French count, Henri de Saint Simon, is reported to have charged his valet with the responsibility to wake him each morning by saying, "Awake, my lord, you have great things to do today." I have no valet to get me going; but, one morning I awoke with a premonition. Before the day was over, I had agreed to go to Mexico for the Olympic Games in October as a press liaison staff member for the International Olympic Committee.

This was rather a turn of events: I was quite anticipatory, yet sometimes, almost appalled at the prospect. We made a few false starts, due to Mexican bureaucracy; finally, a group of us gathered at Kennedy International Airport on September 8 for the non-stop flight to Mexico City. In all, our group from New York, Washington, France, Spain, Holland, India, USSR, Israel and Argentina numbered about 30. There were to be 4,000 news writers, TV and radio men covering the Games: we were out-ratioed from the start.

We were thrown into mad confusion at the airport when we arrived in Mexico City. It seemed our work permits—or whatever they were—for us to enter Mexico were dated September 14: we arived on the 8th. So, we were smuggled into Mexico, herded together and taken by bus to the Hotel El Romano, a second class or worse, establishment in the heart of the city. There was a pleasant roof garden restaurant; but, it was a struggle to get any service and a battle to get what you had ordered. Whiskey and wines were very expensive by our standards—Scotch, $12 or more, wine about the same price. It was explained that the import taxes were so high.

Locally made products were offered, but we seldom ordered them the second time.

Among the assortment of nationalities in our press gang, I soon took a great liking to Marta Hall, a sparkling widow from New York, formerly from Argentina; her beautiful young daughter, Martita; Juan de la Cruz of Spain, Jorge Villareno of Argentina; Paul Gardner from New York, a renowned sports writer and authority on soccer.

Martita and Juan soon found themselves falling in love, which provided a pleasant counterpart to our hard days and exhausting tasks. Our little group went to the flower market the first Sunday and brought back an armload of flowers for all the ladies in our party, many of the men having brought their wives. The flowers cost so little we could have decorated the whole hotel for a few dollars.

The first weeks were spent in orientation. There was a lot to be learned in order to function efficiently as aides to the press. Each morning, we were carried by bus to the various 'venues' where the Games would take place. There were the formal opening ceremonies in Estadio 68: all the sites had 68 after their names. The next day, athletes took over in the Estadio; baseball began in the Palacio, the Sports Palace; boxing in the Arena; football in Azteca Stadium; hockey at Michuca; weight-lifting in the Teatro; and the modern pentathlon at Campo Militar.

Rowing and canoeing events were held in Xochimilco, the famous floating gardens: special waterways had been built for the Games. Yachting events were held at Acapulco. Football preliminary games were played in Puebla, Jalisco and Leon. The tennis matches were at Guadalajara.

Volleyball was housed at Gimnasio and Cancha; fronton, a popular sport in Mexico, at Fronton Mexico; water polo was at C.U. Alberca; cycling at the Velodromo; fencing at Mixhuca; equestrian sports at Campo Marte and Avandaro; wrestling at Pistahielo; swimming and diving at the Alberca; shooting at Poligono; and gymnastics at Auditorio.

Those of our number who were experts in a particular sport were assigned to help newsmen at the venues where those sports were played: the rest were in an unassigned pool to help newsmen, radio and TV crews in general. We were at first ruled by a 'character' named Islas (a Mexican Vice-Consul in Antwerp) who knew paractically nothing of sports, public relations, diplomacy or handling of staff. His first order to us was that we were not to use the public entrance to Villa Prensa where we worked, but to come in by the employees' entrance. Needless to say, no one ever obeyed that order. There was a great deal of resentment over our having come to Mexico, for Mexican newsmen (and especially politicians) wanted our 'cushy' jobs. Of course, they lacked the qualifications; but, that didn't matter. El Senor Islas finally got a number of his friends employed:

some of us were fired, for trumped up reasons; some resigned; and others, including myself, got re-assigned and saw no more of the 'twirp from Antwerp.'

We were actually in the employ of, and paid by, the Mexican Olympic Committee: their way of handling this bunch of prima-donnas was something none of us can ever forget. The Games went on smoothly enough: the closing ceremony was an absolute triumph for Mexico. But behind the scenes, everything was run the 'Mexican way,' with spies in abundance, scalping of tickets, cheating, rudeness, juggling for position, and all the known sins of omission and commission. Overall, I made some very good and lasting friendships among my Mexican associates. If any of them should happen to read these lines, they'll know the criticism is neither unfair nor in any sense referring to them.

At the top of the Mexican Committee was Pedro Vazquez Ramirez, Chairman of the Organizing Committee of the Games of the XIX Olympiad, to give him his full title. A distinguished architect, creator of many of the finest buildings in Mexico, natably the National Museum of Anthropology, conceded to be the greatest of its kind in the world. Vazquez Ramirez is also a great and many-sided gentleman. Homespun and gentle, he made me think of what Abraham Lincoln was said to be like. The three addresses I heard him give were eloquent evidence of a visionary and peotic mind. It was he who insisted upon bringing the Cultural Olympics back, as they were originally part of the Games in Greece: they had been dropped from the modern Olympics for several decades. I like to think that meeting him was worth all the effort and the misfortunes and the unfortunate aspects of my journey to Mexico.

I was not able, because of my time schedule, to witness many of the Games; but, I spent one evening at the Palacio witnessing three basketball games of positively Olympian style. The match between the USSR and Yugoslavia (which the latter won) was particularly exciting, an even contest which the winners celebrated with the wildest acrobatics and enthusiastic hugs and kisses I ever saw engaged in by an athletic team.

The final day, I saw the equestrian finals in the Estadio before the closing ceremony. Canada had a large team in many sports in Mexico, but had won practically nothing up to that point. The Canadian horse and rider were faultless performers, almost flying as a unit over barriers and water jumps. At last, they came forward to receive the gold medal which pleased me and the crowd—and thrilled the Canadians.

The closing ceremonies were spectacular in the extreme. President Diaz Ordaz of Mexico, who had opened the Games, brought them to an official close. Senorita Enriqueta Basilio, who carried the Olympic torch on the final miles of its long journey from Greece, and lit the stadium torch, re-traced her steps around the stadium, climbed the long flight of steps and symbolically put out the flame. She was the first woman athlete to have this honor.

Prior to this, Olympic officials spoke. Finally, the teams came dashing in—thousands of athletes, happy in victory or proud in defeat, followed by several hundred mariachi musicians. The scene was one of incredible color, movement and music. Silenced for the President's remarks and the dying flame, the moment this was finished, a fireworks display began over the stadium. It showered the happy crowd with fantastic light and sound for an hour. Then, dancing began in the streets and lasted until morning. My colleagues and I were so exalted by the spectacle that we hastened to the Villa Prensa bar and got quietly and thoroughly plastered.

Before the actual Games had begun, our group had moved from the city to the Olympic center. At Villa Olympica, several high-rise buildings were reserved for the athletes, coaches, national members, etc. Villa Prensa was where all press activity was conducted. We were housed in Villa Coapa, another high-rise center five miles farther out. Villa Coapa also housed cultural groups from all over the world: our promenade, in leisure hours, resembled a Tower of Babel, or a costumer's dream. All these buildings were supposedly low-cost housing projects finished by the government in time for the Olympics, and occupied, at once when the Games ended by Mexican buyers. Their construction was poor and the prices were high, I thought, but they all were sold and the purchasers waiting for us to move out.

What I missed in witnessing the Games, I made up somewhat by attending the cultural and social affairs. There were many cocktail parties—one for the opening of Villa Prensa and an enormous one given for all those participating in any way in the Games, with Chairman Ramirez Vazquez as the host. That party was held at the beautiful and historic Hacienda de Los Morales. A reception was given at the Pyramids in Teotihuacan when the Olympic torch arrived there. A sumptuous cocktail and buffet was given the press by the Mexican Businessmen's Council at the elegant new hotel, Camino Real. Here I made friends who entertained me at lunch later at the Hacienda San Angel where I signed the VIP Golden Book. They sent a car for me, returned me to Villa Prensa, and again entertained me at dinner at a magnificent villa in Chapultapec Heights. One chauffeur came for me, another took me back—and they called the dinner, 'pot luck.' That I should always have pot luck like that!

On the cultural side, I attended a German opera presentation of *Orfeo*; the "Magic Lantern Show" from Czechoslovakia; a concert by Duke Ellington and his band at the Palacio de Belles Artes; a Chilean folklore concert; and, two evenings with Maurice Dejart's Twentieth Century Ballet of the Royal Mint Theater of Brussels, Belgium. The first ballet, which marked the opening of the Sports Palace, was a white-tie affair with the President and Mexico City society in attendance. The ballet was the full score of Beethoven's *Ninth Symphony*. The dancing was supurb throughout and, at the finale, the "Ode to Joy," two hundred dancers swirled about the stage to the accompaniment of two hundred vocalists and an orchestra of two hundred instruments. The audience was enraptured: some were in tears; the applause was thundrous after a few minutes of silent tribute.

The following week, I saw this great company at the Palacio des Belles Artes in three short ballets: "Neither Flowers Nor Crowns," a spoof on academic ballet; "Love Scene from Romeo and Juliet;" and the "Consecration of Spring" to Stravinsky's music. All were expertly done: I would believe that the Twentieth Century is the world's best ballet company today.

I attended services at Christ Episcopal church near my hotel; dined at the Mirador, in the tower of the highest building in Latin America; and went with my Spanish friends for an all-day tour to Taxco, the silver capital with its many glittering shops and its famed Church of Santa Prisca, with walls and ceiling lined with gold leaf. Taxco seems to hang on a mountainside and reminds me of Toledo, Spain: Close up, they are not much alike.

I also paid my respects to the national Spanish and Mexican pastime of bullfighting. Our first Sunday, my Spanish friends and I witnessed in Plaza Mexico the unusual sight of one matador killing six bulls. No, not a matador: it was a 'novillero' and an American, at that—Diego O'Bolger who had come to Mexico from Tucson, Arizona six years before. He had four fights of his own and finished off two bulls for other fighters who were injured and removed from the ring. Soon after, he took his 'alternativa' to become a full-fledged matador.

The second Sunday was a special Olympic corida featuring the Spanish matador, Palomo Linares, for his first time in Mexico, along with two other matadors. That afternoon was full of action: one bull jumped over the fence four times, another twice; horses were knocked down frequently; and an 'espontaneo' jumped into the ring and got trampled by the bull. He was taken out to a hospital.

Linares, who was just 19, made an exciting debut. Press comment said he was "very brave, artistic, almost elegant at times, yet boyishly enthusiastic and with a personality which appeals to the crowd." He killed his bulls, was awarded an ear, pelted with roses as he toured the ring twice, and was carried out on the shoulders of the crowd.

After all those days and nights of excitement, I slipped away to San Miguel de Allende, a 400 years old Indian town nestling among the mountains north of Mexico City. Here I stayed at a former convent, Posada de San Francisco, and visited old friends, retired Admiral Alexander Charlton and his wife, Von. They gave a party to introduce me to their friends: I attended about 20 cocktails, luncheons and affairs of one kind or another in five days. We drove out and bathed in a thermal spring where the water gushes up at 120 degrees, but cools as it flows into a large and pleasant swimming pool. San Miguel is just this side of heaven—but a poor place to go to rest.

****

The following spring, Florida seemed to be calling. We set out for Winter Park and a visit with Dixie Ryland which could be a high point in anybody's life. The agenda included a trip to witness the launching of astronauts into space at Cape Canaveral; a weekend at the beautiful islands of Sanibel and Captiva; a dinner at famed Chalet Suzanne; dinner with friends at Merritt Island; a lovely dinner with Milly Bachman (who lives between two lakes and has a pet alligator) at Chuluota; a weekend at Fort Lauderdale, and a fabulous luncheon at Driftwood and a wild night at Rosie O'Grady's on the way home. In between times, we visited 75 Florida towns with Dixie on her real estate trips.

CHAPTER XXI: 1970/71
MEDITERRANEAN JOURNEY

Since my sister was approaching her 75th birthday and had not yet travelled in Europe, we decided it was high time that she should. In a downpour of rain one morning in September, 1970, we loaded our 11 pieces of luggage into a taxi bound for Union Station where we took a drawing room on a train bound for New York. In a few hours, we were safely on board, having been photographed as we crossed the gangplank of the TS *Hamburg*, a new luxury liner built in West Germany and described by authorities as the "finest cruise ship afloat."

We headed into 32 days of sunshine, with a stop at Port Everglades to pick up Florida passengers, then on to Charlotte Amalie; Saint Thomas, where we climbed a mountain and drank a banana daiquiri at Hilltop House; visited Bluebeard's Castle and shopped in attractive stores. Next stop was Funchal, Madeira where we motored up another mountain and then coasted down five miles in a wooden sled with two stalwart Portugese men holding the guide ropes. We had a memorable lunch with fellow passengers, the Jochen Erlers, at Reid's Hotel overlookign the harbor, more shopping—gorgeous embroideries and mellow wine which could be tasted for free.

Across the water to Morocco and, at Casablanc, we were sent aboard a special train which rolled several hundred miles through barren country to Marrakesch. I asked a native why the herds of sheep on the stony fields all had their heads down, seemingly grazing where there was nothing to eat. He said they were suffering form the heat. I believed him when, upon arrival in Marrakesch, we were told the temperature was 115 degrees F.

It was an ordeal walking through the tunnel-like, stuffy souks where everything imaginable was offered for sale. We had a fine lunch at an Oriental-style hotel, Es Saadi, with a beautiful garden; more sightseeing and a mosque or two, a great square with snake-charmers, sidewalk merchants—a mixed bag of sights, sounds and smells along a wide boulevarde reminding one of Paris. Then, back to our air-conditioned train and to the bar, quickly, for a gin and tonic!

After this brief glimpse of Africa, we headed across the sea to Italy and Europe. We edged into the dock among ships from all the world at the busy port of Genova (Genoa) for a two-day stay. Here we said good-bye to many new friends who were debarking at 'first call,' at the same time we welcomed many new passengers, mostly from Germany, who were taking the second two weeks on the Mediterranean. Among these were the charming Becker family: father, mother, two beautiful daughtters and two handsome sons from Hanover, Germany. This family group were joyous and carefree, dancing the hours away each night in the nightclub.

On a sunny Sunday, we landed and drove through the picturesque little town of Santa Margarita enroute to Portofino, snuggled beside a bay with mountains encircling it, a favorite spot for artists and world travelers. Here we took a motor launch to a miserable luncheon on the waterfront at Rapallo. The town itself seemed very charming and I'm sure had other, and better, restaurants.

Accompanied by one of the handsome German ship stewards, I had a night 'on the town' in Genoa which I still remember. Upon returning to the ship in the morning, I found Laura not feeling well, so we passed up a shore trip to Lake Maggiore. Those who went said they couldn't see much because of the fog.

After a day-long stop at the walled fortress of Malta, where we stocked up on Maltese history and Maltese crosses, we went on across the beautiful blue sea to the fabulous city of Istanbul where we trailed endlessly through the sultan's palaces, the Sophia and Blue mosques, and got an idea of the riches of the Orient. We were served a typical dinner in a Turkish restaurant, followed by a nightclub visit where belly dancers did a lot of sensuous writhing. Their so-called dance had a strange effect on a dignified member of our party who crawled across the floor on his belly to get a better view.

The last afternoon, in gorgeous weather, our ship cruised slowly through the Strait of Bosphorus from the Golden Horn to the Black Sea, an exciting and wonderful trip. The next day, we arrived at Izmir in Asia Minor, an early seat of Christianity, and left by bus for Ephesus where we viewed centuries-old ruins and walked the streets of a city deserted almost two thousand years ago. The Third Ecumenical Council was held there in 431 A.D.

The original schedule to visit Yalta and Odessa on the Black Sea was cancelled due to a cholera scare. Instead, we cruised among the fabled Greek Isles which were 'out-of-season' brown masses rising from the sea and hardly justifying the high praise one hears of their beauty. Perhaps, in a greener time of year, they are beautiful? We visited Mykonos, Daelos, and Heraklion (Crete). On the latter island, we came upon the famous temple of Knossos which is almost older than civilization itself. The murals featuring bulls were in bright colors which had survived the centuries. The wealth of ruins on all the islands caused one lady tourist to remark that she didn't want to go ashore "to see anymore broken dishes." The age of the ruins gave us pause and they were exceeedingly interesting to some.

Our day in glorious Athens was exciting, with the first hours spent in climbing the Acropolis and studying the Parthenon, also enjoying the magnificent vistas of Athens on every side, far below. A pleasant cocktail and luncheon, Greek-style, rounded out a perfect day in the sunshine. Coming down from the Acropolis, we visited the age-old Theater of Dionysius, said to be the world's first great house of drama. The front rows of marble seats, still in good condition after the centuries, were carved with the names of Athenian senators and other 'VIP's' of the long,long past. How amusing to compare this with society leaders today fussing over having the same seats every season at the opera or symphony concerts!

Landing at Catania, Sicily, we found patient tour buses to take us up the shore and into the mountain town of Taormina where, on clear days, one gets a marvelous view of Mount Etna and its several snows. Alas, we had a cloudy day and had to satisfy ourselves with wandering up and down the one important street lined on both sides with colorful shops of every kind, tempting us to load up on huge puppets, toys, embroidery, jewelry and souvenirs.

While our days passed all too quickly in a panaorama of sightseeing, our nights on the luxurious *Hamburg* also raced by with marvelous dinners in a choice of restaurants and great, after-dinner shows and dancing. The entertainment crew included the many-talented Tony Boice who was in charge of music, plays and special events. His beautiful blond wife, Helga, gave German lessons in the forenoons. Others led us in needed exercise— the mile walks twice around the deck before lunch.

One night, the ship's dance team held a waltzing contest: the female partner came over and stunned me by asking me to dance with her. The Viennese Waltz has always been my favorite; so, needless to say, we won (or she won) to great applause. Another night, Tony sang "Me and My Shadow," asking me to be the shadow behind him. I did everything wrong—which proved to be exactly right!

My gorgeous Mexican shawl and a huge sombrero won first prize at the costume ball . . . so many prizes and so much champagne!!

At Naples we set out by private car with John and Esther Layport on a memorable sunny day's trip to Sorrento. Enroute, we stopped at Pompeii and Herculaneum and tramped among the ruins of these great cities of yore. High to our left was Mount Vesuvius which had scattered tons of ashes to bury these cities and their inhabitants in the years 63 and 79 A.D. In those days, these cities were peopled by wealthy Romans: great riches of historical and actual value are still found among the ruins.

After a visit to a fascinating cameo factory on the way, we rounded the great bay of Naples, looked across to the Isle of Capri, and came to the delightful town of Sorrento, built on hills overlooking the sea. Soon we found a shop making inlaid furniture which was irresistible. To my astonishment, the fine Italian proprietor, when I explained that I did not have enough money or travelers' checks with me to buy anything, said (with evident sincerity), "I'll send your purchases to your home address. you can send me a check when you get there." I've never had such a vote of confidence: it all worked out. The tea cart arrived in fine condition, was paid for and is the envy of all who see it.

Our Italian gentleman (driver) escorted us to a beautiful and exclusive restaurant for lunch with not an American tourist to be seen. After the food won our high praise, the proprietor wrapped up all we did not eat and gave the package to us with a smile "for later pleasure." We sailed for Genoa and 'second call', going on deck at midnight to pick up the flares of the volcano Stromboli on shore. The last night out, we gave a champagne party to use the bottles which had been given to us—or won—enroute. Our guests included the tour director, Tony Boice and his Helga; the two song birds, Gene Reed and Marcia King; the incredible Bill Carlsons from Atlanta; the Axel Wars from Mexico; and the Erlers from Germany. Our faithful cabin steward handled all the details. It was a grand party. The only missing guest was Chief Steward Guenther Stein who was detained by official duties.

Having rather sadly packed our bags and set them in the corridor the night before (according to instructions), we were awakened for an early breakfast and hustled ashore, through customs without any delay and on to waiting taxis which carried us to a vast, gloomy edifice (the Genoa Railroad Station) to board a train for Milan.

Here ensued an experience which I wish never to repeat on this planet! I had invested an extra $2 in a pair of tickets on a 'Rapido', an express train which I was told, rather confidentially, was the luxury train to take, instead of the regular train which left at 9:23 and made stops enroute. The waiting room was vast and chilly; there were no signs to indicate trains or tracks; no one spoke English, except at the information booth, where I went and learned exactly nothing.

We were standing in utter confusion when a friend from our journey came up and offered to help us with our luggage. He said he had found the right track. Two or three trips up and down stairs, through hallways and tunnels, and we found many of our former shipmates waiting for a train. I have no idea what became of the 'Rapido.' It must have left by another track. The 9:23 was late: a vast crowd of Italians, as well as tourists, waited as it finally pulled in.

I grabbed some luggage and forced my way, surrounded by a shoving, screaming throng, aboard and into a car where every seat was already taken. The train started to move: I looked out the window to see Laura standing, with a horrified look, amidst our pile of luggage. I wondered if we would ever meet again! The train jerked to a stop after a few feet. My friend came back to help us with the luggage, and into a first class car where we found a compartment occupied only by a frail, quiet lady swathed in black who offered to share it with us.

I scarcely regained my composure during the two hour journey. When we arrived in Milan, there seemed to be no porters. I trudged what seemed a mile down the platform toward another, huge barnlike station where I finally enlisted a reluctant porter who gave me an anguished look as we returned to the platform and I indicated by a sign where we had to go. He managed to make it and, in the course of a half hour, we were at last in a taxi and on our way to the Principe and Savoia Hotel where we had reservations.

We were shown to a palatial suite with a beautifully furnished parlor whose windows opened out on a handsome garden or park with many flowers and green shrubbery. There was a spacious bedroom and bath. We were hungry and descended to the dining room where we had an elegant lunch. **HOW** elegant I learned later!

It was a sunny afternoon, so we started off to the great cathedral, one of the most famous in Europe. All cathedrals in Europe make this claim, however, and who is to challenge the statement? The safest thing to do is to see them all. We found the La Scala Opera House closed so were not able to see its truly famous interior.

The next morning we were to depart on a bus tour of Italian cities. I went to the desk to check out and found our bill was only $65 for the 20 hours or so we had enjoyed their food and lodging. It was a truly beautiful hotel; but, I hadn't meant to buy that much of it! We went back upstairs to await our bus: we saw one standing outside the entrance, but no call came. After a half hour, we returned to the lobby, to find an angry guide who said we were supposed to be "standing by the door."

He summoned us a cab and rushed us to the cathedral where the bus had already gone. There, we found a strike of city employees, on parade, smiling and singing. We could not get through. We had to carry all our luggage across the vast square to where the bus was waiting. Once aboard, we had to wait for the other tourists who were sightseeing in the cathedral. Meanwhile, the strikers decided our driver should be forced to join their march: there was quite a tense moment until the army (or some body of uniformed men) arrived and escorted us out of the city, for which we (and especially our driver) were very grateful.

On this tour, we had aboard two other Americans, Mexicans, Argentinians, Uruguayans, Peruvians, Puerto Ricans, Germans, French—and maybe another nation or two. Our guide, supposedly Italian, was a grinning soul who spoke no language clearly, took no trouble to point out historical or unusual sights, and who was generally a total loss. He took no thought to the need for comfort stops and thus, nearly drove us 'up the wall.'

The drive from Milan to Venice is a beautiful one; in the early evening, we checked in to our gondolas on the canals of Venice and arrived at the Splendide Suisse—which failed to be either of these! Shopping is an exciting experience in Venice, even if you are not buying. But we found a lovely ceramic log with two birds perched on it for dear friends at home: they were thrilled with it.

On the great esplanade in front of St. Marks Cathedral, we found two friends from the *Hamburg* at sunset and settled down at an open air table to enjoy our drinks. Two orchestras played classical music while throngs of people and pigeons swirled around us. The next evening, we met two other friends and repeated the experience which is one of the enchantments of life in Venice.

Enroute to Florence the next morning, we halted for a visit to the great church of St. Anthony at Padova (Padua). Another day, we stopped at Assisi to see the Shrine of St. Francis, the patron saint of birds: the saint's statue stands in beautiful surroundings. There is no dearth of churches in Italy!

In Firenze, we had attractive rooms with a large terrace: the weather was balmy, until it began to rain. We visited the St. Mary Maggiore with the incredible gold doors and the early Renaissance tower, the various Michelangelo works, the courtyards and sculpture and painting galleries, and shopped on the Ponte Vecchio which crosses the Arno.

As we plunged through the many tunnels in the Appennines Mountains on the way to Rome, our passengers, who had by this time become well acquainted, began to sing. A Mexican gentleman led off with a tenor lament: other soloists followed, mostly with a Latin American flavor. Suddenly, the Mexican began to urge me to sing.

Others joined him: my protestations that I couldn't sing were to no avail. They continued to beg me until I finally decided to 'do or die.' I walked to the front of the bus, took the guide's microphone, and waded into "There's a Long, Long Trail A'winding" and sang it through. Applause, which was literally astonishing, greeted me. I ralized one of the outstanding traits of the Latin is his recognition of one who is a good sport. Thus my international debut as a concert singer passed into history among those green and lovely Appennine hills.

Our stay in Rome was marked by lodgings in tthe second class Hotel Napoleon near the railway station. It proved to have good food and wine, somewhat comfortable rooms and a concierge who was the soul of courtesy and kindness. I have found that it pays to get on good terms with the concierges when one is traveling, for they can ease your pathway in a number of surporising ways if they wish to.

We enjoyed the visit to St. Peters on a Sunday morning when the Holy Father appeared at his palace window to bless the "city and world," while a crowd of some 500,000 greeted him below. We drove with a horse and carriage from the Victor Emmanuele statue back to our hotel. We dined in an interesting German restauranrt and a quiet Italian one near our restaurant. We visited the Spanish Steps, the Via Veneto, many fountains and ruins, several other churches, the flower markets and luxurious shops.

A pleasant plane trip carried us to Madrid and the Hotel Ritz where our reservations were waiting: three men escorted us to palatial quarters. Since I had been in Madrid before and knew a thing or two about the place, I asked the concierge to get us reservations at Las Bermejas which has excellent cuisine and the finest flamenco show of any restaurant in Spain, I'm sure. We arrived at 9:30. After our cab had departed, we found the restaurant closed. Eventually, a young man came out and asked if we wished to have dinner there: he told us they would not open until 10. It was a very chilly night, but he left us shivering on the street. A few minutes later, he came and, rather surreptitiously, took us inside, up a flight of stairs and ushered us into a theater box overlooking the stage.

A special show for a large touring group was starting, so we witnessed the entire show, receiving special bows from the artists. Then, we were given a good stageside table where we enjoyed an excellent dinner and saw the performance a second time.

Our departure from the Ritz was was easier than from Milan for, despite the luxury of our rooms, the bill was just $3 more than the reservation deposit! And now we were off across the plains of La Mancha where the ghost of Don Quixote seemed to be lurking in the background, through Arahnjuez to Valdepenas for lunch, and on to our night stop at Cordoba.

As we entered the dining room for lunch, we found most tables full. We stopped where only one gentleman was seated: he invited us to join him. He proved to be a Catholic priest, Father Abraham Azar from Alabama, on a sabbatical leave in Europe. To ours, and apparantly his, delight, we were able to travel together for some time, parting at the Majorca airport just before Christmas when we were leaving for Madrid. He was a jovial companion and shared our food and wines, our complaints and exhilarations, and added much to many incidents of our travel. We three engaged a carriage for a twilight drive about Cordoba, a place all of us found agreeable.

The next stop was Seville—more cathedrals, flamenco, shops, the Giralda, the Alcazar (evidence of the Moorish conquest) and, an astonishing view of the twenty-centuries old stone bridge across the Guadalquivir River.

Father Abraham joked with me over my saying, as each new town in Spain unfolded its charms, that I should like to live there. This was again true in Granada which lies in a valley watched over by the Sierra Nevada Mountains, their tops snow-covered around the year, lying close by. The famous Alhambra Palace, the Generalife Gardens, are wonders that a visitor could never forget. The hills nearby are full of caves which are the homes of gypsies: their flamenco shows are an enticement to the traveler who seeks night life. Life must have been beautiful in the last capital of the Moorish Kingdom in Spain!

On we went, crossing the range of the Sierra Nevada, to Puerto Lumbreras for lunch, through the fertile plains of Murcia, and passing the only palm groves of Europe, to reach Alicante The town was enchanting: our hotel on the seaside was fronted by a mile-long promenade, paved with marble, with tall fountains at each end which were gorgeous, especially when lit at night. Alicante has an elegant shopping street, paved with white marble for several blocks: here we purchased and mailed turrones, a famous nougat which goes from here to all parts of the world. A lovely flower market is nearby with unbelievably low prices.

Our journey continued through fashionable Benidorm and Gandia. Evening found us at Valencia, the heart of the orange-growing zone of Spain. After dinner at our hotel, I could not resist a walk to the flower market in a nearby square, dominated by a statue of Generalissimo Franco. Here I asked at several of the colorful booths and found the price of roses and carnations, to my astonishment, to be ten cents a dozen! How I wished we were staying long enough for me to fill our hotel room with flowers for only about $3.00!

Valencia has many interesting scenes: we toured the city before leaving for lunch in Benecarlo on the shore. We traveled on to Tarragona, which we toured briefly, and then proceeded to Barcelona. To my surprise, for I had always assumed Barcelona to be a drab port city, i found it exactly the opposite. We stopped at the charming Avenida Palace Hotel, one block from the great Cataluna Square with its huge and glowing fountains.

With Father Abraham, we gathered up a fine Spanish car and chauffeur for a trip to Montjuich, a mountain which stands between the city and the sea, beside the harbor with its great statue of Christopher Columbus.

Montjuich has a fortress and an amusement park at the top: the view is supurb in every direction. Then, we crossed the city and ascended Mont Tibidabo, another high point with a great church at the top, surmounted by a sculptured figure of Christ with outspread arms which seem to enfold all of Barcelona in their protection.

The sunshine was beautiful and here, there was another astonishing view of the city and its environs as well as the other mountain ranges leading well into the countryside. The following day, we took the same car and driver for the long trip to Montserratt, a monastery high in the mountains with a cathedral which is noted for the statue of the Black Virgin in its high altar. Here we missed the noon concert of the boys' choir. But, we dined on fresh strawberries. As we left our car and ascended the final heights by cable car, Father Abraham noted that my sister was somewhat perturbed. He said, "Don't worry. I can give you absolution." The ascent and the views atop were breathtaking: an outcropping of huge white rocks climbs still higher above the manastery.

The final day of our stay in Barcelona, the Yochen Erlers, a charming couple who had been on the *Hamburg*, arrived in the harbor on a ship which is a floating university. Dr. Yochen had joined the ship at a German port and given lectures on the United Nations as they sailed around to Spain. We met them as they landed, much to their surprise, and later went with them to a reception by the mayor of Barcelona. After a delightful lunch an Cataluna Plaza, we left for the airport to fly to Majorca.

We stayed at the Melia Majorca for a couple days while we searched for an apartment. We finally found one in Edificio Queen, a new high rise in the suburb of San Agustin, high above the sea. Settled here, we walked down the hill to the waterfront paseo and to Los Candiles for lunch, on a sunshiny terrace. The proprietor welcomed us; when we told him we were going to live in Majorca for six weeks, he said we must celebrate. He brought us a lovely bottle of Rondel champagne, which cost 35 pesetas, or 42 cents American.

This bottle was representative of all prices during our stay on this enchanting island. We found Spanish wines plentiful and inexpensive. After trying many brands, we found that Federeico Paternina, both red and white, was our favorite. It comes from Rioja, one of the best wine districts in Spain.

Food was equally cheap, for we visited many of the outstanding restaurants in Palma and seldom spent more than $2.50 American for a very good, six-course dinner. We enjoyed Tres Coronas for its Swedish smorgasbord; Meson Carlos Primero both for its elegant style and cuisine (this cafe was housed in an ancient castle on a centuries-old block on a long, narrow street whose paving was said to have been laid centuries ago). Here we met the genial and outgoing proprietor, Bob Schultz, who has become a great friend as a result of our many return visits. We also liked Nico's for its Danish menu and Los Candilles for outdoor dining and excellent trout almandine. The dinners at the hotels Victoria and Maricel were pleasing, but on the expensive side.

Our 'studio' apartment in Edificio Queen consisted of a bathroom as small as we could get into, a small kitchen and a large bed-sittting room, quite comfortable, with a balcony where we could watch the ever-changing colors of the sea. I tended the balcony boxes of pink geraniums which had been sadly neglected. Before we left, we were rewarded by a flurry of blooms.

Shortly after we settled down, the U.S. aircraft carrier, *John F. Kennedy* came into the harbor with a salute of many guns. It provided us with a great show of maneuvers for ten days and a beautifully lighted superstructure every night.

We had the good fortune to meet Gary Nelson, an American just graduated from the University of Michigan, who was touring in Europe. He had an apartment near us and shortly hired a car, inviting us to go touring the island. There followed three delightful days of touring and surprises. The first morning, we set forth in a little Seat car, passing the Cathedral and long miles of wide, white beaches at El Arenal, on down the southern coast to Cabo Blanco, Salinas, Colonia de San Jorge; and finally to Santanyi where I asked a motorcycle policman where we could find a good restaurant. "Follow me," he smiled and said in Spanish. So, off we dashed to a hidden-away place (probably owned by his sweetheart) and had good food and wine. The officer stayed for lunch, too. He waved a very cheerful farewell to us as we left.

In the afternoon, we drove through Felanitx (ending in 'itch') to Manacor, the center of the great Majorcan pearl industry. We stopped at a large store selling only pearls and made some purchases. We then drove back to Palma for the night.

The second day, we turned northward, coasting through Santa Maria, Binisalem, and Inca to a stop to view the Campanet caves. While the island abounds in 'cuevas,' these are truly among the most beautiful. The entrance on a hillside was almost covered with flowers: beauty was on every side within, in fantastic colors and shapes.

From here, we hastened on to Formentor and found one of the most beautiful hotels we could imagine. It is situated in a rather lonely spot: a tortuous mountain road, high above the sea with gorgeous views, leads to it. It has enjoyed the patronage of Churchill, Princess Margaret and her bridegroom, Prince and Princess Rainier and other such notables.

We scrambled back over the mountain and shopped for groceries at Puerto Pollensa, a lovely town beside the bay. We stocked up on fruit, meat and other goodies and drove back to Palma as the sun was setting behind the grey mountain ridges. The next morning, we went west through many new settlements along the shore: Palma Nova, Magaluf, on to Playas de Paguera where we sat on a shop veranda and sipped coffee and brandy in the sunshine while high breakers rolled right up to our feet. On to Adraitx—folowing a high and scary mountain road, we rounded the western end of the island and came to Es Grau, a restaurant that seemed to hang directly above the sea on the rocky grey side of Grau peak. Here we lunched superbly, with excellent wine, in a dining room where you could look out to sea in three directions as far as eyesight could reach. On to Banalbufar, a village literally hanging on the mountain (the level of the street sloped down from one side to the other.) As we left the village, the road led round a curve and up another ridge so we could look back. It seemed as if the town had been thrown against the mountain and just lodged there. I shall never forget Banalbufar.

We spent a couple fascinating hours at Valldemosa, the town made famous by Chopin and George Sand who romanced there more than a century ago. The convent where they lived still stands: there is every reason to believe that anyone's romance would flower amidst such beauty.

Our days in Majorca passed quickly, with visits to the great city markets which seemed to have every known vegetable, fruit, cheese, meat and other edible known to man. We hesitated to buy those we did not know well (because of their Spanish names) and not knowing how to prepare and serve them. Other visits to the Cathedral, Castle Bellver, the Yacht Club with Father Abraham, shopping in Gen. Franco paseo, Jaime III and Calle San Antonio, a Thanksgiving dinner with the American Club at a tennis club in the suburbs where I met Riki Lash, a broadcaster and night club owner. He wrote me up in his column in the Majorca daily newspaper. When I appeared at his plush club, My Own Place, he interviewed me on the air.

We also heard the Majorca Symphony in a very good concert; the Police Band (surprisingly good) in two concerts; took in a play and a bull fight. I attended the Anglican church every Sunday, presided over ably by Father Moody, a young and handsome Australian priest. We took our six cents bus to the ceremony of the lighting of the Christmas tree and decorated streets. It was a spectacular sight, although most natives seemed strangely unmoved. We were thrilled; yet, they were nothing to compare with the Christmas lights in Madrid a week later which were absolutely the most fantastic we had ever seen.

We were sad when the time came to bid farewell to our studio and its unforgettable view. We took off by Iberian plane for Madrid and a fortnight's stay at the Castellana Hilton. When the management learned we were staying through the holidays, they gave us beautiful quarters with red upholstered furniture, red covers on the beds, red frames on the pictures. When we added red flowers from the florist shop, we were ready for Christmas.

The maitre'd brought us a large bottle of Cordoniu, Spain's best champagne, and a "gypsy's arm" (ice cream cake) Christmas Eve. We shared them with a nice gal from the TWA office in the lobby. We had a splendid Christmas Eve dinner and later attended services at midnight in a nearby Catholic church. On New Year's Eve, we dined at a fine German restaurant, then crossed the street to the Theatre Zarsuela for a marvelous singing and dancing show. Just before midnight, the show stopped. Everyone was given a bottle of champagne, twelve white grapes (to be eaten as the clock struck twelve to bring good luck in the year ahead) and paper hats and confetti. A party ensued with the cast joining in the great gaiety; then, the show continued for some time to give the new year a fine start.

After sightseeing at the old walled capital of Toledo and the Valley of the Fallen (which I had seen on a previous visit), we flew to Lisbon and stopped at the Hotel Florida near the Marques de Pombal circle and monument on the wide Liberdade boulevarde. We took a city tour, went to the fabulous Gulbenkian ballet and museum, St. Georges castle with its lake crowded with swans and other exotic birds, and to the Flea Market where I bought a boina (beret). We lunched at the elegant Verando Do Chantecler and dined at Fiai with 'fado' songs. We lunched several times at Hotel Ritz, said to be the finest hotel in Europe.

A fine Portugese chauffeur supplied by the concierge took us to Queluz and the Pink Palace, to Sintra and Hotel Palacio de Sertais, one of the most attractive hotels I ever saw, to Cascais, to Cabo da Boca, the westernmost point in Europe, and to Estoril, the playground of royalty. Enroute, we saw Boca da Inferno (the Mouth of Hell) where waves come roaring through the rocks with an unearthly sound.

Finally came "A Dios" to Portugal: we flew to Malaga and a seaside hotel from whence we drove down the Costa del Sol to Torremolinas, Fuengirola and Marbella where we lunched in style (with champagne from the management) at Don Pepe's glittering restaurant. Another day, we made the same drive in bright sunshine to Algeciras where we went to board the Italian Lines great flagship, *Michelangelo*. It was delayed and we spent the night at the Reine Christina, another elegant hotel. In morning fog, we went aboard a lighter to where the queen of the seas was waiting outside the harbor.

The six-days crossing was marked by heavy rain, snow and gale storms, marvelous dinners served by two fine Italian stewards, Joe and Vicente, who anticipated our every wish, a wine steward who kept us well supplied, and background music. We played bingo and generally enjoyed the trip, especially meeting the Marshalls who were returning from extensive service in Morocco. After their vacation, they planned to go out again for the Agency for International Development in Uganda (I wonder if they survived the troubles there?) Others we enjoyed were the Wolfes, delightful Germans coming to America for Bayer Company; Bob Howes and Milton Chapin from Cape Cod's Half House; and the Hardaways from Boston.

Landing in New York in zero degree weather, we were charged $10 for a $1.25 trip to Pennsylvania Station. Then we knew we were home! We had never been overcharged in Europe, to my knowledge. We got a drawing room and had an excellent lunch on the train to Washington.

We had many pleasant memories of Spain and the proud people who are poor by American standards, but who seem to make do with what they have and appear much more content than we are. Life is serene there: we neither heard nor read little mention of crime. We thought of them as an oppressed people living under a dictatorship. They thought of the United States as a place where the colored race are crushed under heel. (A 'triumph' of modern international journalism.) We ate all kinds of food, drank water with neither fear nor unpleasant results. We had not one day's illness in our five-months stay. We should have taken up residence in Majorca!

A year later, the Karl Sottungs and their delightful son, Jurgen, came from Germany to visit their daughter who lived near us in a garden apartment at Hermitage Hill. They enjoyed the swimming pool: we met there almost every day and became quite good friends, with the result that I was urgently invited to visit them soon in Germany.

In 1973, I flew from McGuire Air Force Base by 'space available' and landed in Frankfort. I tried to reach them by telephone in Aschaffenburg, 25 miles away, but failed. I then tried a telegram. While waiting for a reply, I walked to Frankfort Stadium, an impressive home for all sports, where a merry crowd of ice skaters were enjoying a large outdoor rink.

The Sottungs welcomed me warmly and summoned friends of various ages to a 'carnaval' in my honor, it being the carnival season just before Lent. Excellent wine and beer flowed freely: we danced and talked for hours. Jurgen and a friend played guitars: I was coaxed into singing my specialty, "Long, Long Trail" to much applause, just as months before on the bus in Italy. Marianna and Gustave Heike were special fun. The former, a tall blonde, blue-eyed German woman, joined me in the "Rucci Zucci," a popular dance. We howled with laughter, almost danced our shoes off and celebrated close to dawn.

Jurgen and his friend took me sightseeing to castles (at one of which we lunched on trout snatched from the castle moat), fabulous churches and the oldest *gast-haus* in Germany where one mug of the bock beer made me want to settle in Bavaria for life. Eventually, I tore myself away, taking

Jurgen with me to Zurich and to St. Moritz where, amidst the hordes of skiers, the deep snows and the millionaires, I found my friends, Hildegarde Knef and her husband, David Cameron. After we were settled in hotel Post at $50 per day, David drove in and took us to their apartment for a delightful round of martinis and supper. Hildegarde was enchanting in a gown with Oriental touches, and flushed with the world-wide success of her book, *The Gift Horse* which she told me had been translated into many languages. She was at work on another book, *The Verdict*, which has since been published and tells of her battle with cancer.

We traveled on to Geneva for a brief visit with the Adrian Davids. Jurgen and I parted company there, he to return to duty with the German Air Force and I to fly to Majorca where I settled down for a month at the fine old Hotel Mediterraneo whose vast, beautifully furnished lobby and evening concerts spoke of olden times. This hotel has since been permanently closed.

During my stay, I met Captain and crew of the carrier, *Intrepid* and went on board for lunch with the officers' mess. I also had many evenings of fine music, the outstanding one being an all Chopin concert by Artur Rubenstein. Nearing 80 years of age, Rubenstein gave a full program of exquisite Chopin, was called back and gave a Chopin encore and again another. The third time, he gave a very formal bow and walked stiffly from the stage. What a memorable evening! Another exciting night was the flamenco dancers at Pueblo Espanol.

Home again by 'space available' from Torrejon, Spain to Dover, Delaware which seemed like the end of the earth until I found a young chauffeur who delivered me safely to the doorstep of Vinson Hall where we had moved the previous October. It is a retired officers residence sponsored by the Navy in McLean, Virginia.

Each spring and fall the Vinson Hall residents enjoy a day at the races at Bowie track in Maryland. I got home just in time to join my sister for the trip that year. We had a wonderful day with a fine lunch in the clubhouse and reserved seats to watch the horses run. We both enjoyed the sport and tried to join the group on each outing, usually coming home with a fair amount of 'track money.'

In addition to a busy schedule of private entertaining, with morning coffees, luncheons, cocktail parties and dinners appearing on the social calendar, Vinson Hall has art shows, bridge, bingo and poker games. Fine concerts are provided by men and women's groups of the Army, Navy, Air Force, Coast Guard and Marine Corps and their service bands. Each spring, the grounds are beautified by dogwood trees, azalea and rose gardens. Many of the residents are widely traveled and provide interesting slide shows.

For those impressed by military rank, one, two and three star gentlemen and there ladies are everywhere, both as residents and visitors. Frequently distinguished guests such as former First Lady Lady Bird Johnson and her daughter, Lynda Johnson Robb, First Lady of Virginia, are welcomed and entertained.

Our many friends in Florida were clamoring for a visit; so, off we flew to Fort Meyer to see old friends from Washington, Herman and Martha Bly whose luxurious new home in Whiskey Creek Estates had an in-house swimming pool. We also spent a happy evening with the Robert Abbotts, parents of dear friends in Vienna, Virginia; the William Cummings who was U.S. District Attorney for Northern Virginia. I went to Saratoga to spend a day with the Earnest Heils (Lucille was a dear friend of younger days in Columbus, Ohio); then, on to Miami for a few days with Mrs. Chester M. Wright whose late husband was an old friend and public relations associate. She gave us a wonderful visit, topped of by a night at the fabulous Palm Bay Club. We made a long bus trip to Orlando where we were met by Dixie Ryland and well-entertained by General and Mrs. Bruce Holloway at a unique Country Store restaurant.

Col. Oscar Drake, recently home from Korea and now retired, met us here and drove us to their new home in Ocala where he was joining the 'army' of Florida realtors. Later, they drove us to Green Cove Springs to visit Col. and Mrs. Edward Stansell (he is retired from the Marine Corps) who have literally carved a lovely spot from the jungle to build their new home. A pleasant evening flight took us back to Washington.

Highlight of the year 1974—of my whole life, perhaps—was my initiation into Beta Theta Pi, the college fraternity to which I had been pledged 55 years before at Bethany College in West Virginia. I was the only man known to have served as a pledge so long in fraternity history! Psi chapter voted unanimously to 'activate' me at their "Spring Stampede," after I had written to suggest that they had improperly addressed me as "brother" in correspondence asking for financial help. I sent along a check despite the mistake! When some 50 active members who had never met me, voted me in, I felt I was really wanted.

I attended the national convention that year at beautiful Bedford Springs Hotel in Pennsylvania; the following year, at Mackinac Island's Grand Hotel (with the longest hotel veranda in the world); and in succeeding years at French Lick Springs, Tan-Ta-Ra in the Ozarks, again to Mackinac, then to Miami University at Oxford, Ohio (where the fraternity was founded in 1839) and finally at the famous "Homestead" in Virginia.

At these meetings, I've come to know and admire former president Ralph Fey and his successor, Congressman James J. Martin; national vice presidents Richard 'Misty' Shoop and James McMullen III, Reverend Seth Brooks, the 'grand old man' of all the Beta world; Ford Weber, Jonathon Brant and many others. As I write this, the current president is former

Arizona congressman John B. Rhodes, a most distinguished Beta.

At Mackinac I met Ken Rawley of the Penn State chapter who later invited me to visit Alpha Upsilon where I made a speech, won a rising ovation, was royally entertained and 'adopted' by that great group of Betas. I have visited them several times.

While lunching at the Arizona Biltmore some winters later, the maitre'd approached our table and said to me, "Aren't you a Beta Theta Pi?" Imagine my surprise and pleasure when he introduced himself as Brad Feffer of Penn State who was present and heard me speak there some years before.

In the autumn of 1974, I returned to Bavaria with a Bethany College tour to the Oktoberfest in Munich. We were housed in a pleasant little town, Inzell, near the Austrian border. I was most fortunate in staying at Gasthaus Bluml whose young German proprietor, Alois Bluml, took especially good care of me, cooked me gourmet dinners, drove me about in his Rolls-Royce and added much pleasure to my visit.

Tour members were taken by bus to three of Mad King Ludwig's palaces: Neuchwanstein, Herrenchemsee and Linderhof; to Berchtesgaden and the "Eagle's Nest" (where mad Hitler made his plans to rule the world;) to Garmisch-Partenkirchen and Oberammergau; to Salzburg and beautiful Mirabel gardens and many other historic spots; to Die Wiekirche, an amazing country church; to Munich for the Oktoberfest and to see the world-famous Glockenspiel and Nymphenburg palace. A whole new world in eight days!

In February, 1975 I went to Dover and off again on 'space available' to Spain where I spent three pleasant days at the Air Force Officers Club at Torrejon Air Base. Then I flew to Mallorca to find an apartment. When my sister and her friend Vicky Kissel arrived ten days later, I wass settled in El Pelicano, right beside the sea in a Palma suburb, San Augustin. Six busy weeks followed, highlighted by a motor tour around the island with Miguel Mir, a fine young Mallorcan gentleman, as our driver and guide.

We flew to Barcelona for an exciting weekend, a visit to the Sagrada Familia ultra-modern cathedral which will take one hundred years more to finish; the great Picasso museum; and a night at the 'Scala' night club, a worthy competitor to the Lido in Paris. Finally, we celebrated my birthday with a supurb dinner at the palatial Valparaiso Hotel in Palma. Then, en route home, we went sightseeing in Madrid.

After a day trip by motor across the Guadarrama Mountains in a fog so deep we could not see the road ahead, we reached the ancient walled city of Avila, famed as the final resting place of Saint Theresa noted for her contribution to Roman Catholic history as the founder of many monasteries, nunneries, hospitals and churches in Spain.

We moved on to Segovia, visiting enroute the 'fairy castle' where Queen Isabella received Christopher Columbus when he returned from 'discovering' America (or perhaps when she gave him the money to make the trip, I'm not certain) In Segovia, we lunched at the Master Butcher's, saw the twenty centuries old aqueduct still providing water to the city, and drove on to the magnificent castle of San Ildefonso, "La Granja", which is said to house the most magnificent collection of tapestries in the world, literally hundreds of them. Returning to Madrid, we crossed the mountains at another spot deep in snow with magnificent views. As we came down the pass, we could see, far off to the right, the great cross atop the underground cathedral in the Valley of the Fallen; also, the Escorial, the burial place of Spanish kings and queens for several centuries.

After seeing my sister and her friend off on Iberian Airlines at Madrid airport, I taxied to Torrejon, almost immediately got passage by 'space available' and arrived at Vinson Hall via Dover only five hours after my sister's return! I gave my fellow residents a travel talk about our journey which brought out a good crowd and was well received.

****

Later, my sister Laura underwent a cataract operation and, when a letter came from Dixie Ryland urging us to come to Winter Park to 'recuperate,' we both happily accepted. Shortly after our arrival, we met Dixie's great friends and realtor associates, O.C. and Jean Halyard, who wined and dined us, took me to Episcopal services where I met the famous John Medaris (Army general who became an Episcopal priest after retirement). With Dixie and them, I attended a large realtors' luncheon in Disney World. Later, we made an all-day visit to this amazing resort, with lunch at Cinderella's Castle and a much more exciting day than our visit four years before.

The Halyards took us to charming entertainment at the home of John and Florence Leier which resembles Mount Vernon. We also went to visit William and Julie Deutsch in Maitland. I gave them a dinner party at the newly-opened La Belle Verriere, a French restaurant decorated with Tiffany stained glass panels and windows. Later, Dixie took us to the Tiffany glass museum and the Maltby shell museum on the campus of Rollins College. Then, we drove through the wooded park nearby where a flock of peacocks gave us a special show.

Enroute to a weekend with the Oscar Drakes in Ocala, we stopped in Gainesville for lunch with General and Mrs. Russell Ryland, Dixie's brother and sister-in-law.

Back to Orlando and a champagne farewell at the airport with the Halyards and Dixie.

****

Spain called us back in 1976 and we flew a British Airways 747. After a champagne and orchid send-off at Dulles airport by Betty and Jay Seelinger, we survived the tumult at Heathrow Airport in London and arrived at Mallorca to be met by faithful Miguel Mir who drove us quickly to El Pelicano. Here we found next door neighbors from Connecticut, Ed and Agatha Dakin. As Ed was a Beta brother, we got off to a great start and traveled with them to fine restaurants high in the mountains, at Galilea and at another, the Hostal de Muntanya in Oriente, where delicious Spanish food and homemade wine (at 37 cents American per bottle) were served to us by a proprietor who showed us courtesies one would expect at Club 21 in New York. We found a spledid country inn just outside Palma, Foc y Fum (Fire and Smoke in Mallorquinese) which was super in beverages, food and atmosphere. I ordered 'vieja rops' (old clothes) and found it to be a tasty dish of lamb and onions en casserole. Another trip with Miguel and his bride took us to the monastary of Lluch. We arrived too late to hear the famous boys' choir; so, we went on to a mountainside inn for lunch with 'pajamas' for dessert (ice cream with fruit.) Then, back to Palma where Miguel proudly showed us their new home and loaded us with oranges from their garden.

We joined the British-American Club and spent many pleasant hours there, with fine food in the Buttery and an excellent bar. I joined the club's Spanish class and there met Dorothy Diaz. She and her husband, Edmundo, who is a skilled painter, came to be our great friends and are now in New York.

Our old and dear friend, Abby Wood of Washington, wrote us five times from Montreux, Switzerland urging us to leave Palma and join her. So, we scheduled our homeward journey by way of Geneva and Montreux. The Davids in Geneva had just returned from Afghanistan: we divided out time between the two places.

At Montreux, we stopped at charming Hotel Helvetia, journeyed by mountain train to Gstaad (fabulous ski resort of royalty) and by motor to Gruyere, an ancient city with a castle and cheese. At St. Georges Hotel there, I ordered cheese fondue for lunch, only to be told I would have to have lunch in another room because patrons objected to the odor. We had fresh strawberries—even with snow piled up outside! Each morning I hiked along Lake Leman with at least 20 swans following, hoping for a bite of breakfast, The lake promenade runs for miles, bordered all the way by great beds of spring flowers. Spring comes early in the Rhone Valley: the Rhone enters Lake Leman at Montreux. From our hotel windows, we could look across the lake to the snow-crested mountains in France.

We visited the garish Casino, also the Castle of Chillon where Lord Byron did (or did not) write some of his best works, and where he was (or was not) imprisoned and chained to a marble pillar, whichever you believe.

Laura Luanna Brookover

Vinson Hall Handicap at Bowie

183

CHAPTER XXII
HIGHLIGHTS 1972-78

Home again and I resumed my trips every three months to New York where I attended the meetings of the Diocese Investment Trust of the Episcopal Diocese of New Jersey of which I was a member. One of our board memebers was the genial Emlen Roosevelt, notable New Jersey banker. That year, the mid-summer meeting was held, at his invitation, on the Jersey coast. We were his guests at a yacht club for lunch and afterward on an exciting deep sea fishing trip on his boat. We topped it off with dinner at another fine seaside club.

At other times, the trust meetings were held in the luxurious offices of our financial advisers on the 94th floor of the World Trade Building, high above the harbor and the Statue of Liberty.

In autumn of 1977, my sister and I returned to Arizona for a month's visit with the Folkerths. We journeyed to Tucson for Thanksgiving with Mabel Gilliam and dined on turkey at Davis-Monthan Air Force Base. 'Gil,' as all her friends know her, has a charming house nestling at the base of the Santa Catalina mountain range. I returned to Tucson later for a Beta Theta Pi banquet at Tanque Verde guest ranch out in the desert, presided over by owner (and Beta brother) 'Brownie' Cote. It is truly a playground for millionaires. Guests come from all over the States and many foreign countries.

Final event of this stay was a weekend trip with the Folkerth family to Page, Arizona, site of Wahweap Lodge where we stayed. We saw Glen Canyon Dam, one of the highest in the world, and Lake Powell, where

Colorado River waters have formed a 3,000 mile complex of beautiful canyons and shoreline, a marvelously scenic boat journey.

The next summer, we fled from Washington heat to the charming little town of Camden, on Penobscot Bay in Maine. Here we enjoyed the hospitality of Whitehall Inn and its hosts, Edward and Jean Dewing and their engaging sons, Jonathan and 'Chip.' We were delighted with the cool, green woods, the ocean breezes and trips in the family speedboat. We drove to famous Bar Harbor for Laura's birthday and an unforgetable lunch at Jordan Pond. We spent much time with new friends Ben and Ruth Wolfe from Philadelphia and, with them, enjoyed lunches at the Sail Loft in Rockport.

1978 swung me into politics: I became a delegate to the Virginia Republican Convention in June at Richmond, supporting the candidacy of John Warner, former Secretary of Navy and head of the National Bicentenial Committee in 1976. I voted for him consistently for six ballots, but he finally lost the nomination to Richard Obenchain who was later killed in a plane crash. Warner was then chosen as the candidate and won a seat in the United States Senate.

A social highlight of the campaign was a country supper for 4,000 guests at the Warners' "Atoka Farm" in Middleburg. Warner was married to the beautiful and famous Elizabeth Taylor, movie and TV star. I came to know them both quite well during the campaign. I found 'Liz' to be a gentle, sensitive person, quite unlike her image on the screen.

In November, my sister and I cast absentee ballots for John, of course, and hied ourselves again to Phoenix to spend the winter at beautiful Los Arboles on Camelback Boulevarde. We again spent Thanksgiving with Mabel Gilliam in Tucson, drove the day after (in a downpour) to lunch at Tanque Verde Ranch. We were warned about flash floods, but got home safely. We also visited the Arizona-Sonora Desert Museum, the Saguaro National Monument and the desert studio of the famous artist, Jose Grazia.

Dixie Ryland drove from Florida, arriving for Christmas with her Toyota loaded with citrus fruit, pecans and other goodies. With her, we visited Care Free (described earlier) and enjoyed Sunday champagne brunch at Elbow Bend Restaurant; Superstition Mountains; Casa Grande, the 600 years old 'great house' of the Hohokam Indians; St. Barnabas-In-The-Desert, a beautiful Episcopal church where we enjoyed the Christmas service. We also attended the dedication of a new pipe organ in the First Baptist church of Phoenix (which seats 6,000 people) with my old friend, Virgil Fox at the console.

On a lovely sunny day, we drove out to Fountain hills, a new development nestling among the mountains which boasts the highest fountain stream in the world; then on to Lake Saguaro, a scenic spot, ideal for water sports and picknicking. We returned often to Fountain Hills: another new desert village we enjoyed was Rio Verde.

While eating our way through Phoenix, we found Caf'Casino, a typical French cafe (although cafeteria style) to be so much like Paris as to make a Frenchman homesick. We enjoyed the champagne lunches at the Arizona Biltmore Hotel, world famous and luxurious, surrounded by acres of equally grand and expensive private villas, swimming pools, golf course, and tennis courts—all part of the Biltmore complex. Our first lunch there was followed by a limousine tour of the Wrigley mansion, high on the hill above, a monument to the chewing gum king of America, a man who made millions from an unpleasant habit indulged in by his countrymen of all ages. (Perhaps pleasant to do, but quite unpleasant to watch on a bus or in a theater. However, I chewed gum as a child, but never since.)

The Wrigley showplace made a poor comparison with the many palaces I have seen in Europe. But, we were told by a tour guide that since the Biltmore which now owns the mansion began sending paying guests to stay there, many of the original objects of beauty and wealth had been removed. The Wrigley family had other homes, of course, and never spent more than two months in a year at Wrigley Phoenix.

Camelback Inn, also quite famous, has been somewhat spoiled by conversion to condominium style. Lunch there is not so elegant as in the former days. Col. John S. Lynch and his charming Jane took me to Maximillion's Cafe, a hacienda at the edge of the desert now operating as a rambling, charming Mexican restaurant. We also dined at Navarre's, old and popular in downtown Phoenix; Mag's Ham and Bun in Scottsdale, fun and famous; TGIF (Thank God It's Friday) with good food and deafening noise; King's Table and Marie Callendar's, the latter justly famous for unbelievably good pies.

I lunched every Thursday with Beta brothers from the new chapter at Arizona State University and distinguished Beta alumni, of whom there are literally scores in Arizona. Outstanding Betas I met and admired were the Louis Linxwilers, father and son; George Marshall, a retired banker whom I chose to call 'Mr. Secretary'; and Spencer Stewart, who purchased a house for the new brothers at ASU. He and his charming wife gave an all-day party in their mansion at the 18th hole of the Phoenix Golf Club to watch the finals of the Phoenix Open tournament.

We also had a most delightful invitation to lunch with Mrs. Frank Brophy, a dear lady whom a Beta brother described as head of a "royal family, or the nearest thing to royalty that Arizona can provide." She is the widow of the late Frank Cullen Brophy, one of the state's most distinguished pioneers, a man involved in mining, ranching, banking, railroading and all successful pursuits in this case. It was said of him that he was 'too busy' and turned down all requests to run for state or national office.

Mrs. Brophy lived in a gorgeous ranch home, built many years ago on the desert, but now almost downtown. There are sons and daughters living nearby. The family are ardent Roman Catholics and have established a private school for boys and a magnificent shrine, St. Francis Xavier Catholic church, in the center of the city.

We had another invitation to visit our former neighbors at Vinson Hall, Vice Admiral and Mrs. Glynn Donaho, who are now resident at Sierra Vista, a small town in the desert near Fort Huachuca and the Mexican border. Fort Huachuaca is the oldest active Army base in this country, the only one surviving from 70 forts built in Indian fighting days. It is now a world center for Army communications. The Donahos stopped to visit Army friends here, enroute to Mexico for the winter, and decided to stay. They purchased a fine lot with many fruit-bearing trees, gardening and landscaping possibilities and are settled down, and very happy.

They entertained us beautifully, at home and at the Lakeview Officers' Club, at Ricardos for 'chimichanga', a great Mexican dish. We drove to Tombstone and Boot Hill Cemetery, to Bisbee and the Copper Queen mine and famous Lavendar pit, to Naco, located both in the U.S. and Mexico across the border.

As this narrative has progressed, I have looked for a place to end it—in order to get it published within my lifetime and not 'posthumorously'. I finally found a most appropriate place, I think, at 'Sin City', Las Vegas, Nevada. Since the Bible tells us that we were born in sin, it seems fitting to approach the end of my rambling life story at this place.

Early one February morning, we went forth, breakfasted at the Golden Nugget at Wickenburg, passed through Wickieup, Santa Claus, Grasshopper Junction, Kingman, past Hoover Dam and Lake Mead, arriving before evening at the Showboat Hotel where we were to stay. A full-sized showboat in front gives the hotel its name. We made our way through dozens of slot machines to register at the desk, after which we were shown to delightfully furnished rooms.

We passed a rather quiet evening with the losing and winning clicks of the slots. The next day, we drove 'The Strip' and gazed at all the gaudy architectural gems that must house at least a million slot machines. At famous Ceasar's Palace, we could hardly get into the lobby for machines and players. In every hotel and restaurant, it was the same.

The next evening, we were regaled at the Stardust Hotel with the Lido show 'direct from Paris.' Since I have seen it there, I found no fault with the Las Vegas version. Scores of undressed maidens dancing with handsome gents in one beautiful scene after another, prancing down the runway, vieing with an elephant for attention, a Venetian scene with authentic gondolas, gondoliers, and gorgeous dames floating by, a magician who made a lion and tiger disappear in mid-air and then sawed a girl in two in front of us. This was the Lido, with four drinks during the show included in the bill.

We breakfasted in Nevada the next day, lunched in California, and dined in Arizona. Enroute we saw Havasu City (with the London Bridge), Needles, Quartzite, Sore Finger and Litchfield Park. We felt no sadness at leaving 'Sin City' to survive or perish among its slot machines.

'Sin City' proved, however, not the end but more like a prelude to more fun, if not more sin. A long summer return visit to Whitehall Inn in Maine was followed by a second return in October. Chip Dewing joined me for a drive to Orono and the University of Maine where the Beta Theta Pi chapter was celebrating its 100th anniversary with a dinner for four hundred guests. I was honored by being asked to make an impromptu speech which was well received, especially by the ladies present whom I addressed as 'Beta Sweethearts.'

CHAPTER XXIII:1980
VIENNA AND BAVARIA

Came December 14 and I delivered my well-worn speech "A Speech For All Occasions" to the Greater McLean Republican Women's Club to considerable applause and some consternation on the part of those who weren't sure whether I was serious or pulling their legs. When two Beta Theta Pi fraternity brothers of mine from Penn State, Ken Rawley and Chuck McKelvey appeared in the audience, I was quite startled: they claimed they had come to see me off for Europe. The next day, they waved farewell as I boarded Air France for the long flight to Vienna. A pleasant surprise enroute was a luncheon with 23 items of food and beverage. Vive Air France!

My pal, Chip Dewing from Whitehall Inn, was at the airport gate in Wien and hustled me off through falling snow to a comfortable pension where we prepared for an evening tour of several wine kellers for which Vienna is famous. The city was ablaze with Christmas decorations: a glittering tree rose high in front of the Rathaus (City Hall) and the street below was lined by small temporary shops (a Kriskindelmarkt) where 'everything for Christmas' was displayed for sale, making an unforgettable sight.

We first went to the Esterhazy Wine Keller, named for a famous Hungarian patron of music and arts. In his honor, when it came time to eat, we had Liptauer cheese and the famous seven-layer chocolate torte which originated in Hungary, but is quite different from the widely-known Sacher torte of Vienna.

We hopped on to the keller of the Twelve Apostles where we sipped powerful Stierblut wine from the Hungarian border and hopped again to Helga's Bar, a really jumping place presided over by the one and only Helga, Chip's friend from his school days in Vienna. After a few winks of sleep, we rose and hastened to the Spanish Riding School, fortunately having the glorious experience of witnessing the white Lippizaner stallions giving their last performance of the season, dancing and marching in formation to classical music.

On the days following, Chip and I toured the Belvedere, Schoenbrunn and Hofburg palaces, magnificent reminders of days of empire. We went also to the great Kunthistoriches Museum, one of the world's great collections of painting and sculpture. There to my astonishment, I heard my name called out and turned to behold a gentleman from Houston, Texas, a former manager of Vinson Hall in McLean, Virginia, my present home. Inspiring sights ever present in Wien are the dome of Saint Stephens and the Votif Kirche with the many wonderful stained glass windows.

We lunched at Demel's, Vienna's finest coffee house, and dined at Grinzing in the Vienna Woods. We were invited to a delightful evening and dinner at the home of Dr. and Mrs. Peter Jandl (he was a close friend of Austria's chancellor) where choice food and wines ended with a marvelous Saint Laurent, a red dessert wine.

We climbed above Grinzing to the Kloster Neuberg, an ages-old monastery, and enjoyed a brown-bag luncheon on a balustrade with beautiful scenes in every direction. Far below, the Blue Danube (only, it wasn't so blue) wound its serpentine way to the sea. Hiking down the mountain for miles to the village, we found green branches over certain doorways, indicating that the season's new wine, produced locally, was being served.

Clutching our Eurail passes, we reluctantly departed by train for Salzburg where we fell into the arms of Hilde Radich who presided over a pension and whose outpouring of kindness, with a rapid-fire mixture of English and German, was a wonder to behold. We had a short stay: a sightseeing drive behind a team of matched greys, with heavy snow falling to provide a white coat to the glamor of Mozart's statue, was a proper farewell (even though we were overcharged for the ride!)

We hired a car and drove to Inzell, Bavaria (West Germany) where Alois Bluml welcomed us warmly to Gasthaus Blüml where I had stayed on a previous visit. On Christmas Eve, a capacity crowd forced us to share a table with a family from Holland (Boy, Hannie and Molly Brüine). Champagne flowed like water until early morning. On Christmas Day, we drove to Rhulpolding where we climbed Mount Rauchberg and waded in deep snow to enjoy the wondrous views of the surrounding Alps. At the inn, we drank Gluwein, a special Christmas beverage, to warm ouselves.

We drove another day to Berches-Garten, Hitler's " Eagles Nest," but found the mountain roads blocked with snow. Disappointed, we were returning to Inzell and stopped at a small village to have more Gluwein. As we drank, a fusillade of shots rang out from the mountain, Bavaria's answer to the Christmas firecrackers of China. As we passed on, buglers in a high church tower were playing Christmas carols, a thrilling sight and sound.

On a sparkling winter day, we drove to Munich where we enjoyed a typical German lunch in a fine restaurant, Domskeller. Later, Joe Scott, an American friend living in Munich, joined us for a few beers. We saw the famed Glockenspiel and other important sights. Another day, we had an excellent lunch at Oberammergau, a tour of the fascinating wood-working shops there. Then, on to the Weis Kirche in the Fields, a fabulously beautiful church in open country, full speed through Parten-Kircken and home to little Inzell.

We back-tracked to Salzburg and found Hilde's pension full to capacity; but, she handed us on to a friendly house nearby. We attended a glorious mass at St. Peter's Cathedral whose dome rose high above the city. We took a night drive on the mountains high above the city (a bit of enchantment) and attended a puppet show "Abduction From the Seraglio" at the Marionette Theater, a large theater devoted to puppetry. With every seat occupied, we were given the courtesy of chairs in the aisle.

An all-day motor tour of the Lake District tthrough superb scenery featured a pleasant lunch at the picturesque little town of Monsee. Before leaving Salzburg, a couple visits to the vast beer keller, Augustine, gave a new dimension to beer consumption.

On New Year's Eve, we celebrated with a bottle of Henkel's Trocken champagne; then, we abducted Hilde from her husband's arms and fled to Sternbrau, a night spot where we saw the old year out with loud, but stirring, disco and polka music and many beautiful girls.

A long train ride to Geneva began the next morning before dawn. The trains in that region are always on time to the split second. Our Eurail passes were most helpful in avoiding long lines at the ticket windows. We had a compartment from whose windows we watched an endless panorama of pine forests heavily laden with snow—truly a winter wonderland!

The train got tired—or we did—and we stopped overnight at Basel, a very interesting city as all Swiss cities are. We left the next day at noon after winning a furious argument with the pension owner who wanted to charge us for an extra day.

A day was spent enjoying Geneva's sights mentioned before. The next day, we took the electric train to Montreux where we boarded a sturdy mountain train which climbed many miles to famed Gstaad, a playground of royalty. Then we went by cable car to the top of the ski run where we nearly froze in zero degree temperature. Beer and wurst helped us thaw a little.

Old friends in Geneva, Adrian and Anne David (previously mentioned) gave us a great dinner, punctuated with many samples from Adrian's huge wine cellar. On the way to Schladming in Austria the next day, I was very tired and 'hung over.' When we were to change trains, I caught my foot in the car door and, after a long struggle to free myself, I collapsed and was carried to the platform where a railroad doctor (or mechanic!) pronounced I had had a stroke and must go by ambulance to a hospital at Wahlenstadt, miles away. After lying for about an hour on a platform truck in freezing weather with heavy snow falling, the ride began over bumpy and icy roads. It ended at a remarkable small white hospital where Dr. Hans Jorge Keel and a bevy of beautiful nurses who spoke only German nursed me to health in three days (without a stroke) with many glasses of hot mint tea and hours of refreshing sleep.

Dr. Keel had served two years at the U.S. Air Force Hospital in Denver: when he learned I was a retired Air Force colonel, I owned the place! When I was leaving, I was presented with a modest bill and a message from Dr. Keel to " pay at my convenience." Imagine this happening in any American hospital!

Chip had gone on to the ski resort of Schladming and found a comfortable pension. He spent most of the week on the ski slope while I drank beer, read books and took long walks to enjoy the magnificent scenery. On Sunday, we attended a Lutheran church service where the good priest spoke for nearly an hour. There was no heat and everyone else was fur-clad. We shook and shivered, but survived to enjoy the beautiful drive back to Salzburg.

Hilde greeted us warmly and laid on a good breakfast and a tasty lunch for us as we were catching a 4 a.m. train. We were off again tó Geneva, and finally, to Spain where dawn the next day found us in Barcelona. After a day sightseeing, we boarded the night boat to Palma, Mallorca.

We bedded down in Palma at the Santa Ana Hotel at the very edge of the Mediterranean, one of the world's most beautiful and romantic waterways, with its oft-changing colors of blue (bluer than the Danube!), green, gray, tan, red and orange, according to the whims of the wind, tides and time of day. Our balcony, from which you could throw a pebble into the ocean, or enjoy coffee at sunrise or goat cheese and Paternina wine at sunset, was a ringside seat for a giant ocean painting of sheer beauty, dotted by sail boats, steamers and small craft by day, and lantern-lit fishing boats at night.

We hied ourselves quickly to Meson Primero Uno, otherwise known as bob Schultz's bar (mentioned earlier) where a welcoming hug and a free, first drink established our identity. It later was the scene of many happy visits.

Bob, a handsome Swedish gentleman and wartime parachutist with the

Allies, had closed the fine restaurant part of his establishment due to the recession and lesser numbers of tourists. He had kept open the bar where he presided nightly. He did much during the day to spark our stay in Palma.

One day he took us to a country spot where crumbling piles of stone were the remains of a village which had stood there twenty centuries ago, before Christ was born. We lunched nearby at Cafe Diablo on the famous sopa of Mallorca, a huge dish of mixed vegetables and meat, eaten with a large spoon, followed by a large slice of whiskey cake. We had a memorable trip with Bob and his glamorous girl friend to Foc y Fum (Fire and Smoke), a typical Mallorcan country inn owned by an American lady, where we dined on Ropa Vieha (old clothes) a lamb specialty with a fiery Foc y Fum cocktail to wash it down.

We hired a car and toured the mountainous northern shore of Mallorca, never far from the sea, our eyes opened to wondrous scenery as we coasted down to Hotel Formentor, a honeymoon hideaway for famous couples and royalty. At Valdemossa, we relived the love story of Chopin and George Sand. At Binalbufar where the town is laid out in terraces rising high from the water's edge, we quenched our thirst at charming Vent y Mar (Wind and Sea) Hotel and on to a memorable lunch at Es Grau which literally hangs on the mountainside, with fantastic views of the sea in three directions.

Meanwhile, we attended two excellent piano concerts (Claude Kahn and Michael Rudy), saw the great movie, "The Deer Hunter," and tried a variety of restaurants, notable among them Mac's Christina, owned by a delightful former Phillipino movie star, Christine, known informally as 'Mac.' We attended a dinner honoring the anniversary of Robert Burns, the Scottish poet: the bag pipes played as the haggis was brought in. The grand finale, the night before I left for home, was a dinner at the white-marbled, luxury hotel, the Valparaiso—more palatial than some of the palaces we had seen and with sumptuous food and service. Our last lunch was at Sa Presa, the city's oldest restaurant. A Dios, Mallorca!

CHAPTER XXIV:1984
THE PASSION PLAY

Soon after my return, my beloved sister suffered a serious illness, followed by recurring health problems. Our vacation in Maine the next summer was marred by her hospitalization and continual treatment. A month's rest in Fort Meyer, Florida that year did not provide the benefit we hoped for.

A heart-warming happening occured that Christmas time when our beloved and long-time friends, Fran and Jack Owens came from Springfield, Virginia with a complete and bountiful Christmas dinner: a large turkey, sweet potatoes, mashed potatoes, and other vegetables, salad, dessert and coffee. They heated it all and served it to us in our apartment. How could anyone be more delightful and kind?! Dear friends are surely the jewels in the crown of life.

All my travel plans had to be laid aside pending my sister's recovery; but, she grew steadily weaker and passed away in her sleep in March, 1984. My fond hope for a visit to Oberammergau for the 1984 "Passion Play" had been held in abeyance. But now, friends urged me to make the trip as a change of scene.

I joined a tour for two weeks in Germany and Switzerland. We had a miserable flight over! I had a nearly-disastrous fall on a stairway and an incredibly unpleasant roommate. However, I was able to enjoy Lake Lucerne, Rothenberg, Heidelberg, a boat trip on the Rhine—and, I saw the "Passion Play!"

So many Americans have seen or read about the play, so I shall not attempt to describe it, except to mention the finale which was a magnificent tableaux of Jesus Christ in Heaven, surrounded by angels. However, as the curtains closed and the audience of 4,800 people rushed for the doors, they were halted by a blinding flash of lightning and a crash of thunder, a cloudburst—a literal wall of water which lasted a half hour—giving way to a hail storm which coated the streets with the white stones.

The earthly finale was eclipsed by a grand finale from Heaven—which I shall consider appropriate as a finale for this book.

Paul and Olga Roebling

EPILOGUE

Before finally ending my story and already, no doubt, being accused of name-dropping (which concerns me not in the least for I've only mentioned people I actually knew), I beg leave to speak briefly of many colorful persons I have encountered through the years.

To the Presidents already mentioned, I'll add the names of President Aleman of Mexico, President Somoza of Nicaragua and President Alberto Lleras Camargo of Columbia who, before becoming president, served in Washington as head of the Pan American Union. There were others whose names escape me who ruled their countries after a tour of duty in their Washington embassies.

I knew U.S. Vice Presidents Charles G. Dawes, Charles Curtis (and his controversial sister and official hostess, Dolly Gann), John Nance Garner, Hubert H. Humphrey and Alben Barkley. The latter, known widely as 'The Veep,' married, late in life, a charming widow whom I kept supplied with drinks at a small party given by Mrs. Arthur McArthur, a sister-in-law of General Douglas McArthur and a beloved Washington hostess for many years.

On many occasions, I've talked with Speakers of the House Longworth, Rayburn, Martin and McCormick; Secretaries of State Stimson and Hull; J.Edgar Hoover of the F.B.I.; W. Averill Harriman, Henry Cabot Lodge, John Lodge and other ambassadors of this country and other nations.

The governors I especially remember include four executives of New Jersey (Walter Edge, Charles Edison, Robert Meyner and Richard Hughes); Governors Donahey and Davey of Ohio; Dewey and Rockefeller of New York; Rockefeller of Arkansas; Knight of California; Folsom of Alabama; Chandler of Kentucky; Talmadge of Georgia; and Dalton, Holton and Almond of Virginia.

I had direct contact with almost all members of the U.S. Senate in the late 1920's and early 1930's. I have pleasant memories of the late John McClelland of Arkansas, Henry Amhurst of Arizona, Everett Dirkson of Illinois, Reed of Missouri and Taft, Fess and Willis of Ohio. I've known a trainload of congressmen: among them, I was especially interested in the late John Ashbrook, a rising Republican conservative from Ohio; Helen Meyner of New Jersey, wife of the former governor; and James G. Martin (formerly mentioned) who went from Congress to become Governor of North Carolina.

Military leaders I've known and admired are Generals Jack Pershing, Omar Bradley, George Patton, Patrick Ryan, Cornelius Ryan, Clinton Robinson, Mark Clark and Bruce Clarke of the Army; Arnold, Stratemeyer, Stone, Lavelle, Holloway and Dany of the Air Force; Admirals King, Radford, Wood, Copping, Charlton, Christie, Burlingame, Laurence, Pugh, Roberts, Donaho, Dodge, Holloway, Royar, Moeller, Kirby Smith, Richard Byrd and Commodore W.C. Wallace of the Navy.

I've feasted my eyes on a bouquet of "Miss Americas", met burlesque queens Gypsy Rose Lee and Ann Corio (with whom I visited while she was ironing costumes in her hotel room); met with two famous international playboys, Aly Khan and 'Baby' Pignatelli, and the latter's glamorous ex-wife, Princess Ira Furstenberg. I've talked with 'Jersey Joe' Walcott, the prize fighter; Louis Armstrong, the trumpet tooter; Roy Howard, news tycoon and Spyros Skouras, movie tycoon; also aviation presidents William Patterson, United Airlines; C.R. Smith, American Airlines; Jack Frey, TWA; and Eddie Richenbacker, Eastern. Also, I've met the aircraft manufacturers, Donald Douglas and Walter Beech.

There have been pleasant visits with Carl Lomen, the 'reindeer king' of Alaska, and his wife Laura, the daughter of Andrew Volsted who invented Prohibition. I called upon Dr. George Washington Carver, the great Negro scientist in Alabama. I've met and heard the late, controversial Episcopal Bishop Pike and the Reverend Norman Vincent Peale.

Society leaders I've known include the prominent Washington hostesses Mary and Elizabeth Howry, Mrs. McCeney Werlich, Mrs. Margaret Nohowel, Mrs. Marjorie Merriweather Post, Miss Jessica Fremont, Mrs. John Allan Dougherty, Mrs. Gwendolyn Cafritz, Mrs. Lily Vogel who threw open her beautiful house for parties for servicemen all during World War II, 'Polly' Logan, the former wife of Col. Robert Guggenheim and at that time, chatelaine of a great estate, "Firenze" in Rock Creek Park and Perle Mesta, the "hostess with the mostest."

Famous and prominent friends elsewhere were the late Daniel Ravenel III and wife Ruth of Charleston, South Carolina; Mr. and Mrs. Louis Marron of Brielle, New Jersey and Palm Beach, Florida; the late Albert M. Greenfield 'Mr. Philadelphia' and his charming wife, Elizabeth; Ambassador and Mrs. Walter Annenberg, Ben and Ruth Wolfe—all of Philadelphia—; Mr. and Mrs. S. Carl Mark of Tulsa, Oklahoma; Mr. and Mrs. Peter Van Brunt of Lake Placid; Mrs. Edward McIntyre of "Killeybegs Plantation", Montgomery, Alabama; the late Mr. and Mrs. John Rogers of New York; and their son, John Bond Rogers, married and living in Stockbridge, Massachusetts. (He flew Air force planes 'over the Hump' in World War II.)

One of the more spectacular and finally tragic figures on memory's wall is the late Daisy Breaux Calhoun, a New Orleans belle in her youth, who married wealth and presided over a great Charleston mansion where she carried off President Theodore Roosevelt and entertained him while the committee in charge of his visit was searching for him everywhere.

She later married Clarence Calhoun (a Washington Lawyer and Scotsman by birth) who built stately Rossdhu Castle in the Capital suburbs and proudly ensconced Daisy there while he pursued his suits in Federal court for millions of dollars claimed due American Indians. At home, Daisy entertained lavishly for some years; but, after her Scotsman died, her fortunes dwindled. I last saw her, a pathetic old lady, sunning herself in a downtown park. She often discussed with me the writing of her life's story, which certainly would have been of 'best seller' material.

A bachelor, and somewhat of a philosopher, at nearly 86, I am inclined to be quite fond of other men's wives and other people's children. People are my greatest delight and a subject for inexhaustible research, for there are no two persons exactly alike.

But, I'm also fond of the theater, music, books, sports, travel and swimming. As you have read, I've moved around a bit for 50 years. Now that I'm retired—after a fashion—I still travel whenever I can.

My loves in the theater have covered a wide range since that long-ago night in Philadelphia when I saw "Little Women" to today's erotic and psychotic outbursts of so-called entertainment. My home town had a theater for one-night stands: there, long ago, I saw a great play, "The Circle", with Mrs. Leslie Carter and John Drew playing the leading parts. As a young man, I naturally found much pleasure in Ziegfield's Follies and George White's Scandals. I shall never forget Maude Adams in "The Merchant of Venice," nor Alfred Lunt and Lynn fontaine in "There Shall Be No Night" and "The Visit." I've made several successful talks reviewing the latter as an unforgettable evening of theater. I enjoyed the "Roar of Grease Paint" the most of any recent plays; also, "Hello, Dolly," with Carol Channing whom I had met at Perle Mesta's previously.

Actors who have provided me enjoyable hours, and most of whom I've met, include George Arliss, Dennis King, Elliot Nugent, Burgess Meredith, Ray Bolger, Yul Brynner, Van Heflin, Peter Ustinov, Orson Welles, Bert

Lytell, Cary Grant, William Powell, Rudy Vallee and Glenn Hunter. Marcel Marceau, the French pantomimist is in a class by himself. Paul Roebling, a young actor, gave great promise in recent plays, notably "The Lark": I hope to hear more of him.

He is not letting the millions left to him by his grandfather (John A. Roebling who built the Brooklyn Bridge) stand in the way of his career. He, his charming wife, Olga, and their son, Kristian, are a very happy family. For Christmas, they sent me a three-ring, standing cardboard circus, the likes of which I'd never seen before.

To have lived in these times and not to have seen Ethel Barrymore would have been sad, indeed; but, I had that pleasure. There were other joyous moments with Bea Lillie, the erstwhile British bomber; Lady Peel, Kitty Carlisle, Katherine Cornell and Irene Bordoni (who can forget that throaty voice singing "The Land of Going To Be"?) There were also Peggy Wood, Margaret Sullavan, Cornelia Otis Skinner, Tallulah Bankhead, Katherine Hepburn, Mary Martin, Helen Menken and Louisa Horton. I watched Louisa grow up. She used to give me a hug when I visited her home and ask eagerly, "Do you think I'll ever be an actress?" On Broadway in "The Voice of the Turtle," she answered this question! Sophie Tucker was one who commanded my admiration and affection as a great trooper, with sure and lasting box office appeal.

Among the opera stars whose voices have thrilled me are the aforementioned Eleanor Steber; Lucrezia Bori; Kirsten Flagstad; Maria Jeritza, Dorothy Kirsten, Licia Albanese, Rosa Ponselle and Heidi Krall. Heidi is the wife of my good friend, Dr. John Preece: they are charming hosts at their country estate in Bucks County, Pennsylvania. The male stars whom I've enjoyed hearing and liked as friends are George London, Giovanni Martinelli, the late Lawrrence Tibbett and Brian Sullivan.

I had the rare privilege on November 24, 1964 of hearing four great divas in concert together at the Metropolitan Opera House, an occasion which happens once in a century. They were Elizabeth Schwarzkopf, Lisa Della Casa, Renata Tebaldi and Joan Sutherland, all sopranos, singing arias from "Der Rosenkavalier," "La Boheme," and "La Traviata." As delighted as I was in hearing and seeing this musical history created before us was my companion, Roberto Ayala, my aforementioned Spanish pal. The divas sang their best, which is the best there is—anywhere.

Always an ardent follower of the dance, I've watched many ballet companies: The Danish Royal, Twentieth Century Royal of Belgium, Joss, Moiseyev, Ballet Russe de Monte Carlo, Ballet theatre, National, Washington, New York City Center and many others, including the Mexican and Chilean folk ballets. I've been delighted by the footwork of Argentinita, Escudero, Ted Shawn and Ruth Denis, who danced around the world; Foster Fitz Simons and Mimi Winslow; Jose Greco and Jose Limon. Backstage at

Greco's concert one evening in New York with Danton Walker, the 'Broadway' columnist, Dan looked straight at the artist and asked him, "Are you a native of Spain?" Apparently undisturbed by the question, Greco answered simply, "No, I was born in Brooklyn!" That has never been a handicap, for he is recognized everywhere as one of the foremost exponents of Spanish dance.

Musicians I've loved hearing and meeting were Sergie Rachmoninoff, who shook hands after his concert wearing woolen mittens to keep his fingers warm; Arthur Schnabel, Artur Rubenstein, Igor Stravinsky, Rudolph Serkin, Wanda Landowska, Yehudi Menuhin, and Mme. Juliette Chautemps, wife of the former Premier of France. One of the great contemporay pianists, I think, is pianist Agustin Anievas, of Spanish ancestry, who grew up in New York, now lives in Brussels, and is playing in European capitals. He has given many brilliant concerts in Washington, New York and other American cities.

My favorite conductors have been Toscanini, Stokowski, Ormandy, Bernstein, Howard Mitchell, and Hans Kindler who was my close friend for many years. He built the National Symphony from only an idea and a hope into a great organization; then, he was ousted, after 18 years, by a cabal within the board of directors. His successor, Howard Mitchell, was a fine conductor.

Now, let's talk about authors and books. The day that man walked upon the moon was certainly history-making for all the world; but, I would say that the men who invented printing, reading, and wireless communication left their marks, also. How many books have been printed since the first one came out? How many millions of people are reading books at a given moment in time? Who was the greatest author of all? I'm sure no one can say with certainty.

My favorite authors and their works are these: Anatole France (*Penguin Island* and *The Red Lily*); Thomas Wolfe (*Look Homeward Angel, Of Time and the River, The Web and the Rock*); James Michener, (*Iberia, Hawaii* and *Chesapeake*); Taylor Caldwell (*Dear and Glorious Physician*, and *Dialogues With the Devil*); Thornton Wilder (*The Bridge of San Luis Rey*, and *The Eighth Day*); Pearl Buck (*The Good Earth*); Thomas Costain, (*The Black Rose*); Phillip Gdedella (*Palmerston*, one of the greatest of all biographies, and *Wellington*).

Marcel Proust's books are timeless, as are *War and Peace* and *Anna Karenina* by Leo Tolstoy. Jules Romain's *Verdun* is a great book; so is Lin Yutang's *Moment in Peking*. Winston Churchill's *Blood, Sweat and Tears* belongs on the immortals list, as does Cervantes' *Don Quixote*, Charles De Coster's *Legend of Ulenspiegel* and T.E. Lawrence's *Revolt in the Desert.*

How can one overlook *The Agony and the Ecstacy*, Irving Stone's moving story of Michelangelo which I have reviewed for several audiences; Papa Hemingway's *The Old Man and the Sea*; Shellabargar's *Captain from Castile*—the list goes on and on. Dante Aligherie's *Divine Comedy* will live forever. So will the works of Shakespeare and Dickens, most of which I haave read.

The *Bible* is admittedly the most-read book of all; others in the religious category are *The Man Nobody Knew, The Listener,* and *The Thirteenth Apostle.* Poetry books one must read are the collected works of A.E. Housman and Robert Frost; also *Leaves of Grass* by Walt Whitman. Robert Service is another of my favorite poets.

Ernie Pyle's war correspondence is literature apart. *The Quest of the Tropic Bird* by John Wilson is one of the greatest short stories I have ever read. The motion pictures I remember most are "Disraeli" and "Abraham Lincoln of Illinois." Both brought tears to my eyes. For top TV billing, I choose Lunt's portrayal of Oliver Wendell Holmes in "The Connecticut Yankee."

What makes an actor, a musician, a play, a book or a short story great? I suggest that great response is the answer, usually, but not necessarily with today's books or plays. Many of the so-called 'best sellers' quickly made into movies today are absolute trash, and rotten as well. Each of us has a right to his own special definition of greatness and lists of 'the greatest.' I would guess that the books which appear the oftenest, and last the longest on all the lists might qualify for greatness. No one alive surely has read all the books in print. We should use care in making comparisons and limit our superlatives to the books we've read which stirred and affected us the most.

And now that my tale is told, I suppose I should (in the manner of James Branch Cabell whose books were a source of great delight to me in bygone days) return to my childhood home and plunge again headfirst into that sparkling spring where the story began. But I should prefer, I think, to say " A Dios" to my dear readers with a few lines of poetry which appeared many years ago, without an author's credit, in Ted Robinson's "Philosopher of Folly" column in the *Cleveland Plain Dealer*:

If, when you die, your mind without a question
Holds death to be an everlasting sleep,
You will sleep ever. For by self-suggestion
That timeless slumber must immerse you deep.
But if you tell yourself a lovely story
Of landscapes where the sun forever gleams,
Why should you not pass into all the glory
Wherewith you have informed your endless dreams?
I'm apt to think that as the dreams we cherish
So must our everlasting dreamland be;
"The spirit that believeth not shall perish"—
That's clear enough for anyone to see.
No grisly devil ever tempts or haunts one
Who doth not in the dark for demons grope;
There is no hell except for him that wants one,
Nor any heaven for him who has no hope.